# Real Estate: Investment and Financial Strategy

# Real Estate: Investment and Financial Strategy

**Peter Chinloy**

**Kluwer Academic Publishers**
**Boston/Dordrecht/London**

**Distributors**

for the United States and Canada: Kluwer Academic Publishers, 101 Philip Drive, Assinippi Park, Norwell, MA 02061

for the UK and Ireland: Kluwer Academic Publishers, MTP Press Limited, Falcon House, Queen Square, Lancaster LA1 1RN, UK

for all other countries: Kluwer Academic Publishers Group, Distribution Centre, P.O. Box 322, 3300 AH Dordrecht, The Netherlands

**Library of Congress Cataloging-in-Publication Data**

Chinloy, Peter, 1950–
Real estate.

Bibliography: p.
Includes index.
1. Real estate investment. 2. Mortgages.
3. Housing—Finance. 4. Real property. I. Title.
HD1382.5.C475 1987 332.63'24 87-3249
ISBN 0-89838-233-5



**Kluwer Academic Publishers,** 101 Philip Drive, Assinippi Park, Norwell, MA 02061

**PRINTED IN THE UNITED STATES.**

# Contents

# Preface

This book has evolved from an interest in formalizing theories of real estate financing and investment. While real estate has characteristics of illiquidity and heterogeneity, recent developments have created markets for financial claims on property assets. These financial claims render real estate similar to other assets. These financial claims render real estate similar to other assets. Yet real estate markets retain degrees of inefficiency, suggesting possibilities for arbitrage opportunities. Such possibilities are examined in the book.

If sellers are prohibited by statute from transferring existing financing to buyers, they tend to hold properties longer when contract interest rates on loans exceed those prevailing in the market. Methods are required to account for and measure the quantity of mortgage equity arising from such favorable financing. Holders of mortgage backed securities face risks on both sides of interest rate movements. Should interest rates fall, debtors refinance. If interest rates rise, debtors do not refinance, and the holders of mortgage backed securities suffer capital losses. Hedging strategies are required. Mortgage warrants and option pricing mechanisms are discussed, and various equity unlocking mechanisms, such as collateralized mortgage obligations.

Real estate is the subject of get rich quick seminars, proposing strategies for obtaining millions. These strategies are discussed. A timing framework is developed. The rate of return after tax on cash invested is expressed as a function of inflationary expectations and various exogenous policy variables such as taxes and interest rates. The holding period is not exogenous, but subject to choice by the investor.

The objective is to integrate quantitative procedures with real estate practice, and to include financial instruments capable of rendering liquid claims against illiquid and immobile property. All the formulas are derived, to permit widespread applicability. The target audience is the researcher in real estate, as well as the real estate investor, appraiser, broker, developer, financier, securities and financial analyst, planner, and other professional who seeks to develop an underlying strategy for investment in physical and financial assets and liabilities of real estate markets.

## Acknowledgments

In preparing the manuscript, I am grateful to several people for research assistance and transcribing the material. Richard Brems, Terry Cooper, and Marian Cork assisted in the preparation process, by checking references, and organizing the material. Terry Cooper also assisted with the preparation of the index and references. The manuscript was written using the Vokswriter Deluxe 2.2 word processing package, Regression Analysis of Time Series (RATS) to perform statistical analysis, and Lotus 1-2-3 for spreadsheets. The editor, Zachary Rolnik of Kluwer Academic Publishers was very helpful and provided encouragement in developing the manuscript. This book is part of a series on real estate markets edited by James Kau and C. F. Sirmans, and their editorial work is appreciated.

The manuscript has been developed over two summers. During the first summer, the work was carried out in Palo Alto. During the second summer, I performed some of the work in Merriam, Kansas, in the Kansas City suburbs. The work completed while I was a Fellow at the Institute for Finance and Governance, Center for Educational Research at Stanford (CERAS), Stanford University. I am grateful for the financial support of a Leavey Grant from the School of Business and Administration at Santa Clara.

The advent of word processing technology has made the home a workplace, and the cottage the source of industry once more. My son Christopher has had to endure this procedure when fishing might have been more pleasurable for him.

# Real Estate: Investment and Financial Strategy

# 1 INTRODUCTION

## Motivation

The motivation for this book is the development of a strategy in real estate investment and holdings. The approach is relatively quantitative, but the appeal is to both researcher and practitioner. Investments in real estate are defined to include the physical holding of property and claims, through financial securities. Where there are problems with current practice, some modifications are suggested. The objective is to prepare the investor or researcher to make decisions on the strategy involved with real estate.

Real estate is illiquid, nonportable, and heterogeneous. Real estate markets are imperfect, and it is possible to beat the market with the appropriate strategy. The further implication is that arbitrage models from the theory of finance are likely to be more relevant than efficient markets models. The book features a unified theory of appraisal, financing acquisition, and holding. The strategy is supported by appropriate spreadsheets. The sequence of steps follows as closely as possible the steps actually used in carrying out a real estate investment: The method of holding title and the legal ramifications of title holding are considered; property appraisal is investigated; financing is examined; alternative financing costs are calculated; and closing costs are detailed. The first sequence is for the principal resident.

Active real estate investment in the physical asset consists of the holding of an interest in a title. The optimal holding period, with rate of return, depends on a number of variables. Passive real estate investments through real estate partnerships and syndications and financial real estate investments in securities markets are examined. hedging strategies are included, as well as the management of risk. The real estate investor—and the borrower who provides the funds for the project—is concerned about interest rate risk, or the fluctuation of borrowing costs over the long term. The long term is relevant because of the long life of real estate. Inflation risk arises. Refinancing risk reflects the prospect of having a real estate loan prepaid before the term. Default risk reflects the prospect of not receiving payments, or of payments delayed. Illiquidity risk creates variation in prices of similar properties, and arises from information differences between and within borrowers and lenders. Divisibility risk arises with the large size of mortgage loans, limiting diversification.

## Method

This book develops a strategy for the acquisition and management of physical and financial real estate assets. For physical assets, the sequence of actual investment is followed. The phases are research, appraisal, financing, acquisition, development, and management. For financial assets, sources of funds, and methods of liquefying real estate are examined. The research method applies mathematical and quantitative statistical analysis.

In the analysis of the physical asset holding, there are four principal features. First, for appraisal, we examine the three conventional approaches to valuation: the market, cost, and income capitalization approaches. In the market approach, a problem is the typically small sample size used for examining comparables. With three observations, there are an insufficient number of degrees of freedom to estimate prices for characteristics. In appraisal as applied, the estimation of prices for the characteristics of land and structures is frequently not based on statistical method. A hedonic procedure, where prices are estimated by regression equations, is incorporated. This procedure, in which properties are relatively overpriced and underpriced—given their characteristics—permits identification of potential outliers.

Second, for financing, the effective cost of financing for alternative real estate loans is developed. The effective cost of financing is a function of the term of the loan, the contract interest rate, frequency of payment and compounding, points, fees and prepayment penalties. A method is presented for comparing the effective cost of funds for alternative lenders, to develop the financing strategy. In financing, explicit calculation of effective costs per dollar borrowed are included, and shown to vary with duration of holding, if points and prepayment penalties are included. The choice between fixed and variable rate financing is a quantal decision, and this process is modelled as one on the degree of risk to be assumed. A strategy to determine the appropriate financing vehicle, given loan conditions, is developed.

Third, the acquisition process for real estate, is examined here in detail. Conventional search theory posits that the distribution of offers is uniform over time, and not serially correlated. This assumption implies that the expected price to be received from longer duration on the market, for a seller of real estate, increases with duration. This assumption is at odds with the real estate dictum that "the first offer is the best offer." The theory presented here reconciles these views with a serially dependent offer distribution which penalizes the seller for remaining on the market. In this and other areas, rules of thumb, common to practitioners, are examined as to their optimality.

Fourth, for investment, the rate of return is prospectively calculated based on the holding period and the price the investor is willing to pay. Alternatively, the maximum price an investor is willing to pay to obtain a target rate of return is estimated, and this price varies with the projected holding period. A strategy on the holding period is derivable. Prices and holding periods also depend on costs and expenses, and the tax and depreciation regimes in place. Real estate investments for owner-occupied residential, rental residential, and nonresidential properties are included.

The financial side of real estate markets includes mortgage banking, real estate and mortgage brokerage, and real estate securities markets. Strategies for hedging a real estate loan portfolio, to insulate against interest rate risk, are discussed. Potential markets in this sector arise, and the cost of creating markets for financial claims on real estate—to reduce the inherent illiquidity—are examined.

In the financial sector, the role of the supply of funds is presented. For mortgage banking and the investor, a model of qualifying standards and underwriting is obtained. The problem is one of asymmetric information, between lender and borrower, on credit risk. Strategies on using the financial markets to hedge the risk of interest rates, by using mortgage securities are developed. The book integrates the physical and financial sides of real estate markets, and attempts to apply quantitative method to the practitioner of real estate, including the individual investor, financial intermediary, real estate broker and developer.

The book is divided into four parts. Part I covers the institutional and legal background, and discusses the research required prior to search for either financing or investment. Part II discusses financing and methods for comparing loan packages at alternative institutions. Part III discusses real estate investments in holding the physical properties. Owner-occupied residential, investment residential, and investment nonresidential projects are discussed. These alternative investments include the effects of depreciation and tax regulations. In Part IV, financial real estate investments are discussed. In part I, chapter 2 examines the legal and specific characteristics of real estate. Legal issues include property rights, public-use control, and alternative methods for taking title to property. Real estate markets, at least for physical properties, are imperfect and inefficient. Chapter 3, on valuation and appraisal, discusses the market, cost, and income capitalization approaches; and problems with appraisal. Some of these problems can be reduced, at least if sufficient degrees of freedom are available, by the application of a hedonic procedure for appraisal. Such a procedure, with statistical application, can be performed with data based on transaction. A price index for real estate, with its movements over time, indicates both the risk and return for such investments. If a price index is artificially smoothed between appraisals, the risk of real estate investments is understated.

In part II, chapter 4 develops the various formulas for mortgage payments, the mortgage multiplier per one dollar of loan, and annuities. The present and future values of annuities are calculated, as are sinking funds. These calculations permit the investor to determine directly the loan payment, to compare alternative mortgages, to obtain the balance outstanding on the mortgage at any time, and to calculate yields on investments.

In chapter 5, the basic fixed rate and payment mortgage (FRPM) is developed. This mortgage has a set interest rate and term. The effective cost of funds is calculated, including the effect of points, fees, and prepayment penalties, as well and the frequency of compounding.

Alternative financing methods to the FRPM are developed in chapter 6. The FRPM requires the lender to assume all interest rate and refinancing risk. Inflationary risk is borne by the lender, once the loan is issued. The only response of the lender is to increase the initial interest rate, as an insurance premium. Alternative financing methods involve the borrower in sharing some of these risks. The compensation is lower interest rates and lower payments. Various mortgages involve periodic changes in interest rates and payments, to permit lenders to more completely match loans and deposits. Financing alternatives include permitting family members to share in the investment, and unlocking equity in property.

In part III, chapter 7 examines real estate investments for the residential sector. The investment decision depends on tax policy. Nothing-down strategies, with infinite leverage, are compared with complete cash purchases. The latter case is attractive to those facing zero current tax rates, such as pension fund investors. A hold versus sell strategy for the owner occupier, who faces no depreciation schedule, is developed.

The behavior of the active real estate investor is developed in chapter 8. Active real estate investment in depreciable property involves tax rules. A set of decision rules on holding and selling is examined. A series of financial statements, including a balance sheet for tax and accounting purposes (and economic or information purposes) is constructed. The effective rate of return for holding is compared with the corresponding rate for selling. The active real estate investor can develop a strategy on when to sell.

Part IV, containing four chapters, deals with the financial side of real estate investments. Chapter 9 deals with passive real estate in the form of syndications, limited partnerships, and real estate investment trusts. Since these items are considered securities, they are treated as financial claims on real estate. The same problems of holding strategy arise. The passive real estate investor benefits by not having the management problems. Costs are paid for management fees and sales loads, and for the lack of control over the timing of sales. There are additional risks of illiquidity and of default by the manager, general partner, or syndicator. Passive real estate tends to permit less lumpy investments than does active real estate. Real estate investment trusts are more liquid and diversified, and trade on securities exchanges.

Chapter 10 considers the development of financial claims against real estate, where the investor holds paper instead of property. Mortgage backed securities, and the risk of interest rates and refinancing, are considered. Mortgage backed securities include single-date maturity and staggered maturity securities, collateralized mortgage obligations (CMOs), and real estate mortgage investment conduits (REMICs). Hedging strategies for the reduction or laying off of interest rate risk are considered. For refinancing risk, some possibilities include the use of options markets, mortgage security warrants, and CMOs, though the risk with the last named cannot be completely laid off.

In chapter 11, methods of hedging or speculation in mortgages and mortgage backed securities are considered. Options are placed against various securities. Put and call option prices are developed.

In chapter 12, the supply of funds for real estate development is discussed. Mortgage banking and sources of funds are examined, together with the screening issues in underwriting standards. A set of financial accounts for the real estate lender is developed. On the balance sheet, mortgages are held as assets for portfolio lenders. The effective rate of return on the mortgage is calculated and compared with the cash realization method used to report lender income. On the liability side, there is matching risk where the maturities of assets and liabilities are unequal. Deposits are typically of shorter duration than assets. Mortgage banking companies are nondepository lenders, and their role is examined. Given the imperfection and inefficiency of real estate markets, there is a market for intermediation. The market for mortgage brokers and the problems of regulation are considered.

Some possibilities for reducing the inefficiency and illiquidity of real estate are secondary markets for mortgages and separate markets for the investment and tax-shelter aspects of real estate. By developing these markets and issuing securities analogous to the stripped-coupon bonds in financial markets, some liquidity for partnership and other tax-shelter investments can arise. Greater efficiency arises from the presence of computerized listings of property.

The book follows the actual sequence of steps involved in a real estate investment. Prior to purchase, the property is appraised and a valuation is established. The financing of the project is also examined. The transaction is then completed. Separate decision rules for owner occupancy and investment are developed, together with a holding strategy. Residential, commercial, and industrial properties are compared. The process of purchasing in the residential sector is discussed, including closing and other transactions costs. Residential finance covers two principal financing mechanisms. The fixed rate and payment mortgage (FRPM), the benchmark loan provides for a constant interest rate and periodic, usually monthly, payment over a fixed period, usually 15 or 30 years. The adjustable rate mortgage (ARM) has a variable interest rate and a number of other variables, including fees, a margin, and frequency of payment changes. The methods for calculating payments under various mortgage payments is derived explicitly.

Active real estate investments are discussed first. Active real estate involves the owner as manager. Own versus rent decisions for shelter as a principal residence are first discussed, including the effect of tax considerations. The active real estate investor, holding the physical property, then moves on to other residential and industrial, commercial, and investment real estate. A timing model is used to develop strategy on holding and the rate of return after tax. The effect of risk and leverage is examined, including the consequence of nothing-down strategies. The relation of risk to the leverage of the project is developed. Passive real estate investment in physical assets follows similarly, except that the owner hires a manager for the property.

The financial side of real estate markets is divided into three sections. The first deals with marketing in syndications and partnerships, both income and tax oriented. For passive real estate investors, real estate syndication and limited partnerships provide methods of diversifying and pooling risks. The second section deals with the sources of funds for real estate finance, including both the thrifts, or savings and loans associations and mutual savings banks, and mortgage banking companies (MBCs). Mortgage banking deals with the sources of funds for real estate transactions. Both depository and nondepository sources are examined. The third section discusses the development of securities markets in mortgages, the most explosively growing sector of real estate markets. Secondary mortgage markets involve the packaging of mortgages as securities and their resale to buyers, to provide additional liquidity. Secondary markets permit the laying off of interest rate risk—and some of the refinancing risk—lenders must bear with fixed rate and payment mortgages.

Mortgages are packaged, pooled, and sold to other investors. Mortgage backed securities, even while being guaranteed—in the case of those secured by mortgages supported by the Government National Mortgage Association (GNMA), or Ginnie Maes—are guaranteed only against default risk, not against either interest rate or refinancing risk. The former risk is shared with other obligations issued by the Treasury, but the latter risk is not. The latter arises because the borrower can refinance and prepay the loan prior to maturity. Other securities examined include CMOs and mortgage security warrants. Also considered are the prospects for a mortgage exchange, which creates a direct secondary market for paper secured by physical real estate. The presence of interest and refinancing risk suggests that lenders holding large mortgage portfolios require hedging strategies and vehicles.

Underlying all real estate markets are the basic and possibly unique characteristics of land. Since real estate markets are shown to be relatively inefficient, the efficient markets theories from other areas in finance may not be completely appropriate. Under efficient markets, one cannot obtain a superior-to-average return, except by accident. In real estate markets, local characteristics, at least of the physical assets, render the possibilities of making arbitrage profits or profits based on superior information. Such possibilities can extend to the financial side of real estate markets, where mortgage backed securities reflect the underlying heterogeneity in properties and borrowers.

Market efficiency in stock, bond, and foreign exchange cases remains a hypothesis. The possibility arises that insider information or trading on a specific strategy will lead to long-term profits. Even more likely is the case for such a strategy in real estate markets. As a specific case, technical analysis is not appropriate if markets are efficient, where individuals attempt a buy or sell timing strategy based only on a time-series type analysis. Technical analysis can be appropriate in real estate markets. The timing strategy examined here is embellished by the application of time series models.

Compared with financial markets as a whole, real estate physical and financial markets are relatively inefficient. There are clear differences in information between players in real estate markets, particularly on the physical side. Real estate markets for physical property are local, not national, in scope.

The presence of the inefficiency is what leads to potential profit making, and corresponding loss making, opportunities. With financial assets, each unit is homogeneous. With real estate physical assets, there are differences in characteristics. Even with reale state financial assets, such as mortgage backed securities, there are differences between similar assets, because of heterogeneity in the underlying borrowers and properties.

The presence of the heterogeneity leads to the need for valuation and appraisal. Were there complete markets, no appraisals would be required. Real estate transactions for physical property are typically large and indivisible. This indivisibility leads to transactions costs for brokerage and search, complexity, and potential inefficiency. Indivisibility also leads prices to be more flexible. There are transactions costs of both entering and leaving real estate markets.

Physical real estate is illiquid, though the presence of mortgage backed securities has increased marketability for the underlying claims, or liabilities or borrowers. The illiquidity immediately conveys inefficiency.

Real estate, both physical and financial, receives specific treatment from various levels of government, sometimes favorable, and sometimes not. Zoning and land-use controls, building codes and regulations, environmental impact reports, and planning restrictions restrict the supply side for physical real estate. The regulations may have a benefit to society as a whole, but there are increased costs of supplying improvements to land. Rent regulations and controls on the residential side, and sometimes on the commercial side, create subsidies and property rights to tenants. There are subsidies to create residential and other construction. The enforcement and maintenance of these regulations lies mainly with local governments.

Governmental regulations at the state and federal levels affect the return from residential properties. For the principal resident, the deductibility of mortgage interest and property taxes, and whether imputed rent, the opportunity cost of not paying a landlord for use of the same residential services, is taxed, both affect the choice between ownership and rental or tenure choice. For the investor in physical real estate, the extent of differential between permitted for tax purposes and economic depreciation, the deductibility of losses against other income, and the treatment of capital gains affect the decision to become a passive or active player in these markets.

For the financial real estate investor, capital gains taxes and the taxation of the interest income, as well as the degree of government guarantee, affect the decision to hold claims secured by mortgages. The presence of tax expenditures, or subsidies in the tax system, for real estate implies that the rate of return received depends on the tax rate of the investor. This heterogeneity in returns creates a threshold marginal entry tax rate for the investor.

# I VALUATION

# 2 REAL ESTATE—INSTITUTIONAL AND LEGAL ENVIRONMENT

## Characteristics of Real Estate

Several characteristics of real estate distinguish it from alternative investments. Real estate does not uniquely possess these characteristics, but they are important in determining the prices and quantities transacted in markets. These characteristics include:

1. Differences in information: In a real estate transaction, there are differences in information between parties—buyer and seller.
2. Localized markets: Markets are local in scope for the physical properties, and trading on a national bourse does not take place.
3. Heterogeneous properties: All properties are not the same, with numerous differences in characteristics.
4. Illiquidity: Real estate is not mobile or portable, and transaction is difficult because of legal institutions, and the large individisibility of size.
5. Tax treatment: Real estate is accorded favorable or unfavorable tax treatment, and tax advantages can be key factors in an investment decision.

6. Depreciation and appreciation: According to tax laws, land does not depreciate. In practice, land can depreciate because of changes in locational patterns and demand. The improvements on the land depreciate, and tax laws can provide rates of depreciation in excess of the underlying physical depreciation.
7. Supply restrictions: It is often noted that "they aren't making any more land." Land is in relatively, if not perfectly, inelastic supply.

There is asymmetric information between buyers and sellers of real estate. Those who are licensed real estate brokers are required by law to disclose whether they are purchasing on own account, but the presence of multiple-listing services and the absence of wide publicity for nonresidential listings renders real estate subject to differences in information. Similar properties transact at differing prices.

Real estate markets are inherently localized. The local market is subject to legislation on land use and controls, zoning, building codes and restrictions, entry to the real estate profession, and access to listings. The properties themselves cannot move. The local nature of real estate markets creates returns to those with internal knowledge of the market.

Properties are heterogeneous. The three factors influencing the price of real estate are argued to be "location, location and location." Location itself is unique, and there need not be a perfect substitute nearby. Other characteristics of real estate can exist, but no two parcels of land with or without their improvements are exactly alike.

Real estate in physical form is illiquid. It cannot be transported. As a store of value, it is useful, but is subject to risk on changes in the economic or social climate. It cannot easily be converted into cash.

Time passes while real estate is listed for sale. The passage of time introduces an element of uncertainty into the prospect of having a transaction, and the price to be paid. The decision to purchase real estate is not marginal, but lumpy and indivisible. The investor requires time to investigate and evaluate the heterogeneous characteristics of real estate.

Real estate receives favorable tax treatment not accorded to other assets in some areas. The tax treatment includes the handling of depreciation on improvements. If the tax laws permit a depreciation rate greater that the rate of economic deterioration of the property, real estate can provide a source of additional returns.

## Holding Title to Real Property

### *Joint Tenancy*

The potential investor or investors must determine the most appropriate method to hold title. Individual owners can take title as joint tenants or tenants in common. Married couples are permitted in some states to take title in community property, or tenancy by the entirety. Other legal persons permitted to hold title to property are trusts, partnerships, and corporations.

One method of holding title among individual investors is that of joint tenancy, which automatically conveys right of survivorship. If one joint tenant dies, the surviving joint tenant owns the cntire property without probate proceedings. A joint tenancy is immediately broken if one joint tenant files for bankruptcy.

Joint tenancy involves four unities: time, title, interst, and possession. It must be created at the same time, and by the same joint instrument. Each owner has equal interest, and has the same right of possession. Express declaration is required, so the document of title specifies—if A and B are joint tenants—"to A and B as joint tenants."

Joint tenancy need not be restricted to spouses; it can include any group of owners. To clear the title of the deceased joint tenant's interest, all that is required is to record an affidavit of survivorship and a copy of the deceased joint tenant's death certificate in the county where the property is located.

The right of survivorship with joint tenancy can prove to be a disadvantage. The provisions of a decedent's will, leaving the property to party other than the joint tenant, are automatically overridden by the survivorship. A will is nevertheless recommended, to allocate the property in case all joint tenants die simultaneously.

Joint tenancy can be dissolved without the consent of all parties, and one joint tenant can convey his or her interest to another without permission. Such conveyance includes selling or giving away the joint tenancy interest without permission of the remaining joint tenants. Where a joint tenancy interest has been conveyed to another not originally part of the tenancy, a tenancy in common is created. The new co-owner and the previous joint tenants are tenants in common. Joint tenancy is also dissolved if any one tenant is declared a bankrupt, in which case the property is vested in the remaining joint tenants and the trustee in bankruptcy as tenants in common.

Regarding taxes, a transfer of a joint tenancy interest can be considered a deemed realization for capital gains tax purposes, with the basis being the original cost of acquisition, plus any improvements. The acquiring joint tenant is thus liable for the payment of capital gains taxes. While some estate and probate costs are saved, these may be small by comparison with potential capital gains taxes, particularly if long-term capital gains are treated as ordinary income.

### *Tenancy in Common*

Tenancy in common is the residual method of holding ownership. It arises as the default option when there is no joint tenancy or partnership under individual ownership. Under tenancy in common, interests can be unequal and acquired at different times, by comparison with joint tenancy.

There is no right of survivorship, and the interest transfers to the heirs of the tenant in common. Upon death, a tenancy in common interest triggers a capital gains realization, based on the original purchase price. Capital gains taxes are levied on the differential between the market price at death, and the purchase price originally, plus any improvements, the basis, less any depreciation taken.

The interest is freely transferable. The ownership is of an undivided interest, not to a specific portion of the property. On the deed, the fraction of ownership of each is spelled out.

### *Restricted Ownership Between Spouses*

**Community Property.** The concept of community property arises from the premise that a married couple should have equal ownership of property acquired during espousal, and is based upon Mexican and Spanish civil law. For example, in California, it survives from the Treaty of Guadalupe Hidalgo in 1848. Other community property states are Idaho, Washington, Arizona, New Mexico, Texas, Nevada, and Louisiana. Community property can only be an interest between spouses, and requires permission for transfer.

Community property is defined as possessions acquired by either spouse during marriage, when not acquired as the separate property of either. Separate property, as opposed to community property, includes assets and accumulations acquired prior to marriage, subsequent to a legal separation; payments in settlement of an injuries damages claim; assets acquired as gifts or bequests; or property conveyed by one spouse to another with the intent of creating separate property.

Community property, as opposed to separate property, is subject to equal interest and rights. Neither spouse can transfer or encumber community property without the consent or signature of the other, and each has the right of testamentary disposition of one half of the community property. If there is no will, all community property goes to a surviving spouse. By comparison with joint tenancy, there are probate costs.

For tax purposes, all community property is revalued upon termination of the community property arrangement at current market prices for capital gains tax purposes. The property receives the current market price as basis, and no capital gains tax is payable. The cost of community property, as opposed to joint tenancy, is the payment of some legal and probate fees. A will is recommended, as otherwise the law of the state determines allocation of the interest. Under joint tenancy, no current market basis applies. Death is a deemed realization, and capital gains tax is payable on the differential between current market value, and the initial purchase price plus the cost of improvements.

Suppose in a community property state a married couple bought a property for $50,000. On the death of one, the market value is $120,000, and there have been no improvements. If the title were held as community property, the new basis of the property becomes $120,000, and no capital gains tax is payable. Under tenancy in common, half the capital gain is attributable to the deceased, or $35,000, and this amount becomes taxable income.

**Tenancy by the Entirety.** Some states permit tenancy by the entirety, to reduce some of the problems caused by the liquidity that results from joint tenancy. Tenancy by the entirety, as with community property, imposes restrictions on the transfer of the ownership interest of property held by spouses. An interest cannot be transferred without the consent of the other. The interest is protected against creditors.

### *Partnership*

A partnership is an association of two or more persons carrying on business for a profit. In a general partnership, each partner is liable for all debts, while in a limited partnership, the limited partner is restricted to only the loss of the initial investment, and is limited in the management.

Such an arrangement must be recorded at the office of the county recorder in a statement of partnership. The property can be owned by the partnership as a single entity.

### *Corporation*

A corporation is an organization having the status of a legal person, with limited liability for shareholders to the amount of their investment. A corporation is permitted to hold property, but not as a joint tenant. When a corporation owns real property, who is permitted to act on behalf of the corporation becomes an issue.

### *Trust*

A trust is an arrangement providing for the care and well-being of another person. Title to real property is transferred by the owner to another party, the trustee, who holds the title and manages the property for the benefit of the beneficiary. A living or inter vivos trust is effective during the lifetime of the creator, and a testamentary trust is effective after the death of the person creating it. A common trust form is the real estate investment trust (REIT). The REIT uses the funds of many investors to acquire real property.

### *Title Issues*

Issues and controversy surround the holding of title on both a corporate and individual basis. For individuals, since joint tenancy conveys right of survivorship and can be transferred without permission of all tenants, problems on title holding arise.

As an example, suppose parents A and B assist a child C and spouse D to purchase a property, placing all names on the title as joint tenants. The allocation of initial contribution to the down payment or of continuing contribution is irrelevant, since joint tenancy conveys equal interest. If parent A dies, then parent B, together with child C and spouse D remain joint tenants, dominating the provisions of a will and involving no probate. Each has equal ownership interest. If subsequently there should be a divorce between C and D, spouse D has an entitlement to one-third of the property, as one of the joint tenants, regardless of contribution. Spouse D can transfer the interest to another party, without the permission of the spouse C, or the surviving in-law B.

A potential solution to problems of joint tenancy is to hold title as tenants in common. The tenancy in common provides for unequal allocations of the holding, registered on the title at the applicable land title office with the county recorder. Costs with tenancy in common arise from wills and probate proceedings being required to assign interest. Disputes between individuals, with frequent tragic circumstances, revolve around the method of holding title. Such a decision requires care, and possibly legal advice.

## Acquiring Title

Title to property can be acquired by will, succession, accession, occupany, or transfer. Will or succession involve the acquisition of title through death. Accession involves the addition of property by natural circumstance, or the addition of improvements of fixtures. Occupancy involves adverse possession, or without permission of the owner. Transfer, the method most of relevance to real estate investment, can be through voluntary alienation by the seller; passing title; or involuntary alienation, such as through bankruptcy. Transfer of title is typically through a deed.[1] The deed, as with other real estate documents, must be written to be valid. The suffix "-or" applies to the giver, and the suffix "-ee" to the recipient. The grantee must be capable of acquiring title. The document must have operative wrods, such as "grant," and a legal description of the property. The deed must be executed by the grantor and delivered and accepted by the grantee.[2]

A deed conveys the property. A bill of sale conveys personal property, such as furniture and equipment not attached and not considered fixtures. An agreement for sale, or contract for sale, or interim agreement, is the document stipulating the conditions under which sale takes place. The execution and delivery of an agreement for sale typically conveys equitable transfer of title, even if legal title remains with the seller until the deed is delivered. In an installment sales contract, or land contract, the seller agrees to convey title after the buyer has complied with some terms.

The possession of equitable title means that the buyer can sell the interest to another party without taking legal title, a tactic known as *flipping*. The buyer can secure the property with a small consideration, and then sell to another party. In the United States, Canada, and Scotland, equitable title can be acquired prior to legal title. In England, they are acquired simultaneously. Hence a seller in a rising market can pay no attention to an already signed contract for sale, if title has not been delivered, and sell the property to another party. This practice is known as *gazumping* in England.

The holding of a contract for sale can be viewed as a call option, or option to buy, while legal title has not been delivered, provided equitable title has been transferred. Direct options can be placed on physical real estate. An option provides the right to buy on specific terms during a specific period. The optionee, or recipient, can compel the optionor, or owner, to comply with the terms, in exchange for consideration. The optionee pays a fee for receiving this right. The optionor does not have the right to compel the optionee to perform. If the optionee does not perform, the option lapses, and the optionor receives the fee only. Such options arise frequently in long-term leases, or in rentals with options to buy, where the rent is increased by the fee.

These options are all of the buy or call variety. Although a put option, which conveys the right to sell at a given price and to hedge against falling markets, has not been applied in physical real estate markets, it permits additional flexibility and liquidity.

### Encumbrances as Loan Security—Mortgages and Deeds of Trust

An encumbrances is a lien or charge against a property. For real estate finance, liens of relevance are those indicating evidence of debt, such as promissory notes, mortgages and trust deeds, contracts of sale, and land contracts. Real estate can be encumbered voluntary by the owner, or involuntarily by the creditor exercising statutory rights.

A negotiable instrument is a written promise to pay money. It can be in the form of a promissory note, promising to pay principal and interest. To be negotiable, a note must have an unconditional promise or order, be in writing, be made by one person to another, be signed by the maker, agree to pay on demand or at a definite date, be for a certain sum, and be payable to a named payee or to bearer. A promissory note in real estate is typically secured by a mortgage or deed of trust.

A promissory note can contain a clause adding legal fees and court costs if litigation becomes necessary for collection. An acceleration clause provides for the entire amount of the loan to be due at the election of the holder under certain circumstances. Upon sale, the applicable acceleration clause is a "due on sale" or "alienation" clause. Other circumstances other than sale triggering such a clause is default on loan payment, failure to maintain the property or to failure to maintain insurance. In a straight note, the principal is due at a specific time. In an installment note, the principal and interest are paid in blended amounts, with the interest calculated on the principal outstanding.

The term *mortgage* arises from the French words *mort* (dead) and *gage* (pledge). Once paid off, a mortgage becomes a dead pledge. In early mortgages, documented during the Saxon period in England, the borrower conveyed title to the lender as security to the loan.

There are two parties to a mortgage, the lender, or mortgagee, and the borrower, or mortgagor. Title rests with the mortgagor, or borrower, with a mortgage note as evidence of the debt. A mortgage contract provides that the real estate is the security for the debt. To foreclose against the property in the event of default requires court action by the mortgagee, since title remains with the mortgagor. Upon foreclosure proceedings being commenced, the owner can redeem by bringing payments current. After a foreclosure sale, the owner has up to one year to redeem the property. The mortgagee, or lender, has the right to obtain a deficiency judgment against the borrower. The lender can take action against the person, as opposed to the property, if payments are not made. Conveyance is by a warranty deed. Upon discharging the debt, a satisfaction of mortgage is recorded at the county recorder's office. There is a four-year statute of limitations from the due date of the collection of funds. There are costs of court action, litigation, and interest charges, or opportunity costs of funds while the procedures are continuing.

A deed of trust involves three parties, the borrower, termed the trustor, the lender, or beneficiary, and the trustee, a neutral third party. This neutral third party can be a title company, an attorney, or any agreed party, and is usually the first named. Title to the property rests with the trustee. The borrower, or trustor, permits the third party, or trustee, to hold the title to the property in trust, while an unpaid loan balance from the lender remains a claim against the property. A trust deed, is used to convey the title. Upon failure of the trustor to meet the terms, the beneficiary has the option of foreclosure as with a mortgage, which involves court proceedings.

Since the title does not rest with the borrower, there is another alternative, termed the *trustee's sale.* The beneficiary can order a notice of default, where the owner has the option of bringing payments current, usually within three months. If there is no compliance, a notice of sale is posted, and the trustor, or borrower, must make good on the entire debt owed. The beneficiary can then order the trustee, or title company, to sell the property at a trustee's sale, against which there is no redemption by the borrower. The borrower does not have recourse against the lender, but only against the property, so no deficiency judgment is possible. If the entire debt is repaid, a *recorded* deed of reconveyance transfers the title from the trustee to the trustor, or borrower.

Mortgage is used generically to describe mortgages as well as deeds of trust and other negotiable instruments secured by real estate, the term is so used throughout this book. A standard mortgage document requires the borrower to maintain the property in good repair, and to take no action that would jeopardize the security of the lender. Fire insurance is to be maintained, at the expense of the borrower, and also title insurance. Taxes are to be paid, including all obligations incurred prior to taking title. The provisions are binding on all heirs and successors. These clauses are general. In addition, there are alienation clauses, prepayment penalty clauses, and clauses on variable interest if there is an adjustable rate mortgage.

An open-ended clause provides for an increase in the amount borrowed, upon demand by the borrower, and applies particularly in construction loans. The alienation or due on sale clause provides that in the event of transfer of the property by the borrower, the lender can require that the loan balance outstanding be repaid immediately. Such a clause was tested in *Wellenkamp v. Bank of America* in 1978, where the United States Supreme Court ruled that a due on sale clause was not enforceable, and that a mortgage could be sold to another buyer with the property. Subsequent mortgage contracts have provided tighter clauses to restrict the transferability of mortgage financing.

A prepayment clause specifies the penalties due to the lender if the loan is paid prior to the date specified. A typical amount is three months of interest, with no penalty after five years of payment. ARM loans must contain a clause specifying the mechanism for calculating the interest rate payable, and the frequency of adjustment. A late-charge clause applies if the payment is not made on time. A subordination clause determines the priority of the sequence of payments.

## Land Use and Regulation

Real estate is subject to regulation on usage, particularly at the local level. Regulation arises from concerns for "public health, safety, and general welfare." In urban areas, a community plan sets out the overall land usage for the area. Zoning restricts the land use of a property by the police power of the state. Zoning regulations include restrictions on height, density, and coverage of the site. Zoning applies to single- and multiple-family residential, commercial, and industrial property.

A condominium provides for single-family ownership within a multifamily structure. Common ownership applies to land and common areas. Fees to support the common ownership are levied on either a proportional square foot or value basis.

Advantages of a condominium include the delegation to others of maintenance of grounds and common areas. The tax advantages of homeownership for owner occupiers is retained. The tax shield, where some expenses for mortgage interest and property taxes are paid from before-tax income, applies. The costs of purchasing housing or office services from the improvements on land are reduced, because there is no individual land ownership.

The condominium poses certain risks for the lender. Maintenance is not provided by the borrower, but by a third party over whom the lender does not have any direct control. Maintenance may not be sufficient. There are problems until all, or a substantial number of units in a project are sold. At the beginning, the ratio of rental to owned units is larger than when all units are sold. Partly, the high rental ratio arises from regulations on registration of condominium projects, and where the developer is not yet able to cede control to an owners' association. If rental units are less well maintained than owned units, the lender faces greater than average risks than lending on detached units.

Uncertainty arises as to the future increase in supply by the developer. If more units are planned, or units are released at random rates, current purchases, and the prospects of capital gains, are reduced. Payments and deposits for initial purchase, at the beginning of the construction phase, are typically placed in escrow accounts not available to the developer until the end of construction. Yet because a larger proportion of condominium units are new, there is construction, delay, and completion risk on lending in this area. There is the risk of conversion, from both rental units to a condominium, and vice versa.

There is risk to the developer, who is building units without firm purchase commitments, or speculative (spec) construction. By preselling the units, prior to construction, and having a deposit paid into escrow, the developer is able to obtain financing more easily and reduce the risk.

A cooperative provides another alternative form of land and structure ownership. A corporation is established to own the entire property, typically of multifamily residential units. Each unit is allocated a number of shares in the corporation. One basis for allocating the shares is the number of residential square feet, as a percentage of the total in the project. Height and location can be used in allocating the shares.

The prospective owner must purchase the shares in the cooperative from a seller. In some instances, the corporation by-laws permit the remaining owners to vote their shares in approval or disapproval of new owners. This procedure permits residents to have some control over their neighbors. The cooperative form provides the tax benefits of homeownership.

## Concluding Remarks

This chapter is of necessity a sketch of the legal ramifications in the ownership of real estate. The focus is on areas where financial implications arise, as for mortgages. Further legal detail on th specific jurisdiction of purchase is required in the investment decision.

Title can be held in various forms. Financial documents related to real estate include both the claims by the lender—the mortgage or deed of trust—and the claim by the buyer on undelivered property. This claim, as summarized in a written contract for sale of purchase, can serve the same function as an option for purchase of real estate. The paper claim of a mortgage or a purchase contract can be resold, thereby increasing the liquidity of real estate.

## Notes

1. Various types of deed exist. The grant deed contains two implied warranties: (1) that thte grantor has not previously conveyed the property or interest to another person and (2) that the property is free from encumbrances. A quitclaim deed contains no implied warranties, and is usually applied to clear restrictions. Where trust deeds are used instead of mortgages, they convey the title of the owner to a third party, or trustee, as security for the payment of a loan against the property. A gift deed is one where there is no consideration.

2. An executed contract is one where there are no terms left to be performed. Delivery involves giving possession of a document, such as a deed, to convey title from the grantor to the grantee. Acceptance means that the terms of the contract are satisfactory and agreed to. Acceptance is usually preceded by an offer of one party, and acceptance by the other.

# 3 VALUATION AND APPRAISAL OF PROPERTIES

## Introduction

With the heterogeneity of property markets, disagreements arise as to the value of real estate. Such disagreements imply a demand for appraisal to determine the price. The basic rationale for appraisal is to protect a party in a real estate transaction.

Appraisals are required because in addition to the buyer and seller, there is frequently a third party, a lender, involved in the transaction. This third party neither directly surrenders nor receives title, but is involved in advancing funds for the purchase. To protect the interest of the lender as third party, and to guard against fraud and misrepresentation, appraisal is sought. With the presence of other parties in real estate transactions, including secondary holders of mortgages, more parties require protection against loss. Appraisal has the objective of providing insurance to protect third parties, and sometimes the two direct parties to a transaction.

An appraisal is a subjective opinion of value of property at a point in time. As applied, appraisals are not objective, since reliance is placed on opinion about prices. There are several problems in real estate transactions that appraisal attempts to minimize.

The lender or secondary-market intermediary—the packager of mortgage securities against the property—seeks an appraisal to protect itself against moral hazard. The buyer and seller can conspire, as they have interest in conflict with the interests of the lender and packager. By agreeing to a higher price than might otherwise obtain, a seller can obtain more financing and leverage. Practically, a buyer is limited in liability to the down payment. A severe reduction in equity by the buyer leaves the lender with little or no security. Agreements between buyer and seller could take the form of agreeing on one price for official, or loan document purposes, and on another price for the actual transaction, by the provision of other direct or indirect rebates from the seller to the buyer. The lender is thus exposed to additional risk, and the risk of high leverage is shifted to the lender or ultimate holder of the mortgage. An appraisal, by providing an alternative estimate of the price, provides an insurance policy for the lender. The lender can lend on the minimum of the agreed transaction or appraised price.

Risk of default is shifted from the lender to the buyer with the appraisal process. The lender requires the buyer to pay this cost of purchasing insurance, in effect reducing the risk of default and permitting the funds to be advanced.

Appraisals also serve the purpose of objectively reassuring a buyer or seller. While the dominant rationale is to protect a lender, a buyer or seller with an all-cash transaction may require an estimate, presumably prior to signing an interim agreement of offer to purchase, that the price being paid is appropriate, as compared with other similar and substitutable property.

If the appraiser carried out the task blind, without knowledge of the price being offered, the appraisal can be completely objective. If the appraiser knows the price being paid, then there can be a tendency to produce an appraisal close to that of the property being assessed.

As applied, there are three basic approaches to appraisal and valuation, the cost, market, and income capitalization methods. The cost approach attempts to determine the replacement price of a property or the construction cost of a new building on a given lot. The market approach measures the price payable by a buyer willing and able to carry out a transaction. The income capitalization approach estimates the price of a property based on capitalizing the annual income stream produced. In the income-capitalization approach, a multiplier similar to the price-earnings (P-E) ratio in the stock market is developed. This multiplier is applied to the gross income to produce an appraised value, and is termed the *income multiplier*. The price is developed from a capitalization (cap) rate. The limitations of these procedures are discussed, and alternatives suggested.

One problem with real estate markets is thinness. The number of transactions in particular markets is small. Such incomplete markets increase the problems of accurate estimation of prices and creates the demand for appraisal. With complete markets, there would be no need for appraisal.

## The Basic Problem of Appraisal

The underlying inefficiency of real estate markets creates the need for appraisal. An appraisal is a statement of market price at a point in time, using all available information. Appraisals are procedures to provide information to buyers, as to what is the appropriate price to pay, and to lenders, to determine whether a mortgage can be appropriately secured by the property. With the emergence of secondary mortgage markets, appraisers provide information to holders of securities that the price of the property is appropriate. So powerful has become the requirement to satisfy this secondary market that many appraisals require conformity with guidelines set in advance. These guidelines frequently include the selection of an approved appraiser.

Some problems with appraisal are posed by inflation and its presence or absence: whether regulation of the industry is appropriate; the potential conflict of interest in appraisal; the level of fees; the type of comparable properties; and the interaction with agencies involved in secondary mortgage markets, such as the Federal National Mortgage Association.

In an environment with a high inflation rate, an appraisal at a point in time that is overstated can soon be rendered appropriate. Any error in the initial appraisal underlying the financing is corrected by subsequent price increases. With a reduced rate of inflation, and particularly if there is a decrease in prices, problems arise with appraisals. The appraisal industry benefits from high inflation rates. When inflation rates are high, a given appraisal is more likely to be validated by subsequent events. Conversely, if subsequent inflation rates are negative, high appraisals can cause the mortgage debt to exceed the value of a property. On income property where there is frequently negative cash flow in early years and positive inflation rates are required to achieve target rates of return on which the loan is predicated, positive but low inflation rates can cause appraisal problems.

Appraisal is an occupation not requiring a license for entry. In other real estate or related professions, such as real estate brokerage and the law, state licenses are required. There are costs and benefits of regulation on appraisers. The costs of obtaining an appraisal would increase were there to be increased regulation, as the supply of potential appraisers is reduced. Whether the quality of appraisal would increase depends on the treatment of incumbents and the standards for entry.

Although the appraisal fee is paid by the borrower, there is an incidence problem, in that part can be paid by the lender.[1] If the borrower or developer hires the appraiser, there is a potential conflict of interest. The appraiser can generate a valuation that the employer wants to hear. The degree of research in an appraisal report depends on the fees payable. In a residential appraisal, where fees are relatively low, the appraiser is unable to perform extensive research.

All appraisal requires the collection of data on comparable properties. Sample selection bias is a problem. Some properties have creative financing, to reduce the monthly payment by the borrower, to permit loan qualification. The method by which the seller receives payment for the concessionary financing is through the receipt of a higher price. The higher price must be adjusted downward by comparison with a property where no creative financing is involved. The appraisal must be based on actual transactions prices, not on asking prices.

Liability problems arise with appraisal. An appraisal is only an opinion of value at a point in time. With declining property prices, some lenders face losses on loans. The lenders seeking to recover losses can bring legal actions against the appraisers. A comparative negligence standard can apply, in that an appraiser could be liable for damages only if failure to measure and estimate the prices of characteristics correctly in the original appraisal is provable. An appraiser cannot easily be held liable for a decline in the overall rate of inflation, but could be liable for failing to note potential structural damage and neighborhood change. The risk of default, of absence of security for the loan if property values decline or fail to appreciate at projected rates, is shifted to the mortgage holder. To reduce the risk in holding mortgage holder. To reduce the risk in holding mortgage securities, secondary market packagers, require lenders selling nonperforming loans—where no payments have been made for three months—to buy them back. The default risk is shifted to the originating lender. Wherever the risk is shifted, accurate appraisal attempts to provide a method of minimizing the default risk arising on the specific property. The risk on the borrower is not an appraisal issue.

Underlying all appraisals is the problem of land valuation. Markets for undeveloped land are more incomplete than those for properties. Some markets have few transactions, and some of the transactions may not be at arm's length. In land sales, the seller frequently assumes the financing, or concessionary financing, which requires adjustments in prices. If there are special circumstance, such as foreclosures, estate sales, or public-sector restricted transactions, adjustments are required. There are shortages of vacant land in developed areas, and so comparables are relatively difficult to locate. These problems affect all appraisal procedures.

### Appraisal Information

In valuation and appraisal, the investor requires background information on prices and locations. The information sources vary for different investments. For rental residential real estate, the nature of the apartment, cooperative, or condominium must be verified.

Income data on apartments are published in *Apartments, Condominiums and Cooperatives* (Chicago, IL: Institute of Real Estate Management). This publication collects data on revenues and expenses on residential properties in different locations and provides information on apartments, condominiums, and cooperatives.

For office buildings, the *Office Building Experience Exchange Report* (Washington, DC: Owners and Managers Association International) publishes data on comparable rents and prices for office space and buildings. For the investor, selecting a site across the country requires comparison of alternative locations. The *Site Selection Handbook* (Atlanta, GA: Conway) provides information on industrial parks, and *The Dollars and Sense of Shopping Centers* (Washington, DC: Urban Land Institute) supplies data on shopping centers.

The cost, market, and income capitalization methods of valuation each have advantages and disadvantages, but all suffer from the fundamental problem that statistical inference cannot easily be drawn from them, and that subjectivity is required in estimation. Real estate markets are thin and heterogeneous, and so any appraisal method is likely to lead to errors.

### Cost Approach

The cost approach to valuation is frequently used for the purchase of a new property or building. Costs can be divided between hard and soft costs. Hard costs are direct construction expenditures; soft costs include costs of services such as financing, fees, and permits. The appraisal value from the cost approach is the sum of the hard costs, soft costs, and land costs. The valuation can include a profit markup over costs.

The cost approach to valuation derives from the cost or supply side of real estate and neglects the demand side. The market equilibrium in price occurs where demand and supply are equal. The approach is only valid if the construction is on a specific performance or contract basis, where the owner is willing to pay costs plus a markup. With speculative (spec) construction, where the buyer is not known in advance, using costs of estimate price can be erroneous, and usually leads to overstated appraised values.[2]

The cost approach obtains the production price, not the transaction price. On new construction, the costs can be obtained with facility. On older properties, a depreciation rate must be applied to derive a cost approach appraisal. Another problem with the cost approach is that the builder is assumed to be the most efficient. If a builder is inefficient, with higher than minimum average costs, the procedure overstates appraised value.

In practical application, hard costs include those for excavation and foundation, framing, electrical, plumbing, heating, finishing work, and parking. Soft costs include the services of architects, attorney, and accounting; interest and permit fees; and developer and contractor profits. These costs plus those for land produce the cost appraisal estimate.

On older properties, a depreciation rate is applied to each characteristic. The depreciation rate selected adds a subjective aspect to cost appraisal. For residential property, separate depreciation rates can be applied to the roof, plumbing, wiring, and framing.

### Market Approach

In the market approach, the property is appraised by surveys of comparable properties (comps). The characteristics of the property to be appraised, or subject property, are tabulated. For residential property, characteristics include aspects of location; number, type, and sizes of rooms; dimensions; and construction form. Similar data are collected on the comparables. Usually, in market appraisal three comparables relatively close to subject property and having transacted recently are selected.

The comparables should have no concessionary financing, or if present, information can be included to adjust the price. No arm's length transactions are normally included; prices usually reflect transactions of willing participants.

In the market approach, the data on the three comparables are placed in a spreadsheet or other tabular form. The data on the comparables are averaged on a weighted basis. For owner-occupied dwellings, the selling price, on a square-foot basis, is averaged in weighted form over the comparables.[3] For rental property, both rent and selling price are included.

This average price and rent are initial estimates applicable to subject property. Adjustments are made for the time between the transaction date for subject property and a weighted average of the dates of sale for the comparables. Other adjustments are made for location and differences in characteristics.

In effect, the value of the property is defined as the product of a price and a quantity. The price is of an aggregate unit of housing and a quantity of real estate services. Real estate services are constructed from the quantities of the characteristics, such as for residential housing, bedrooms, bathrooms, and type of construction. A price, or weight, for each of these characteristics must be constructed; this price is subjective. The estimation of quantity is not without subjective problems. The quality of construction, effect of depreciation, and soil conditions are subject to interpretation by different appraisers. Hence, the weighting method can be subjective.

The major problem lies in estimating the price of the characteristics. Suppose subject property has four bedrooms, while each of the three comparables has three. There is a difference of one bedroom, regardless of averaging procedure. What is subjective is the increase in value over the others for having an additional bedroom. The market approach does not have a uniform method of estimating, and the price of a bedroom is based on considerations of the appraiser.

If the difference between subject property and the comparable weighted average for a given characteristic is $\Delta X_i$, and the price is $P_i$, the contribution of $i$ is $P_i \Delta X_i$. Here the level of the characteristics for subject property is $X_{i,s}$ and weighted average over the comparables is $\bar{X}_i$. So the differential is $\Delta X_i = X_{i,s} - \bar{X}_i$. If subject property is better than the weighted average of the comparables $\Delta X_i > 0$. Another subjective consideration arises for the appraiser, for with the small sample size of three, the probability of inaccuracy in estimation is high: the possibility of one large or small observation (outlier) makes the mean subject to unstable estimation. If subject property is better than the weighted average, $\Delta X_i > 0$, and $P_i \Delta X_i > 0$. The sum of all adjustments, including time as one of the characteristics $i = 1, \ldots, I$ is $\Sigma_{i=1}^{I} P_i \Delta X_i$. If $\bar{V}$ is the weighted average price from the comparables, then

$$V = \bar{V} + \sum_{i=1}^{I} P_i \Delta X_i$$

where $V$ is the market-approach appraisal.

### *Issues with the Market Approach*

A number of problems arise with the market approach:

1. Subjectivity on prices: The subjective view of the appraiser is required to determine the prices to use for the characteristics. Such prices vary between appraisers.
2. Subjectivity on weighting on comparables: The appraiser can use any weighting scheme over the comparables. If a simple average is used, the weights are (⅓, ⅓, ⅓). The appraiser has the option of using only one of the comparables, with weights (1, 0, 0).
3. Insufficient sample size: With three observations, there is an insufficient or negative degrees of freedom to estimate the prices for the characteristics. A larger sample size, even if including transactions not in the immediate neighborhood and not in the recent past, provides more degrees of freedom and more accurate estimation of the prices or weights. In industrial or commercial transactions, where markets are thin, it may be infeasible to obtain a large sample size; but for residential transactions, data are readily available. Statistical inference cannot be drawn on a sample size of three. The accuracy of estimates is increased substantially with at least 20, as opposed to 3, degrees of freedom. Degrees of freedom are observations less the number of characteristics.
4. Land values: There remains the problem of appraising the price of land, as with all appraisal techniques.
5. Leveling effects: In the absence of information, there is a tendency in appraisal to update a previous appraisal by a given percentage factor, and to appraise properties at whatever was a last-transaction price for that property, particularly where no recent sales have occurred. This leveling imparts stability and smoothing in asset values, and can miss sudden downturns in real estate markets caused by changes in actual and expected interest rates, inflation, and demand. Market-approach appraisal also tends to neglect strictly financial variables.

Suppose an appraisal of an income producing property is being carried out. (See table 3-1.) In dollars, comparable #1 sells for 1.2 million, comparable #2 sells for 1 million, and comparable #3 sells for 0.8 million. The gross annual rent on a triple-net (net net net or NNN) basis is 0.2 million for the first property, 0.1 million for the second, and 0.12 million for the third property. Tenants pay property taxes, maintenance, and insurance

**Table 3-1. Worksheet for Market-Value Appraisal—Basic Data**

| | *Subject Property* | *Comparables* | | |
|---|---|---|---|---|
| | | *1* | *2* | *3* |
| Sale date (current date less month of sale) | 0 | −4 | −1 | −1 |
| Price (million dollars) | | 1.2 | 1 | 0.8 |
| Gross annual rent (thousand dollars) | | 200 | 100 | 120 |
| Gross square feet (thousand) | 10 | 20 | 15 | 10 |
| Percent leaseable | 80 | 90 | 90 | 90 |
| Price/square foot (gross) | | 60 | 100 | 80 |
| Rent/square foot (dollars) | | 10 | 10 | 12 |
| Proximity (miles to subject property) | | 4 | 5 | 6 |
| Frontage square feet | 120 | 200 | 150 | 250 |
| Parking spaces | 40 | 50 | 60 | 70 |
| Number of floors | 2 | 2 | 2 | 2 |
| Number elevators | 1 | 1 | 1 | 1 |
| Age (years) | 0 | 3 | 4 | 2 |

fees. The areas in thousand square feet are 10, 20, and 15. From these gross square feet of building, the percentage rentable is determined in each case. Both the price and the rent are determined per rentable square foot.

Adjustments are then made for proximity, parking space, number of floors, age, and various characteristics. The price and rent per square foot for the comparables provides the base appraisal. In this particular example, suppose a simple average is used over the comparables on all data. (See table 3-2.)

A list of the differences between subject property and the average of the comparables is made, and the $\Delta X_i$ is obtained by subtraction. At this stage, the market-value appraiser makes estimates as to the prices of each of the characteristics. A typical worksheet for a market appraisal involved obtaining data on the prices and characteristics of three comparables, and the characteristics of subject property. The example data are for a commercial property.

The worksheets (tables 3-1 and 3-2) illustrate some other problems with the application of the market method of appraisal. The averages used for the comparables are constructed as unweighted means, not means weighted by the sizes of the properties. The initial average prices are also unweighted means. The sample size of three for this appraisal has nega-

**Table 3-2. Worksheet for Computation of Market-Value Appraisal**

| | *Subject Property* | *Unweighted Mean Comparable Data* | *Difference* $\Delta X_i$ | *Prices* $P_i$ *Asset* | *Rent* | *Values* $P_i \Delta X_i$ *Asset* | *Rent* |
|---|---|---|---|---|---|---|---|
| Sale date | 0 | −2 | −2 | | | | |
| Price (million dollars) | | 1 | | | | | |
| Gross annual rent (thousand dollars) | | 140 | | | | | |
| Gross square feet (thousand) | 10 | 13.33 | −3.33 | | | | |
| Percent leaseable | 80 | 90 | 10 | | | | |
| Price/square foot (gross) | | 80 | | | | | |
| Rent/square foot (dollars) | | 10.67 | | | | | |
| Proximity (miles to subject property) | | 5 | −5 | 0 | 0 | | |
| Frontage square feet | 120 | 200 | −80 | 0.1 | 0.01 | −8 | −0.8 |
| Parking spaces | 40 | 60 | −20 | 0.2 | 0.02 | −4 | −0.4 |
| Number of floors | 2 | 2 | 0 | 0.1 | 0.05 | 0 | 0 |
| Number elevators | 1 | 1 | 0 | 0.1 | 0.02 | 0 | 0 |
| Age (years) | 0 | 3 | −3 | 0.1 | 0.05 | −0.3 | −0.15 |
| Total adjustments | | | | | | −12.3 | −1.35 |
| Unweighted average estimate | | | | | | 80 | 10.67 |
| Adjusted estimate per square foot | | | | | | 67.7 | 9.32 |

tive degrees of freedom, since there are six characteristics—proximity, frontage, parking spaces, number of floors, number of elevators, and age.

## Income Capitalization Approach

The income capitalization approach is frequently used in the appraisal of income producing property, such as commercial, industrial, or investment residential real estate. Suppose the investor is buying an office building that will be rented. For the present, depreciation and tax-shelter advantages are not considered. The income capitalization method involves three variables, the income produced, the capitalization—cap rate—and the appraised value.

The cap rate is defined as

$$r_e = y/V$$

where $V$ is the value of the property and $y$ is the income produced per period. The value of the property is obtained by rearranging

$$V = y/r_e$$
$$= yG$$

where $G = 1/r_e$ is the income multiplier. The appraised value of the property is the income times the income multiplier. Properties with a low income multiplier cover the investment more rapidly. The cap rate can be compared with rates of return on alternative investments.

One limitation of the procedure is that the cap rate or income multiplier is assumed to be constant over the appraisal period. In practice, the cap rate varies with market interest rates, inflationary expectations, and economic conditions. The cap rate varies over types of property. Properties in high-growth areas, where overall values are expected to increase, tend to have a low cap rate and a high income multiplier. Properties in slow-growing or decaying areas—where the annual income, and not the prospect of capital gains, is the motivating factor in the investment decision—have a high cap rate and low income multiplier. The cap rate varies over types of investments, location, and quality of the real estate. The cap rate is set by the appraiser on the basis of current information on similar properties.

The assumption of stable cap rates also contributes to the leveling effect of appraisal. If cap rates or income multiplier estimates do not change, and the income is predetermined by a long-term lease agreement, typical on commercial and industrial properties, then the appraised values of the asset are stable for real estate. By comparison, financial assets, which are traded regularly on securities markets, are subject to shifts and fluctuation in valuation. The income capitalization method imparts a smoothing to otherwise potentially fluctuating market values.

Another controversy lies in the definition of income to be used for $y$. Gross income, or total revenue received per period, excludes all expenses. Capital gains expected are excluded, but these may be important components of the investment decision. Effective gross income adjusts gross income downward, with an allowance for vacancy and collection costs. Collection costs include bank charges, administrative fees, and legal fees.

Net operating income is another candidate for $y$, being effective gross income less operating costs. Operating costs include labor, materials, utilities, and property taxes incurred for current servicing.

The appraiser determines the annual gross income. This gross income is total rent collections over the year, less an allowance for vacany and collection costs, less operating expenses. In some appraisals, gross income is defined without subtracting operating expenses. From this calculation, the income $y$ for the appraisal is obtained. Operating expenses include personnel, building maintenance, utilities, property management, painting, real estate taxes, and fees. Subtracting operating expenses from gross income less vacancy and collection costs produces net operating income.

Interest expenses are not subtracted, nor are depreciation charges. The argument on interest expenses is that they are not operating expenses, and the cap rate will apply as an effective interest rate. In actual calculation of the rate of return for the investor, as opposed to the appraisal calculation, net operating income is capitalized; and the resulting internal rate of return is compared with the interest rate charged on borrowed funds. If the internal rate of return exceeds the interest rate on borrowed funds, the investment is undertaken. If the investor or corporation has a target rate of return on investments to be undertaken, an adjustment is made for risk and illiquidity.

The pro forma income statement is:

Gross potential income
Less: Vacancy and collection
Equals: Effective gross income

Less: Operating expenses
 Personnel—wages
 Utilities
 Management
 Painting and decorating
 Repairs
 Insurance
 Real estate taxes
Equals: Net operating income

Less: Interest expense
Equals: Net income after interest (before-tax cash flow)

Less: Depreciation permitted for tax purposes
Equals: Income for tax purposes

Less: Income taxes
Equals: Net accounting income
Add: Depreciation tax shield (tax rate times depreciation permitted for tax purposes)
Equals: After-tax cash flow

Economic depreciation, or the rate of actual physical decay and obsolescence of the property, is excluded in the calculation. It could be included by adjusting the allowance for appreciation in the property downwards. The net effect of time includes capital gains net of depreciation. Capital gains are not a cash flow item until a realization, which involves either a sale or a deemed realization through an ownership termination.

Direct interest expenses on loans or mortgages are not the only costs of funds. An opportunity cost of the down payment can be added as a cost, and also the time spent in managerial or supervisory activity on the property. The return on equity should at least cover these last two costs for the investment to be considered.

The income capitalization method does not use present-value calculations, but rather the formula $V = y/r_e$. There are problems with both components, $y$ and $r_e$. The estimation of $r_e$ frequently does not rely on statistical method, but rather on interpolation of current transactions. The calculation of $y$ depends on assumptions regarding the vacancy rate and the cost of collection. It is based on a single period, with current rent. Future rent increases need not occur at current rates of change.

A variant of the income capitalization approach uses a present-value calculation, with the cap rate selected in advance. If the income variable used is $y_t$, in period $t$, and $r_e$ is the cap rate, then

$$V = \sum_{t=1}^{N} \frac{y_t}{(1 + r_e)^t} + \frac{L_N}{(1 + r_e)^N}$$

is the appraised value of the property. Here $L_N$ is the value of the property at time $N$. Some estimate of this value is required, as the sum of the value of the land and the depreciated improvements. If $r_e$ is measured in real terms, net of inflation, and the same rate of inflation applies to land, improvements, and all goods in general, further adjustments for prices are required.

### *Issues with the Income Capitalization Approach*

Using net operating income as $y_t$ in the present-value calculation, or $y$ in the one-period capitalization, implies that variable profit or quasi-rents are used in the calculation. This net operating income does not reflect the return to the owner since depreciation and personal taxes are excluded. Since people have different tax situations, and these affect the expenses chargeable, appraisal on this basis varies with the individual.

As with any long-term investment, income must be projected over an uncertain future. Annuitizing a constant $y$ makes an assumption as to the future course of net incomes. The value of the property, if annual income is constant, is

$$V = A(r_e, N)y + L_N/(1 + r_e)^N$$

where $y$ is constant, $A$ is an annuity, and $L_N$ is the terminal value of the land and improvements.

The current income may not obtain over the long term. The appraisal of $V = y/r_e$ is extremely sensitive to the choice of the cap rate or income multiplier. For a property producing $10,000 in income, and an income multiplier of 8, the appraisal is $80,000. For an income multiplier of 9, the appraisal is $90,000. As interest rates change, the income multiplier can vary substantially.

The above assumes that $r_e$ applies equally to debt and equity. Let $B$ be the debt, or total mortgage and loan balance outstanding. Equity, or property value less debt is $E$; and $r$ is the interest rate on the debt. The project may have favorable below-market financing, so an alternative $r_e$ is

$$r_e = (B/V)r + (E/V)g$$

where $g$ is the return, in alternative activity, on equity. This includes adjustments for risk and liquidity.

Another method of appraisal by the income capitalization method is to impute the equity $E$. The value is

$$V = B + E$$

$$= (B/V)V + E$$

Assume that $B/V$ is a constant, such as 0.8. Then $V = 0.8V + E$. Once $E$ is determined, then $V$ can be appraised. Now

$$E = \sum_{t=1}^{N} \frac{y_t}{(1+g)^t} + \frac{L_N - B_N}{(1+g)^N}$$

where $y_i$ is the net income after interest expense (quasi-rent) and $g$ is the return on equity. The terminal value of land and improvements is $L_N$, and the value of the loan debt outstanding is $B_N$ at date $N$. This return on equity depends on inflationary expectations, the marginal product of capital, risk and liquidity of investment, and taxes and government policies. Further, if $y_i = y$, or the income is constant and the loan-value ratio is constant, at $b$

$$V = bV + yA(g,N) + \frac{L_N - B_N}{(1+g)^N} \quad \text{or} \quad V = \frac{1}{1-b}$$

$$\times \left[ yA(g,N) + \frac{L_N - B_N}{(1+g)^N} \right]$$

is the value of the property. The value of the property is the sum of the capitalized income stream $yA$, where $A$ is the present value of one dollar per period at interest rate $g$ over time period $N$, plus the net equity at the end of the period being considered $N$, discounted at rate $g$. All are multiplied by $(1 - b)^{-1}$, the leverage multiplier. The loan-to-value ratio is $b$, so as $b$ increases, $1 - b$ decreases, and its inverse increases, raising the value of the property. The discount rate $g$ is a real rate of interest, after netting out the rate of expected inflation.

The above appraisal assumes that income is measured net of interest payments, and that the loan balance at $N$, $B_N$, is discounted in an identical manner as the property. The nominal value of the loan does not change with prices, and payments on financing are constant. Let the nominal interest rate, with no adjustment for prices, be $a$, and the rate of inflation be $\rho$. Then

$$V = (1 - b)^{-1}\left[\sum_{t=1}^{N} \frac{y(1 + \rho)^t}{(1 + a)^t} + \frac{L_N(1 + \rho)^N - B_N}{(1 + a)^N} - BA(r,N)\right]$$

is the appraised value of the property using the income capitalization method. The constant mortgage payment is $M$. Income $y$ is measures as before-tax cash flow plus interest payments. If the owner is a tax free of tax-deferred entity, such as a pension fund of insurance company, no taxes enter. The income definition can exclude all depreciation charges. The appraised value of the property is the sum of the discounted income $y$, adjusted by a constant percentage factor for inflation $\rho$, and discounted by the nominal interest rate $a$. The equity in the property at time $N$ is the improvements and land, net of depreciation, but adjusted for inflation, less the loan balance, which is in nominal unadjusted dollars. The interest payments are capitalized using the nominal interest rate.

### Hedonic Approach

The hedonic approach entails a modification of the market approach; it involves collecting a sample of transactions and forming a regression equation to estimate the predicted price. The characteristics of subject property are substituted into the fitted regression equation—the fitted value is the appraised price. The statistical and subjective problems of appraisal are reduced.

Suppose the only characteristic affecting the price of real estate is distance from the central business district (CBD). If all properties were identical, except for distance from the CBD, a gradient can be developed to determine how prices and rents rise or fall with proximity. The distance from the CBD is measured for each property. On the scatter of prices against distance from the CBD, the line most closely fitting the data is fitted. The estimates from this line indicate an objective measure of the effect of distance on prices or rents, termed the rent gradient in the latter case. The relation need not be linear.

The three methods of appraisal have problems. The two most critical are the small sample sizes used in estimation, with three being a typical number used, and the degree of subjectivity in obtaining data and estimates. Statistical method is not without subjectivity, in imposing prior beliefs as to appraised values, and in determining sample selection. Existing procedures involving subjectivity and small sample sizes do not provide mechanisms by which statistical inference can be applied to place confidence intervals around the appraised values. What is required is an appraisal technique using available statistical data. This procedure reduces the likelihood of obtaining two different appraisals from two appraisers. Differences can be narrowed to statistical procedures and selection, as opposed to subjectivity.

The hedonic approach to appraisal requires data on transaction prices and information on characteristics. Using residential property, neighborhood characteristics such as location, school quality, the nature of the police and fire departments, and the crime rate can be included. This approach also includes structural and lot characteristics, financing, and an adjustment for the time of sale. The information is the same as that for the market approach.

The market value of any commodity, including real estate, is the product of a price and quantity. Let the real estate be described by characteristics with levels $X_i, i = 1, \ldots, I$. These characteristics include neighborhood features, the quality of the structure, and financing. If an index of characteristics can be constructed, the real estate index of the property is $Q(X_1, \ldots, X_I)$. The index $Q$ aggregates the characteristics into a category of residential or commercial real estate quality. It is a quantity index, quality adjusted. The quantity of real estate in a given property is a function of the characteristics. The market value $V$ of the property is

$$V = PQ(X_1, \ldots, X_I)$$

where $P$ is the price of one unit of real estate quality. Data on the market selling price are available as $V$; data on the characteristics $X_i$ can be obtained directly. Taking logarithms of both sides,

$$\ln V = \ln P + \ln Q(X_i, \ldots, X_i)$$

If $P$ is the price of one unit of real estate quality, it ought to be constant over properties, and can be viewed as an intercept term in a regression. One specification for the ln $Q$ term is for linearity in the $X_i$ variables, or

$$\ln Q(X) = \sum_{i=1}^{I} \beta_i X_i$$

Data are on the observed transaction value $V$ and the $X_1, \ldots, X_I$, and regression of the market price on the characteristics is determined:

$$\ln V = \beta_0 + \sum_{i=1}^{I} \beta_i X_i + \varepsilon$$

where $\varepsilon$ is an additive error. The estimates of $\beta$ are the prices of the characteristics. The $X_i$ variables can include date of sale, by month if necessary, and characteristics such as frontage square feet, number of floors, number of elevators, age, construction, and landscaping. For each property, data on $X_i$ are known.

The fitted value of the house price is obtained by taking the estimates of the $\beta_i$, which are the estimated prices of the various characteristics, and multiplying these by the corresponding $X_i$ for a given property. If $X_1$ denotes the number of bedrooms, $\beta_1$ is the increase in price, in percentage terms, of adding one more bedroom. If the estimated coefficient for bedrooms is 0.02, a four-bedroom house adds 8 percent to the value of the property.

If the regression estimates of the prices of characteristics are $\bar{\beta}_i$, $i = 1, \ldots, I$, then the fitted value of the price for a property with known characteristics $\bar{X}_i$, $i = 1, \ldots, I$ is

$$\ln \bar{V} = \bar{\beta}_0 + \bar{\beta}_1 \bar{X}_1 + \cdots + \bar{\beta}_I \bar{X}_I$$

Here $\bar{\beta}_0$ is an estimate of $\ln P$, the constant term. Taking the exponential of $\ln \bar{V}$, the predicted, or appraised, value using the hedonic procedure is

$$\bar{V} = \exp\left(\sum_{i=1}^{I} \bar{\beta}_i \bar{X}_i\right)$$

the appraised value of a property with characteristics $\bar{X}$. Suppose the characteristics $\bar{X}$ describe a standard property. For residential housing, the standard house could have three bedrooms, two bathrooms, an attached garage, be 7 years old, and have wood frame construction, among other characteristics; and these are included in $\bar{X}$. Then $\bar{V}$ is the estimated value of a standard house. Such standard houses are frequently priced in various areas to obtain comparisons. Coldwell Banker in the United States and Royal Lepage in Canada both attempt to define a standard house, and to compare prices across cities nationally. The price index, obtained by pricing the standard house at alternative dates 0 and 1 is

$$\frac{\bar{V}_1}{\bar{V}_0} = \frac{\exp\left(\sum_{i=0}^{I} \beta_{i,1}\bar{X}_i\right)}{\exp\left(\sum_{i=0}^{I} \beta_{i,0}\bar{X}_i\right)}.$$

The index is the relative price of the standard house at time 1, as compared with time 0. This is a price index, since the quantity or quality of the house is held constant.

Once the price for a standard house is given or known, a hedonic quality index can be constructed for any other house. Suppose there is another house with characteristics $X_1, \ldots, X_I$. This housc is to be compared with the standard house $\bar{X}_1, \ldots, \bar{X}_I$. Using the prices estimated from the regression equation, the hedonic appraised value is $\Sigma_{i=0}^{I} \bar{\beta}_i X_i$. Then the relative quality of the house, as compared with the standard house, is

$$\frac{\bar{V}_1}{\bar{V}_0} = \frac{\exp\left(\sum_{i=0}^{I} \bar{\beta}_i X_i\right)}{\exp\left(\sum_{i=0}^{I} \bar{\beta}_i \bar{X}_i\right)}$$

This is a quanity or quality index, since the prices are held constant at some date. The ratio of the value of another house to the standard house is an index of the quality of the house. If the ratio is greater than one, the house is of better quality than standard. If the ratio is less than one, the house considered is of lower quality than the standard. The prices of characteristics being used are the same, only the characteristics differ. Hence the ratio is an estimate of $Q$ in index form.

The characteristics of any house can be included as the $X$ variables, and the hedonic appraisal then derived. The use of a standard house permits the construction of a hedonic price index, so that the rate of real estate inflation is obtainable. By pricing the standard house at two different periods of time, a measure of price change is derived, correcting for quality.

There are problems with the hedonic appraisal procedure. Markets for some properties are thin, with insufficient transactions data and few degrees of freedom. The hedonic equation can be misspecified, or have a large error. If the goodness of fit of the regression to the data is poor, there is inaccuracy in predicting the price. Some characteristics may be missing. The missing characteristics, particularly those regarding neighborhood, may be important in determining price. Characteristics—construction quality, for example—can be measured with error. Any appraisal procedure faces these problems.

The missing or mismeasured variables are reflected in the error term. Estimation is more imprecise and the prices are subject to bias if the error contains effects correlated with the measured characteristics. A prediction error arises in estimating the price of the property, reducing the predictive power of the procedure. Market data can be subject to self-selection. Houses on the market may be the ones that trade frequently because they are lower quality and less-well maintained than average. The sample of transacted properties may not be representative of the underlying population. Traded properties overrepresent newer structures, which are on average more expensive and differ in style and characteristics from older properties. The direction of overall bias is unclear. The coefficients for the hedonic model must be regularly updated.

The hedonic procedure also has some advantages. It is not subjective, and does not require appraisers to form individual opinions on prices (of characteristics of properties) without direct procedures for statistical verification. The hedonic method produces a single appraisal of price, rather than three. The relevant price is what a person would be willing to pay for the bundle of the property's characteristics.

## Appraisal of Income Properties

Cost, income capitalization, and market approaches are used in the appraisal of income producing property. The hedonic procedure has advantages for income property, despite thin markets. For the cost approach, there is a possible difference between market prices and the price of replacement, so the latter need not be appropriate. The Tobin $q$-theory of investment is based on the relationship between the price of existing capital assets and the price of replacement construction.[4] As this ratio increases, there is more investment.

Real estate markets have certain characteristics that are distinct from other markets. These characteristics increase the problems of appraisal and valuation of income properties. There is incomplete information in real estate markets, with some individuals as insiders having more than others. There are local restrictions that create monopoly rents for some players. Such restrictions include the requirements for real estate licenses. Real estate licensing differs across jurisdictions, and brokers have relatively little geographical mobility. Other restrictions include zoning, building codes, and access to listings. There is less information for income property than for individual residential property, where there are multiple listing services.

For income producing properties, there is one index of overall price trends. This index is prepared quarterly by the Frank Russell Company of Seattle, for the National Council of Real Estate Investment Fiduciaries. The index maintains a record on all income and expenses, and the transaction prices of 1048 properties owned by institutional investors. The same properties are followed, and the index is published on a quarterly basis. Hence quality differences and heterogeneity problems are minimized. The Russell index provides a benchmark for office buildings. The Russell index covers industrial and office buildings, but not apartments.

There are problems with the overall Russell index. The coverage is limited by the exclusion of apartment buildings. Only a small number of properties actually transact—are bought or sold—during a quarter. Prices for the remainder, for use in constructing the index, are based on appraisals. Evidence on the properties in the Russell index suggest that there is systematic bias in the appraisal. The most recent appraisals understate on average the sales price on an all-cash basis.[5] Appraisals exhibit a large variation in comparison with the transaction prices. Since the majority of price observations in the Russell index are based on appraised prices, the systematic errors and the variation in appraisals cast doubt on the stability and accuracy of the Russell index of industrial and office building property.

An attempt to finesse the appraisal problem arises in the index of overall income property prices published quarterly as the *National Real Estate Index,* by the Liquidity Fund, Inc., Emeryville, California. The Liquidity index is constructed by obtaining information from institutional buyers and sellers. The same properties are not covered from period to period on a transaction basis. The appraisal problem is removed, but there may be a problem of self-selection or sampling bias in the actual properties entering the market, in the willingness to participate in the sample, and in the properties selected. Apartments are covered, but not industrial property. Since the sample and data are confidential, outside verification of prices is not possible.

Appraisals on income producing properties tend to be biased toward stability through the leveling effect. There is a tendency in appraising to apply the previous estimate, if information in unknown, or the previous estimate plus an add-on for inflation. With the income and expenses also increasing at similar rates, it appears that the rate of return to holding real estate investments is relatively stable, and exhibits a low variance. The price of the real estate asset remains not determined by market factors, but by appraisal.

By comparison with physical real estate, the prices of financial assets such as stocks and bonds are not determined by appraisal, but by markets. Even if a firm has a smooth increase in earnings per share, its stock price, and hence rate of return, can fluctuate widely. The appraisal process in real estate may impose an artificial smoothing, and hence a dampened variance, of the actual rate of return in real estate holding.

## Concluding Remarks

There are three conventional methods for appraisal and valuation of property—the income capitalization, cost, and market approaches. If the sample size for an appraisal procedure produces few or negative degrees of freedom, the statistical reliability is questionable. The use of statistical procedures in the hedonic method of appraisal, once the characteristics of a property are known, removes many of the sampling problems.

For residential property, particularly single-family dwellings, there is a large sample size of transactions available; and the prediction of prices is feasible. For commercial and industrial property, the sample size is smaller; and data can be more difficult to collect. Yet even here, there are potential gains for the improvement of statistical technique.

All conventional appraisal methods require subjective guesses on the part of the appraiser as to the comparability of subject property. These procedures create the potential for error, and liability problems. The use of statistical method produces more objective estimates, which can more readily be corroborated. The assembly of data bases on real estate transactions facilitates application of the statistical procedures.

All three of the approaches are applied in appraisal of a given property. The cost approach is applied to new structures, the market approach to residential and sometimes commercial properties, and the income capitalization approach to income producing properties. The cost approach give the highest appraisal of the three. If the three procedures produce different estimates, one must be selected. Some weighted average of the three is used in practice, such as taking the median estimate, where the highest and lowest count with zero weights. An averaging compounds the problems with conventional appraisal. An accurate appraisal of price ought to be independent of the procedure used. The market approach, by using observed data, should dominate. In small samples, appraisers are obliged to rely on the income and cost approaches.

## Notes

1. The appraisal fee acts as a tax. The cost of completing a transaction is increased, and so the demand for transactions shifts downward. The point at which the supply and demand for transactions is equal determines the equilibrium number. The allocation between the borrower and the lender depends on the elasticities of the demand and supply functions for transactions.

2. The cost method may not always overstate the price, particularly if there has been substantial inflation during the construction period.

3. The weighted average is included to cover the various alternatives applied in practical appraisal. Subjectively, a simple average can be used, or any combination of information on the three comparables.

4. Tobin [1969]. The existence of such a theory suggests that the ratio of existing prices to replacement costs, the latter being the cost appraisal estimate, need not be equal to one, and can be above or below one.

5. Miles [1986]. The overall understatement of the most recent appraisal, as compared with the transaction price on an all cash basis is 9.5 percent. The appraisal on some property differed from the actual transaction price by as much as 25 percent in the largest absolute value case. It is argued that appraisal error is partly responsible, in that the market had shifted without the appraiser being aware of it.

# II FINANCING

# 4 INTEREST RATES, FINANCING, AND MORTGAGE MULTIPLIERS

## Introduction

This chapter examines the issue of financing, including the comparison of costs across lenders. Real estate loan payments frequently entail constant dollar amounts per period. Annuity formulas are applied directly in the computation of mortgage payments. Each mortgage payment is a blend of principal and interest. In a mortgage, the borrower is liquidating an investment. A sinking fund is the reverse of a mortgage. The objective is to build up a fund to achieve a certain sum at a given future date.

Real interest rates are defined as nominal (or contract) interest rates, less the rate of change of some price index. A historical observation is that the differential between interest rates on long-term government bonds and the rate of inflation, as measured by the Consumer Price Index, is approximately 3 percent annually. This observation gives rise to the Fisher [1930] theory of interest, that real interest rates are constant. The expected rate of inflation is inferred by subtracting a constant real rate of interest from the current nominal interest rate. There remain problems of determining the appropriate interest rate to be used. Long-term interest rates on government bonds, mortgages, and corporate bonds need not move in tandem. Mortgages entail more risks to the lender, because an individual homeowner or corporation has less security than a government. Bonds issued by the federal government are usually not subject to recall or refinancing. The differential between long-term interest rates and the rate of inflation is not stable. Nominal interst rates move with expected inflation rate changes. The expected inflation rate determines the prospects for increases in the price of a property, in rents, and in operating expenses. If the expected rate of inflation is $E(\pi)$, and the nominal contract interest rate is $r$, then under the Fisher theory

$$r^* = r + E(\pi)$$

where $r^*$ is the real rate of interest. Since $r$ is observed, and $r^*$ is arguably constant, the expected rate of inflation can be inferred as

$$E(\pi) = r - r^*$$

This equation makes no adjustment for taxes, though the effective tax rate applicable to a holder of a long-term security varies. Some institutions, such as pension funds, insurance companies, and investment funds distributing a large percentage of income, face no taxes. Individuals and corporations face positive tax rates. If taxes are included, a higher nominal interest rate is required to obtain a given after-tax return.

The stability of the real rate of return to capital $r^*$ is unclear. Capital is heterogeneous; and rate of return, and the probability of attaining a given return, varies between real estate and other investments. Real estate constitutes only a portion of total capital, which includes equipment, structures, inventory on the physical side. There are other fianncial investments in securities available in the economy. Hence it is possible for the real rate of return to capital to be low or negative, while that for real estate is high, and vice versa.

Some factors, such as inflationary expectations and energy price increases, cause substitution of structures and real estate for machinery and equipment, within the aggregate capital stock. Investment tax credits and accelerated depreciation provisions tend to favor an increase in the equipment-structures ratio. As a specific example, energy is required to power equipment, but is not required for land, or the requirement is low. If energy prices increase relative to prices in general, the demand for equipment falls, and existing equipment is more costly to operate and consequently less productive. With a lower marginal productivity of capital, and with equipment constituting most of capital, real interest rates decline, and can become negative. Property investors are facing the same capital market with reduced or negative real interest rates and returns unaffected by such a crisis. If real estate is an inflationary hedge, the returns can be enhanced. It is unclear whether the Fisher theory is applicable in general, or to real estate investments in particular.

Historical data indicate that there have been fluctuations in the differential between the rate of return on long-term government bonds and the rate of inflation, though there is controversy as to whether the constant real rate theory is invalidated. There have been periods where long-term interest rates are below the rate of inflation, and others where long-term interest rates are more than 3 percentage points above the rate of inflation. Such differences have substantial impacts in planning real estate investments.

A general increase in prices has a neutral effect only if all prices increase proportionately. There are redistributive effects of inflation, as relative prices are not constant. The real rate of return is not unaffected by inflation. There are resource costs of inflation, such as the transactions costs of reprinting price lists, and litigation over honoring fixed price contracts.

## Interest Rates and Mortgage Multipliers

There has been variation in measured real rates of interest, and negative real rates have been observed. In principle, real rates of interest should be positive. There is a resource cost in borrowing money. A positive interest rate arises because the future is uncertain and the present is certain, and a positive real interest rate compensates for risk.

The initial discussions of interest rates are for real and positive rates of interest. Inflation is considered subsequently. An investor prefers one dollar today versus one dollar tomorrow, and must be paid to defer today's dollar of consumption. The discount rate is the real interest rate used to construct present values of future dollars of consumption. Discount rates vary between investors. Individuals, with finite lives, are likely to have higher discount rates than corporations, with infinite lives.[1] The discount rate used affects the decision to carry out a project.

### *Future Value*

In determining interest received on a deposit, let $r$ be the real rate of interest, net of inflation, $N$ be the number of periods a deposit is held, and $B$

be the balance on deposit. Suppose a depositor has placed $B$ in a depository institution, such as a bank. Interest is received on a compounded basis. Compound interest is the effect of earning interest on interest. Deposits are assumed made at the beginning of the period, and interest is assumed paid or received at the end. For mortgages, the typical first payment is at the end of the first period. The balance on deposit at the end of $N$ years, here years, is

$$B_N = B(1 + r)^N \tag{4.1}$$

Interest can be compounded more than once yearly. Let $k$ be the frequency of compounding per year, where $k \geqslant 1$. The loan balance at time $N$ is

$$B_N = B(1 + r/k)^N \tag{4.2}$$

where $N$ is the number of periods, the product of the number of years $T$, and the number of compoundings per year $k$. Here $N = Tk$. If $k = 12$, compounding is monthly, and if $k = 365$, then compounding is daily. The balance at the end of the year, with $k$ payments per year is

$$B_k = B(1 + r/k)^k$$

The effective annual yield $r_e$ on the investment is

$$\begin{aligned} r_e &= (B_k - B)/B \\ &= B_k/B - 1 \\ &= (1 + r/k)^k - 1 \end{aligned} \tag{4.3}$$

Some compounding procedures include 365-day years and 360-day years divided into 12 months of 30 days each. Monthly compounding on one dollar at 6 percent annually produces

$$\begin{aligned} r_e &= (1 + r/k)^k - 1 \\ &= (1 + 0.06/12)^{12} - 1 \\ &= 0.061677 \end{aligned}$$

Once annual compounding produces

$$\begin{aligned} r_e &= (1 + r/k)^k - 1 \\ &= (1 + 0.06)^1 - 1 \\ &= 0.06 \end{aligned}$$

The differential between monthly and once-annual compounding is 0.061677 − 0.06 = 0.001677. The yield is higher the more frequent is the compounding. The balance $B_N$ is a future value (or the balance at some date subsequent) for a deposit at the initial date in time. Future values have a subscript for future date in time.

### *Present Value*

Individuals have a time preference for current as opposed to future consumption. Figure 4–1 indicates consumption of goods or services today, $x_1$,

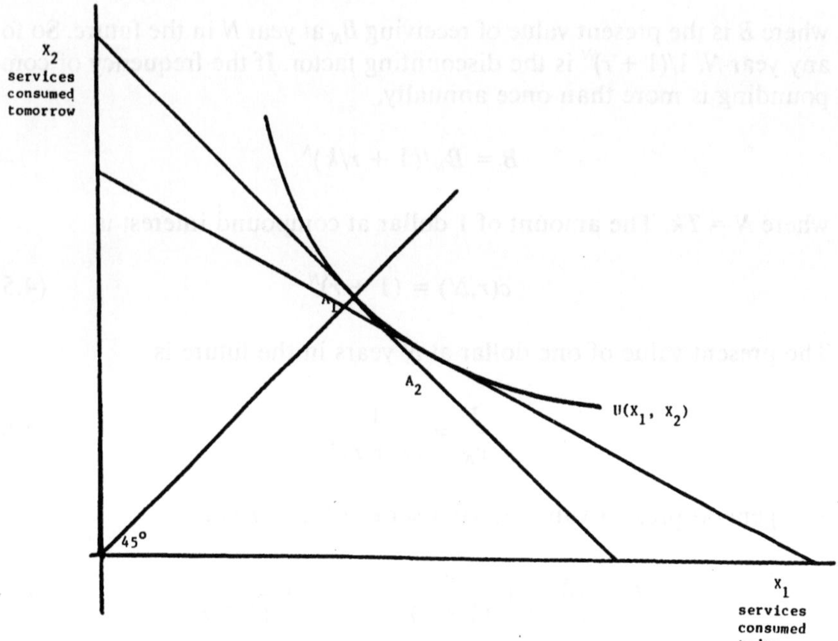


Figure 4–1. Consumption Choices

and goods or services tomorrow, $x_2$. A combination of the two has a level of utility indicated by the indifference curve $u(x_1,x_2)$, which is tangent to the 45° line if current and future consumption are perfect one-for-one substitutes. Otherwise there is a bias toward the present. The bias toward the present arises even if there is no inflation, although positive inflation increases this tendency. Capital markets are imperfect, as is the future. Individuals prefer certainty or current consumption to uncertain future consumption. There is risk of not surviving into the future. For these reasons, the real interest rate $r$ can be expected to be positive.

The present value is the value at current date of a balance or series of incomes over the future. The present value requires an interest rate for discounting the future. Present value compares payments or receipts made over a future time period with payments or receipts made today. An interest or discounting rate is required. One dollar in the future is worth less than it is today. Discounting is the inverse of compounding. Rearranging (4.1),

$$B = B_N/(1 + r)^N \tag{4.4}$$

where $B$ is the present value of receiving $B_N$ at year $N$ in the future. So for any year $N$, $1/(1 + r)^N$ is the discounting factor. If the frequency of compounding is more than once annually,

$$B = B_N/(1 + r/k)^N$$

where $N = Tk$. The amount of 1 dollar at compound interest is

$$c(r,N) = (1 + r)^N \tag{4.5}$$

The present value of one dollar at $N$ years in the future is

$$\frac{1}{c_N} = \frac{1}{(1 + r)^N} \tag{4.6}$$

The general present value is, for a series of incomes $y_i$,

$$P = \frac{y_1}{1 + r} + \frac{y_2}{(1 + r)^2} + \cdots + \frac{y_N}{(1 + r)^N} \tag{4.7}$$

if the interest rate is constant. The internal rate of return is the interest rate $r$ which sets the present value to zero. It is solved by iteration. If the present value is negative for a given $r$, then $r$ is reduced and tried again. If the present value is positive, $r$ is increased. As the interest rate increases in $r$, the present value $P$ decreases. The discounting of future returns is greater because of the higher interest rate. As the term for number of years increases, the present value $N$ increases, for there are more years to discount.

### *Annuity—Present Value*

An annuity is a payment stream of equal constant amounts. A fixed rate and payment mortgage (FRPM) is an annuity. Consider a payment of one dollar per period. A mortgage agreement has been signed providing for the payment of one dollar this year, one dollar next year, and one dollar annually up to $N$ years. The borrower wants to determine the value at date of agreement (the present value) of the mortgage payments. Once the present value of a one dollar per year annuity is determined, it is multiplied by the amount of any annuity.

An annuity involves the payment of one dollar per period. If the period of payment is $t = 1, \ldots, N$, the present value of an annuity of one dollar is

$$\begin{aligned} A(r,N) &= \frac{1}{1+r} + \frac{1}{(1+r)^2} + \cdots + \frac{1}{(1+r)^N} \\ &= \sum_{t=1}^{N} \frac{1}{(1+r)^t} \end{aligned} \tag{4.8}$$

The formula for an annuity is alternatively expressed. If the annuity $A(r,N)$ is as in (4.8), adding one year gives

$$A(r,N+1) = \frac{1}{1+r} + \frac{1}{(1+r)^2} + \cdots + \frac{1}{(1+r)^{N+1}} \tag{4.9}$$

Multiplying both sides by $(1 + r)$

$$(1+r)A(r,N+1) = 1 + \cdots + \frac{1}{(1+r)^N} \tag{4.10}$$

Subtracting (4.9) from (4.10)

$$rA(r,N+1) = 1 - \frac{1}{(1+r)^{N+1}} \tag{4.11}$$

whereupon

$$A(r,N+1) = \left(\frac{1}{r}\right)\left[1 - \frac{1}{(1+r)^{N+1}}\right] \tag{4.12}$$

or

$$A(r,N) = \frac{1 - 1/(1+r)^N}{r} \tag{4.13}$$

The present value of an annuity at interest rate $r$ and term, or number of years $N$ is $A(r,N)$. As $N$ becomes large, the term $1/(1 + r)^N$ becomes smaller, and in the limit, and $N$ tends to positive infinity $A(r,N)$ tends to $1/r$. An approximate estimate of the capital value of an annuity over the long term is the inverse of the interest rate. This annuity provides the justification for the use of a capitalization rate, or cap rate, in real estate analysis, as the interest rate $r$. The value of a property, as in one version of the income capitalization approach to appraisal, is the product of the annual net income and the cap rate. As $r$ increases, $A$ decreases, since the future is being discounted more heavily. As $N$ increases, $A$ increases, since there are more periods over which payment is made.

An annuity permits the calculation of future returns for a constant payment. Suppose the cost of an investment today is $C$, and the return is $y$ per period. The investment has a positive net present value at interest rate $r$ over $N$ years if

$$yA(r,N) - C > 0 \tag{4.14}$$

This criterion, positive net present value, is applied to test the feasibility of an investment. In real estate investments, the interest rate is locked in typically for the long term.

### *Mortgage Multiplier*

Annuities permit mortgage payments to be determined. A standard instrument is a fixed rate and payment mortgage (FRPM) contract, at a given interest rate and term, such as 15 or 30 years on residential contracts. The borrower is obliged to make payments of a constant number of dollars per month, for 360 months on the 30 year contract. The frequency of compounding here $k = 12$ is part of the standard contract.

With a constant payment over a given period of time, at an initially stipulated and constant interest rate, the payments on a FRPM constitute an annuity. The monthly payments over the term of the loan must liquidate the initial loan balance.

If the annuity is annual with payment $M$, then

$$MA(r,N) = B \tag{4.15}$$

or the mortgage payment multiplied by the annuity is equal to the initial balance. For frequency of compounding other than once annually, $k$ times per year, and $N = Tk$,

$$A(r/k,N) = \frac{1 - 1/(1 + r/k)^N}{r/k} \tag{4.16}$$

is the present value of a series of payments for $N$ periods at $r$ percent annually.[2] For the typical mortgage, the borrower knows the initial loan balance $B$, the contract interest rate $r$, and the term $T$, with $k$ the frequency of compounding per year. The borrower calculates the annuity of the mortgage from (4.16), and knows the balance, but the monthly periodic payment $M$ must be determined.

The monthly payment is

$$\begin{aligned} M &= \frac{B}{A(r/k,N)} \\ &= m(r/k,N)B \end{aligned} \tag{4.17}$$

where

$$\begin{aligned} m(r/k,N) &= \frac{1}{A(r/k,N)} \\ &= \frac{r/k}{1 - (1 + r/k)^{-N}} \end{aligned} \tag{4.18}$$

is the mortgage multiplier, or the amount converting one dollar of loan balance at the given interest rate, frequency of compounding, and term, into the periodic payment. For a FRPM of 30-year term, interest rate 12 percent annually, and monthly compounding

$$m = \frac{\frac{0.12}{12}}{1 - \frac{1}{(1 + 0.12/12)^{30\times 12}}} = \frac{0.01}{1 - \frac{1}{(1.01)^{360}}} = 0.010286125 \qquad (4.19)$$

The mortgage multiplier is increasing in the interest rate $r$, increasing in the frequency of compounding $k$, and decreasing in the term $N$.[3]

### *Annuity—Future Value*

The payment of one dollar per period accumulates to form the future value of an annuity, over a given term. Let $A_N$ be the value at date $N$ of an annuity of one dollar per period over $N$ periods. If $r$ is the annual interest rate, the deposit of one dollar per year over $N$ years produces

$$A_N(r,N) = 1 + (1 + r) + (1 + r)^2 + \cdots + (1 + r)^{N-1} \qquad (4.20)$$

The dollar is deposited at the beginning of the period. Interest is not earned until the end of the period, it is credited to the account, and another dollar added at the end. The $N$ periods cover the first period, where no interest is paid—even if earned—until the end of the period, and an additional $N - 1$ period where a one-dollar deposit per period is made.

In the first year, interest is earned at rate $r$ on the initial one-dollar deposited. In the second year, another dollar is added, and the initial account earns interest at rate $r$. The future value of an annuity is used to determine the balance at retirement, if a constant dollar amount per period is deposited in a pension account, where the individual is guaranteed to receive a constant $r$ percent interest rate annually.

If the future value of an annuity holds for $N$ periods, it applies for $N - 1$ years or

$$A_{N-1}(r,N - 1) = 1 + (1 + r) + \cdots + (1 + r)^{N-2} \qquad (4.21)$$

measured at the beginning of the first year. Multiplying (4.21) by $(1 + r)$,

$$(1 + r)A_{N-1}(r,N - 1) = (1 + r) + \cdots + (1 + r)^{N-1} \qquad (4.22)$$

Subtracting (4.21) from (4.22), then

$$rA_{N-1}(r,N-1) = (1+r)^{N-1} - 1 \tag{4.23}$$

Dividing by the interest rate $r$,

$$A_{N-1}(r,N-1) = [(1+r)^{N-1} - 1]/r \tag{4.24}$$

whereupon, altering $N-1$ to $N$,

$$A_N(r,N) = [(1+r)^N - 1]/r \tag{4.25}$$

Then $A_N(r,N)$ is the future value of an annuity. This future value is the compounded value of one per period over $N$ years. The annuity is paid once annually. If the frequency of compounding is not once annually, with $N = Tk$, and $k$ not equal to one, then

$$A_N(r/k,N) = [(1+r/k)^N - 1]/(r/k) \tag{4.26}$$

The total future value of a periodic payment of $M$ per period for $N$ future periods is, at date $N$,

$$B_N = MA_N(r/k,N) \tag{4.27}$$

where $M$ is the periodic payment, at annual interest rate $r$. Suppose an investor places \$2000 once annually in a pension account investing in long-term securities, with a guaranteed interest rate of 12 percent annually. The investor is aged 30, and wants to know the balance at age 65. The balance is

$$\begin{aligned} B_{35} &= \left(\frac{(1+0.12)^{35} - 1}{0.12}\right) \times 2000 \\ &= 863{,}326.99 \end{aligned} \tag{4.28}$$

In real estate investments, future values of annuities are applied in determining the balance outstanding on a mortgage if it is repaid prior to term. Since the great majority of mortgages are prepaid, when a property is refinanced or sold, a future-value calculation is required to determine the loan balance at this prepayment date. Mortgage payments are a blend of principal and interest. Only interest is a deductible expense, for either the owner occupier or investor. The future value of an annuity determines the loan balance each month, which will permit accurate calculation of interest expense and separation of payments between interest and principal for tax planning and reporting.

### *Loan Balance*

The initial loan balance on a mortgage amount $B$ is to be liquidated over the term $N$ by periodic payments of principal and interest. The future value of an annuity at a future date $t$, at frequency of annual compounding $k$ and annual interest rate $r$ is

$$A_t(r/k,t) = [(1 + r/k)^t - 1]/(r/k) \qquad (4.29)$$

Periods are measured by $t$, the product of years completed, including fractions of a year, and frequency of compounding per year.

Now $A_t$ is the cumulative sum of an annuity of one dollar paid periodically at frequency $k$ per year, for $t$ periods or

$$A_t = 1 + (1 + r/k) + (1 + r/k)^2 + \cdots + (1 + r/k)^{t-1} \qquad (4.30)$$

In the first period one dollar is paid, and no interest accumulates until the end of the payment period. At the second payment date, another dollar is paid, and interest at rate $r/k$ is added on. There are $t - 1$ payments involving interest, and one, the first, where only an annuity payment is made, for a total of $t$ payments.

If $t$ were equal to $N$, the total number of periods of payment, the loan balance would be completely repaid. The ratio $A_t/A_N$ is the fraction of the loan balance paid off at time $t$. On a 30-year term, with monthly compounding, the loan balance paid off after 30 months is $A_{30}/A_{360}$. The fraction of balance unpaid is

$$b_t = 1 - A_t/A_N \qquad (4.31)$$

At the end of the loan term, at $N, A_t = A_N$ and $b_t = 0$, that is, the outstanding mortgage balance has been completely discharged. The denominator $A_N$ is constant in the calculations. At the beginning of the loan term, $A_t = 0$, as no balance has been repaid, and $b_t = 1$. Hence $b_t$ exhibits a path decreasing from 1 to 0 over the period of the mortgage. At the beginning of the mortgage term, payments are largely interest as opposed to principal; and the balance unpaid, $b_t$, declines slowly over time. As the mortgage nears the end of the term, principal repayments account for a larger proportion of the total and $b_t$ declines rapidly.

The fraction $b_t$ is the balance outstanding on a FRPM of contract interest rate $r$, compounded with annual frequency $k$, and term $T$ in years, after $t$ periods, per one dollar initially borrowed. The number of payments to be made is $N = Tk$. The total dollar amount outstanding after $t$ payment periods is

$$\begin{aligned} B_t &= b_t B \\ &= (1 - A_t/A_N)B \end{aligned} \tag{4.32}$$

The loan balance can consequently be calculated directly for any interest rate, frequency of compounding, future period before term $t$, and total number of payments.

### Sinking Fund

The calculations thus far are based on an initial present-loan balance $B$ at the present time. There are occasions in real estate financing where a given future balance must be achieved. A real estate agreement can specify a purchase price of a property at some date in the future. A long-term lease can specify a purchase option at a particular price. A fixed payment each period is made, to liquidate a loan at some date in the future, as opposed to a current balance. A sinking fund calculation involves the making of a payment over $N$ periods to liquidate a balance $B_N$.

Suppose the payment is made once annually, and the loan balance to be liquidated, or sunk, is $B_N$ at date $N = Tk$. With $k = 1$, a fixed once per year payment is $M$ and the payments receive annual interest rate $r$. Then

$$M \sum_{t=1}^{N} (1 + r)^t = B_N \tag{4.33}$$

with compound interest accruing on the payment. The payment $M$ is to liquidate a future balance. The investor knows the future balance requirement $B_N$, the interest rate $r$, and the number of payments $N$, and also knows that the frequency of compounding is once annually. The first interest payment is at the end of the period. Financial institutions operate with interest payments on deposits made at the end of the deposit term, and loan interest paid at the end of the period. The required payment is

$$M = B_N / \sum_{t=1}^{N} (1 + r)^t$$
$$= S(r,N)B_N \tag{4.34}$$

where

$$S_N(r,N) = 1/[1 + (1 + r) + (1 + r)^2 + \cdots + (1 + r)^{N-1}]$$
$$= 1/A_N(r,N) \tag{4.35}$$
$$= r/[(1 + r)^N - 1]$$

is the sinking fund multiplier. The sinking fund multiplier is the amount of periodic payment required to liquidate one dollar of loan balance at future date $N$, given interest rate $r$. The periodic payment $M$ is the product of the balance and the sinking fund multiplier. The sinking fund multiplier over period $N$ is the inverse of the future value of an annuity valued at date $N$.

If the frequency of compounding is not annual, then $N = Tk$, and $k$ is not one, so

$$S_N(r/k,N) = \frac{r/k}{(1 + r/k)^N - 1} \tag{4.36}$$

is the sinking fund multiplier. The sinking fund factor converts a future value to a constant periodic payment.

### *Installment*

The sinking fund multiplier is used to construct the installment to amortize one dollar. This installment is the product of the accumulation of one dollar per period, or the future value, $(1 + r)^N$ for once-annual compounding and the sinking fund multiplier. The installment is

$$i(r,N) = (1 + r)^N S_N(r,N)$$
$$= \frac{r(1 + r)^N}{(1 + r)^N - 1} \tag{4.37}$$

For frequency of compounding more than once per year, $N = Tk, k > 1$, is

$$i(r/k,N) = \frac{(1 + r/k)^N}{(1 + r/k)^N - 1} \tag{4.38}$$

## Summary of Formulas

The various formulas can be summarized, at constant annual interest rate $r$, and term $T$ in years, with frequency of compounding $k$, with $N = Tk$. In the first instance, $k = 1$, and compounding is annual. In the second instance, $k$ is arbitrary. In practical application, $k > 1$, and $N = Tk$ as before. For monthly compounding, $k = 12$, and for twice a month compounding on a 12-month, 30-day per month year, $k = 24$.

### *Present and Future Value*

The future values of one dollar at compound interest are

$$c_N = (1 + r)^T \quad \text{and} \quad c_N = (1 + r/k)^N$$

The present values of one dollar are

$$z = \frac{1}{(1 + r)^T} \quad \text{and} \quad z = \frac{1}{(1 + r/k)^T}$$

The future values of one collar per period are

$$A_N(r,N) = \frac{(1 + r)^N - 1}{r} \quad \text{and} \quad A_N(r/k,N) = \frac{(1 + r/k)^N - 1}{r/k}$$

### *Sinking Fund Multiplier*

The sinking fund multipliers to liquidate a balance of one dollar at time $N$ are

$$S_N(r,N) = 1/A_N$$

$$= \frac{r}{(1 + r)^N - 1}$$

and

$$S_N(r/k,N) = \frac{r/k}{(1 + r/k)^N - 1}$$

### *Annuity and Mortgage Multiplier*

The present values of an annuity of one are

$$A(r,N) = \frac{1 - (1 + r)^{-N}}{r} \quad \text{and} \quad A(r/k,N) = \frac{1 - (1 + r/k)^{-N}}{r/k}$$

The mortgage multipliers converting a loan of one dollar into a periodic payment are

$$m(r,N) = 1/A(r,N)$$

$$= \frac{r}{1 - (1 + r)^{-N}}$$

and

$$m(r/k,N) = \frac{r/k}{1 - (1 + r/k)^{-N}}$$

The constant periodic payments to amortize an initial loan of $B$ at interest rate $r$ and term $N$ are

$$M(r,N) = m(r,N)B \quad \text{and} \quad M(r/k,Nk) = m(r/k,Nk)B$$

The balances outstanding on a loan, per one of balance, at time $t < N$ are

$$b_t = 1 - \frac{A_t(r,t)}{A_N(r,N)} \quad \text{and} \quad b_t = 1 - \frac{A_t(r/k,t)}{A_N(r/k,N)}$$

The installments to amortize the future value of one-at-time $N$ are

$$i(r,N) = (1 + r)^N S_N(r,N) \quad \text{and} \quad i(r/k,N) = (1 + r/k)^N S_N(r/k,N)$$

## Notes

1. This is not a universal proposition. Some corporations can have a pressure to perform in current financial statements, because of accounting regulations, lender insistence, institutional investor holdings, or management with a high discount rate.

2. The actuarial method, rather than the United States rule, is used to calculate the multipliers. Either method can be used by the lender.

3. These results are derived in the appendix to chapter 5.

# 5 FIXED RATE AND PAYMENT MORTGAGE (FRPM)

## Introduction

The fixed rate mortgage provides for the payment of an annuity over the term. The mortgage payment is the product of the mortgage multiplier and the initial loan balance. The mortgage multiplier is the inverse of the present value of an annuity at a given interest rate and term, with a specified frequency of compounding. Included in the calculation are fees charged by the lender—for points, loan and origination fees, and prepayment penalties.

Points are prepaid interest charges, paid at the beginning of the loan term. The lender subtracts the points at the beginning to increase the yield on the mortgage. Points are charged as a transaction barrier, to discourage borrowers on FRPMs from refinancing as interest rates decline. By increasing the yield to the lender, the investment becomes more attractive. For the individual borrower, points are deductible in computing individual taxable income on certain types of transactions.[1]

The effect of points is to alter the mortgage multiplier. The mortgage multiplier for a loan at interest rate $r$ annually, with frequency of compounding $k$, and term $T$ in years is $m(r/k,kT)$. The effective mortgage multiplier inclusive of points but no other lender-imposed charges is $m_e = m/(1 - p)$, where $p$ is the rate of points charged. If 2 points are charges on the loan, then $p = 2/100 = 0.02$. The effective mortgage multiplier permits the comparison of alternative FRPMs.

The lender advances a loan balance to the borrower to finance a real estate transaction. The sources and uses of cash for the lender involve a disbursement (payment) of cash flow out at the beginning of the period. During the term of the mortgage, cash flow in arises from the receipt of periodic payments. At the end of the ownership period of the borrower, typically less than the term of the loan, a balloon payment is due. The borrower has the reverse cash-flow statement. At the beginning of the loan, cash flow in represents the receipts from the mortgage. During the loan term, payments are made, representing cash flow out. The effective interest rate on the mortgage equates the present value of cash flow in for the lender from periodic payments and the lump-sum balloon payment with the initial amount disbursed. The effective interest rate on the mortgage provides a criterion as to whether a loan is too expensive, by comparison with a target cost of borrowed funds. Such an effective interest rate can be derived dependent on all the parameters of the FRPM, including the interest rate, frequency of compounding, term, points, prepayment penalty, and fees.

### FRPM Payment Calculation

The FRPM is the basic mortgage contract. A contract annual interest rate $r$, and periodic, usually monthly, payment $M$ are made, with $N = Tk$ payments, over amortization period $N$, where $T$ is the term of the loan in years, and $k$ the annual frequency of compounding.

The mortgage payment is, for once-annual frequency of compounding,

$$M = m(r,N)B \tag{5.1}$$

where

$$m(r,N) = \frac{r}{1 - (1 + r)^{-N}} \tag{5.2}$$

is the mortgage multiplier. If the frequency of compounding is not once annual, but at some other rate $k$, the periodic, or frequency $k$ mortgage multiplier is

$$m(r/k,N) = \frac{r/k}{1-(1+r/k)^{-N}} \tag{5.3}$$

As $k$ increases, the mortgage multiplier increases. As $N$ increases, the mortgage multiplier decreases; and as $r$ increases, the mortgage multiplier increases.[2]

For a typical FRPM contract, where $N = 30$ and $k = 12$, the mortgage multiplier is

$$m(r/12, 360) = (r/12)/\left[1 - \frac{1}{(1+r/12)^{360}}\right] \tag{5.4}$$

As $r$ increases, the payment multiplier increases.

The mix of payment between principal and interest is indicated in figure 5-1. On the vertical axis is the periodic payment $M$, and on the horizontal axis the term. At the beginning of the mortgage term, the

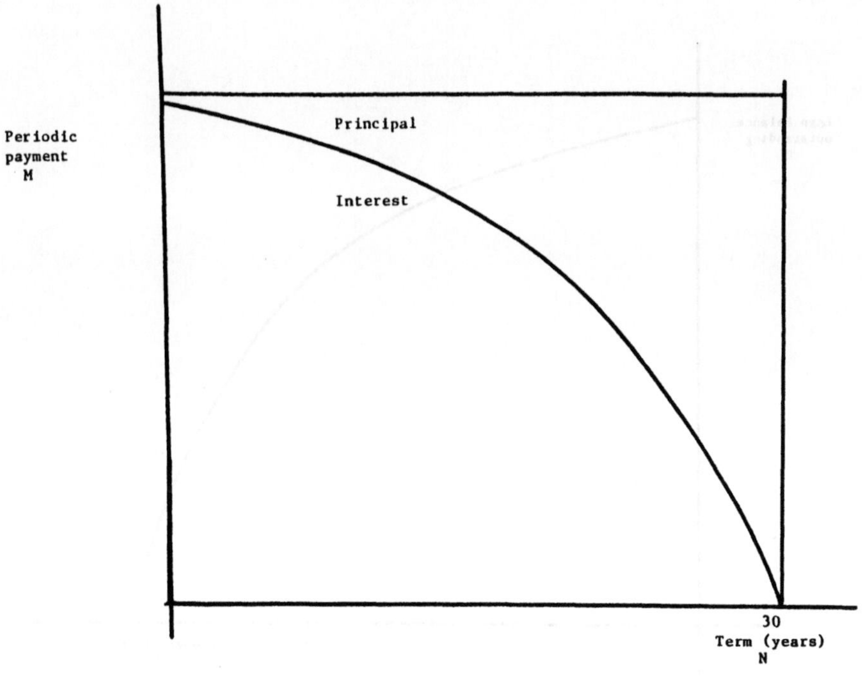


Figure 5-1. Composition of Monthly Payments

payments are almost all interest; at the end, they are almost all principal. The loan balance over time is indicated in figure 5-2. As the number of payments $N$ increases, the loan balance decreases. The table 5-1 is an indicator of loan amortization. Payments are made on a 30-year FRPM at 9 percent annual interest, compounded monthly. Payments are shown in table 5-1.

As in chapter 4, the outstanding loan balance outstanding for a FRPM can be calculated at any point in time using the future value of an annuity of one dollar per periodic payment. The proportion paid on the mortgage, per dollar, at time period $t < N$, with $t$ measured in years, is $A_t/A_N$, where

$$A_t = \frac{(1 + r/k)^N - 1}{r/k} \qquad (5.5)$$

is the value, at period $t$, of the payment of one dollar per period commencing at time 1, and continuing through $t$. The loan balance outstanding is

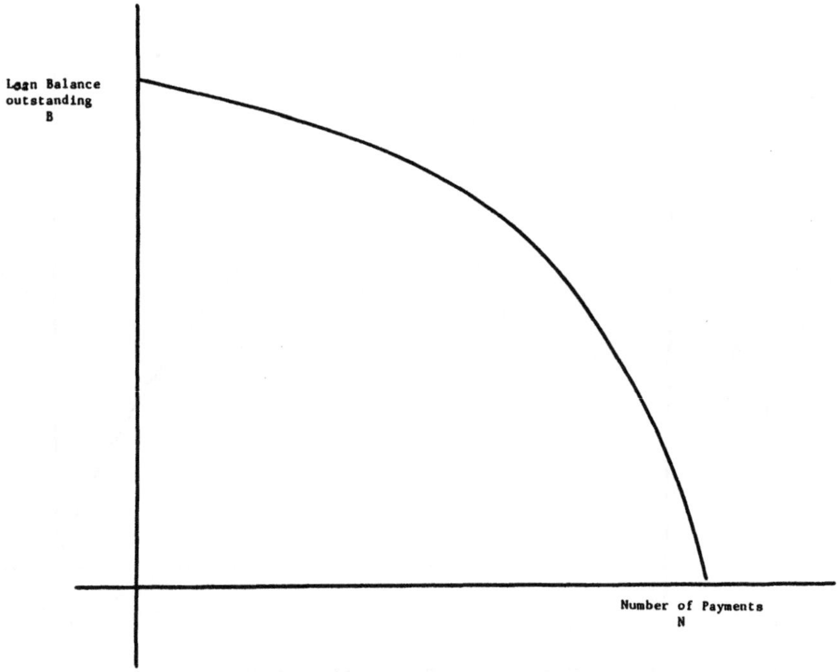


Figure 5-2. Loan Balance

**Table 5-1. Loan Amortization: Payments on a 30-year FRPM**

| *Month* | *Initial Balance* | *Payment* | *Interest 9% ÷ 12* | *Principal Reduction* | *Ending Loan Balance* |
|---|---|---|---|---|---|
| 1 | 32,000.00 | 257.48 | 240.00 | 17.48 | 31,982.52 |
| 2 | 31,982.52 | 257.48 | 239.87 | 17.61 | 31,964.90 |
| 3 | 31,964.90 | 257.48 | 239.74 | 17.74 | 31,947.15 |
| 4 | 31,947.15 | 257.48 | 239.60 | 17.87 | 31,929.27 |
| 5 | 31,929.27 | 257.48 | 239.47 | 18.01 | 31,911.28 |
| 6 | 31,911.26 | 257.48 | 239.33 | 18.15 | 31,893.11 |
| 358 | 761.00 | 257.48 | 5.71 | 251.77 | 509.23 |
| 359 | 509.23 | 257.48 | 3.82 | 253.66 | 255.57 |
| 360 | 255.57 | 257.48 | 1.92 | 255.56 | 0 |

$$B_t = \left[1 - \frac{A_t(r/k,t)}{A_N(r/k,N)}\right]B \tag{5.6}$$

on initial balance $B$. Over the full term of the mortgage, the borrower will have paid an annuity with a future value of $A_N$, over $N$ periods. Hence the proportion paid at $N$ is $A_N/A_N$ or one, and the remaining balance is zero. At the beginning of the loan period, $A_1 = 0$, so none of the balance has been paid off, and $B_1 = B$. The fraction of the initial loan balance remaining unpaid at time $t$ from chapter 4 is

$$\begin{aligned} b_t &= B_t/B \\ &= 1 - \frac{A_t(r/k,t)}{A_N(r/k,N)} \end{aligned} \tag{5.7}$$

The fractional balance outstanding after 24 months, on monthly compounding on the above mortgage, is

$$b_{24} = 1 - \frac{A_t(0.01, 24)}{A_N(0.01, 360)} \tag{5.8}$$

### Closing and Transactions Costs

Suppose an appraisal has been performed along the lines of that in chapter 3, and it is favorable for purchase. The financing is under negotiation. All matters can be negotiated between borrower and lender, including points.

On closing the property, there are statutory payments, such as for property taxes and land transfer fees. Third-party charges include for real estate commissions and legal and title fees. Additional finance charges are for loan application fees, loan origination fees, points, and appraisals.

## Points

The FRPM mortgage is not assumable—that is, is not transferable to a subsequent buyer—unless stated in the contract. FRPM contracts can contain a due-on-sale or alienation clause which makes them callable upon sale, not transferable with either the owner or the property. For those refinancing a FRPM within a specific number of years, there can be a prepayment penalty. The presence of the alienation clause implies that some of the interest rate risk is borne by the borrower, in that mortgage equity, an increase in equity because of favorable financing, cannot be sold directly with the title. The borrower can retain the mortgage equity only by continuing to hold the title.

The due-on-sale clause in the FRPM shifts some risk to the borrower. The borrower bears no interest rate risk, since the rate is held constant. If interest rates rise, the borrower is protected by having the rate and payments locked in. If interest rates fall, the borrower can refinance, shifting this refinancing risk to the lender. By having a due-on-sale clause, this locked-in protection lasts only with the incumbent borrower; the risk of current interest rates must be faced on sale.

A return arises to the borrower only by retaining the property, as the FRPM is not transferable. This nontransferability reduces the liquidity of the FRPM, shifting some risk to the borrower and providing an incentive to hold rather than to sell the property. The period over which the interest risk is borne by the lender is reduced following the inclusion and enforcement of due-on-sale clauses.

The effective mortgage multiplier should equate the actual payment with the payment on the reduced balance. Points are subtracted from the gross loan amount. For every one dollar of loan, the borrower receives only $(1 - p)$, but must make payments on the full dollar. The mortgage payment remains based on the initial balance, without points subtracted. If $B$ is the loan balance, the payment is $M = m(r/k,N)B$. The actual loan amount received is $(1 - p)B$. Since the payment is the same, the effective mortgage multiplier equates the payment with the actual received loan. Hence

$$(1 - p)m_e B = M = mB \tag{5.9}$$

and

$$m_e(r/k,N,p) = \frac{m(r/k,N)}{1-p} \tag{5.10}$$

The effective mortgage multiplier provides a method of comparing mortgages where points are the only lender fees charged, or other fees are negligible. The effective mortgage multiplier is

$$m_e = (r/k)/\left[\frac{1-(1+r/k)^{-N}}{1-p}\right] \tag{5.11}$$

An increase in points increases the mortgage multiplier. The effective mortgage multiplier is $m/(1-p)$, where $p$ is the rate of points per dollar. The effective mortgage multiplier permits the comparison of interest rates and points between lenders.

Suppose one lender quotes a FRPM with a 12 percent contract interest rate and 2 points, and another has a 13 percent FRPM with no points. Both loans are compounded monthly. The effective mortgage multiplier for the former loan is

$$\frac{m(r/k,N)}{1-p} = \frac{m(0.12/12,360)}{1-.02} = 0.010103$$

per dollar borrowed. The effective mortgage multiplier for the latter loan is

$$\frac{m(r/k,N)}{1-p} = \frac{m(0.13/12,360)}{1-p} = 0.0110$$

so the mortgage with the 2 points has a lower multiplier. These multipliers assume that the borrower holds the loan to the full 30 year term. For a shorter term, points are amortized over a smaller length of time, a comparison more favorable to the no-points loan.

The rationale for points (loan discount fees) includes the covering of the fixed costs of the lender, such as for the application, the loan department, and advertising. Points deter refinancing if the market interest rate falls below that in the contract. The risk of loss through refinancing, borne by the lender, is reduced if the cost of altering the mortgage is increased.

Points provide a method whereby the lender can charge a premium to the borrower for bearing the refinancing risk. Since these points are deductible as interest on purchase-money loans and first-time purchases against other income, the effective premium to the borrower is reduced.[3]

Points serve as a credit rationing device. They require the borrower to have more equity in the project by reducing the loan balance contributed. Since the reduction in loan balance occurs up front, at closing, points serve as a screen for ferreting out the more able and better credit risks, given interest rates and underwriting standards.

Points act as a single of the liquidity of the borrower. The payment of points increases the amount of cash a borrower must put into a transaction. Points provide additional flexibility to the lender by adding another variable in the mortgage pricing process. The additional variable is particularly important in the FRPM. There is little observed variability across lenders in $k$ and $N$. The lender adjusts the interest rate and points. The lender substitutes between variable costs to the borrower, $r$, and fixed costs to the borrower, $p$. As $p$ increases, $1 - p$ decreases and $m$ increases, so $r_e$ increases. For $p > 0$, $r_e > r$. The effective rate is higher than the contract rate.

A rule of thumb is that for each 2 points, the $r_e - r$ is about 0.25 percent. This rule assumes that the borrower retains the loan to a full 30-year term. When the mortgage is prepaid—prepayment assumptions of 12 years are used in most mortgage backed securities—the effective rate is higher. The effective rate is the annual percentage rate (APR), which is required disclosure (truth in lending) on mortgage rates and other installment loans, but may be understated by prepayment. The increase in effective interest rate is greater if the borrower is not planning to hold the mortgage to term.

## Prepayment Penalties

Another potential variable for a lender is a prepayment penalty. Prepayment penalties have tended to elicit complaint from borrowers, even though or perhaps because they serve a self-selective function. Those who sell or refinance early pay more penalties. The complaints have resulted in restrictions on or elimination of prepayment penalties on loans sold in the secondary market.

The lender sets a prepayment penalty. Prepayment penalties are charged on FRPM mortgages. On mortgages with adjustable interest rates, prepayment penalties are usually not applied. The justification for prepayment penalties on FRPMs is similar to that for the charging of points. Prepayment penalties discourage refinancing when interest rates decline. There are fixed costs to lenders in loan processing and transactions when a prepayment occurs. If the lender has retained the loan in the portfolio, there are matching problems between assets and liabilities. Long-term deposits continue with interest rates that are likely to be higher than current-deposit interest rates. The lender either loses the borrower altogether, or replaces the mortgage asset with a lower yielding loan. The maturity distribution of assets and liabilities for the lender is not consistent. If the lender has sold the mortgage, the secondary market bears the cost of a reduction in income flow or loss of investment.

Lenders bear refinancing risk. Since the FRPM does not permit any adjustment in the flow of payments or interest rates once the mortgage has been closed, all adjustments have to be made when the borrower is taking out or repaying a loan.

Prepayment penalties are arguably more efficient than points, in that incentive compatibility is served. Those who do prepay are charged. With points, some borrowers are charged, even though they may not prepay, although their points are amortized over a longer period.

## Effective Interest Rates—Pricing the Variables in the FRPM

The FRPM has variables for the contrast interest rate $r$, frequency of compounding $k$, points $p$, prepayment penalty $q$, and number of payments $N$. The effective interest rate on the FRPM, $r_e(r,k,p,q,N)$, is a function of the five variables. Annual percentage rate (APR) charges are required by truth in lending legislation. Such APR financing rates are quoted only for loans taken out to term ($N = Tk$). For loans prepaid prior to term, the effective interest rate faced by the borrower is required. Such an effective interest rate measures the actual cost to the borrower of carrying the FRPM. For decision making, the effective interest rate provides a guide for whether refinancing is appropriate, and is usable in calculating the actual rate of return. For prospective investors, given an expected holding period for the property, the effective interest rate measures the cost of funds; and the target rate of return must be at least as great as this cost.

The lender has paid out initially $(1 - p)B$ to the borrower. This payment is cash flow out from the point of view of the lender. Cash flow in for the lender consists of the payments during the life of the mortgage and the balloon payment at the refinancing date. The loan is not fully amortized if the prepayment date $t$ is less than the number of payments $N$. The balloon payment is the sum of the unpaid balance $b_tB$ on the loan, plus any prepayment penalty. Correspondingly, the borrower has cash flow in at the initial date of the net loan proceeds, $(1-p)B$, and cash flow out (the mortgage payments) up to the date of payment and the balloon payment.

Cash flow in for the borrower is equal to the present value of cash flow out, to discharge the loan obligation. If the prepayment penalty consists of $C$ payments of interest, as of the existing balance, then

$$Q_t = (r/k)B \sum_{i=1}^{C} b_{t+i} \tag{5.12}$$

is the total cost of the prepayment penalty. The prepayment penalty is based on the total initial balance. Payments of the balance are made each month. The borrower has already made $t$ payments. As a specific case, if $k = 12$, and payments are monthly, and $C = 3$—that is, if there are three months of interest as a prepayment penalty,

$$Q_t = (r/12)B \sum_{i=1}^{3} b_{t+i}.$$

Dividing the prepayment penalty by the total loan balance $B$,

$$\begin{aligned} q_t &= (r/k) \sum_{i=1}^{C} b_{t+i} \qquad & t < t^* \\ &= 0 & t > t^* \end{aligned}$$

is the prepayment penalty as a percentage of the initial balance. Prepayment penalties specify a schedule, where the penalty drops to zero after a certain number of payments, here after date $t^*$.

The balance outstanding per dollar of loan is

$$b_t = 1 - \frac{A_t(r/k,t)}{A_N(r/k,N)}$$

where $A_t$ is the future value of an annuity of one dollar, at the contract interest rate $r$, the date of prepayment $t$, and frequency of compounding $k$. The future value of an annuity of one dollar is

$$A_t = \frac{(1 + r/k)^t - 1}{r/k}$$

The balloon payment is $(b_t + q_t)B$, the sum of the outstanding balance $b_tB$ and the prepayment penalty $q_tB$. To match dates for the cash flow statement, either the initial proceeds must be adjusted for the date of prepayment $t$, or the proceeds at the date of refinancing must be adjusted to the date of initial loan. The adjustments are made to the date of purchase, but the methods are equivalent. A prospective investor is making the calculations as of date of initial loan. A refinancing decision is of date $t$. The balloon payment is discounted to date of initial loan by the effective interest rate. The present value of the balloon payment is

$$\frac{b_t B + Q_t}{(1 + r_e/k)^t} = \frac{(b_t + q_t)B}{(1 + r_e/k)^t}$$

At refinancing, the borrower must make a decision based on determination of the effective rate of return (period $t$), thus:

**Cash Flow Statement, Date of Initial Financing**

**Cash Flow In**
Date of initial financing $(1 - p)B$

**Cash Flow Out**
Present value of mortgage payment
During holding
Loan balance $B$
Mortgage multiplier (at loan terms) $m(r/k,N)$
Equals: Periodic payment $M = m(r/k,N)B$
Times: Present value of annuity (at effective interest rate, to be determined, $r_e$) $A(r_e/k,t)$
Equals: Present value, mortgage payments $m(r/k,N)BA(r_e/k,t)$

Plus: Balloon payment
Balance outstanding (present value) $b_t B/(1 + r_e/k)^t$
Prepayment penalty $q_t B/(1 + r_e/k)^t$
Equals: Cash flow out $m(r/k,N)BA(r_e/k,t) + (b_t + q_t)B/(1 + r_e/k)^t$

To solve for $r_e$, the cash flow in and out equation is

$$(1 - p) = m(r/k,N)A(r_e/k,t) + \frac{b_t + q_t}{(1 + r_e/k)^t}$$

Note that cash flow out for the borrower includes the mortgage payments made.

Over the period $i = 1, \ldots, t$, the borrower is making payments $M = m(r/k,N)B$ on the loan amount, where the mortgage multiplier $m = (r/k)/[1 - (1 + r/k)^{-N}]$. The mortgage payment $M$ is an annuity, paid with frequency per year $k$. The present value of the mortgage payments, at effective rate of interest $r_e$ compounded at the same frequency is $MA(r_e/k,t)$, where $A = [1 - (1 + r_e/k)^{-t}]/(r_e/k)$. The effective rate of interest, the only unknown, is compounded at $k$. If $r_e$ is compounded annually, then $k = 1$ for the calculations involving this rate.

Equating the cash flow in of the borrower with the cash flow out,

$$(1 - p)B = m(r/k,N)BA(r_e/k,t) + \frac{(b_t + q_t)B}{(1 + r_e/k)^t} \tag{5.13}$$

where the effective interest rate is compounded with the same frequency as the mortgage. The left side is the payment by the lender. The first term on the right is the present value per dollar of the mortgage payments. The second is the present value of the balloon payment.

The equation can be solved directly. The solution for $r_e$ is iterative. Select an initial value for $r_e$. An appropriate choice could be one percentage point in excess of the contract rate $r$. The remaining variables $r$, $k$, $N$, and $p$ are known constants, and the prepayment penalty is determined once the date of refinancing $t$ is known. The effective $r_e$ depends on the holding period for the mortgage $t$. The holding period can be selected to attain a target interest rate $r_e$. If the left side (borrower cash flow in) is less than the right side (cash flow out) for the initial $r_e$, increase $r_e$, until the differential between cash flow in and out becomes arbitrarily small.

This procedure solves $r_e(t,Q(t){:}r,N,k,p)$, where $r_e$ depends directly on the holding period $t$, the prepayment penalty $Q(t)$, and the variables $r$, $N$, $k$, and $p$. Solving for alternative combinations of holding and $r_e$ produces an optimal holding period, given that $r_e$ is below a certain target interest rate.

The effect of changes in the loan package containing $r$, $N$, $p$, and prepayment penalties can be determined. As the contract interest rate increases, $m$ increases, as does the cash flow out of the borrower. To reduce the cash flow out to the constant cash flow in, the effective interest rate $r_e$ must be increased. As the term increases, $m$ decreases, and the effective interest rate decrases. As points increase, $(1 - p)$ decreases, reducing cash flow in. Cash flow out must be reduced by increasing $r_e$. An increase in prepayment penalty charges increases $r_e$.

The response of the effective interest rate is shown in figure 5-3. The standard FRPM contains a clause restricting transfer of FRPM loans. If

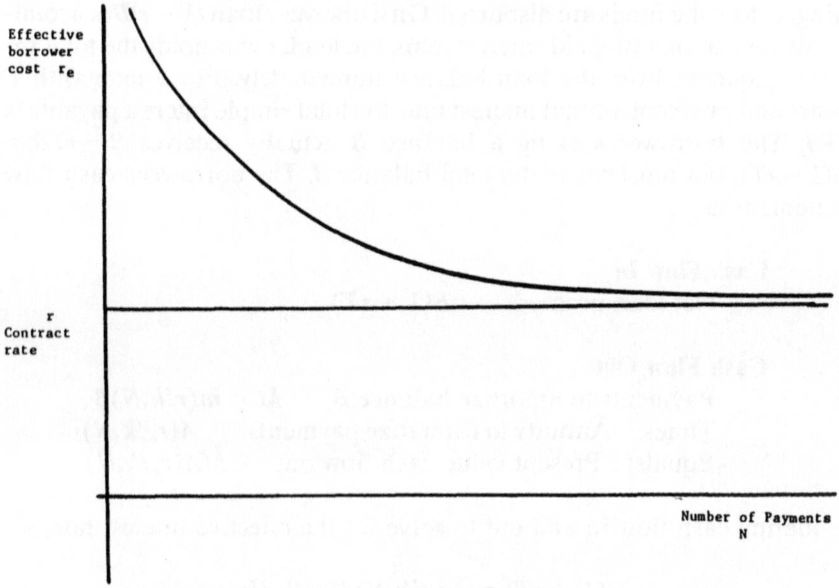


**Figure 5-3. Effect of Prepayment for Given Points on $r_e$.**

prepayment penalties are removed, the contract interest rate increases to maintain the effective rate.

## Short-Term Loans and Interim Financing

In real estate transactions, interim financing is used in construction and development projects while the construction takes place. Once the project is completed, long-term financing can be put in place. Bridge financing of a short-term nature is used when property owners are between transactions prior to closing, or holding one more property than desired while on the market.

### *Prepaid Interest Loan*

The prepaid interest loan obtains is short-term financing provides for the payment of interest only, with no principal repayment. The payment is calculated on a simple interest basis as $rB$. Interest is prepaid at the beginning, before the funds are disbursed. On a one-year loan $(1 - r)B$ is actually disbursed. In a prepaid interest loan, the lender withholds the total interest payment from the loan balance immediately. For a loan with $T$ years and $r$ percent annual interest rate, the total simple interest payable is $rTB$. The borrower seeking a balance $B$ actually receives $B - rTB = B(1 - rT)$, but must repay the total balance $B$. The borrower's cash flow statement is

**Cash Flow In**

Net loan proceeds $B(1 - rT)$

**Cash Flow Out**

Payments to amortize balance $B$ $M = m(r/k,N)B$

Times: Annuity to capitalize payments $A(r_e/k,N)$

Equals: Present value cash flow out $MA(r_e/k,N)$

Equating cash flow in and out to solve for the effective interest rate,

$$(1 - rT) = m(r/k,N)A(r_e/k,N)$$

The effective annual interest rate $r_e$ can be solved by iteration. If $T = 1$, for a one-year loan, then $B(1 - r)$ is borrowed and $B$ must be repaid. The effective rate of interest is

$$\begin{aligned} r_e &= [B - (1 - r)B]/(1 - r)B \\ &= [1 - (1 - r)]/(1 - r) \qquad (5.14) \\ &= r/(1 - r) > r \end{aligned}$$

Prepayment prior to term on a prepaid interest loan increases the effective interest rate further, because the total interest obligation is unchanged, but must be amortized over a shorter period.

### *Add-On Interest Loan*

The add-on interest loan is sometimes applied in real estate financing, but is more typically used for automobile, furniture, and other installment loans. The balance is calculated, with interest for the full period added on, and then divided by the number of periods. For interest rate $r$ and $T$ years, with $k$ payments per year,

$$M = (B + rT)/kT \tag{5.15}$$

With each payment, some of the principal, $B/kT$ is being repaid, on a straight-line basis, but the interest is based on the full amount, which is being borrowed for less than $N$. So the effective rate is

$$MA(r_e/k,kT) = B$$
$$= A(r_e/12, 12T)\left[\frac{(B + rT)}{12T}\right] \tag{5.16}$$

This implies that

$$A(r_e/k,kT) = \frac{kBT}{B + rT} \tag{5.17}$$

from which $r_e$ can be calculated.

If the loan is prepaid, the *rule of 78s* is used to credit the interest. This rebate interest $R$ is, for repayment at month $t$, on a monthly-payment loan where $k = 12$,

$$R = rT(12T - t)\left(\frac{12T + 1 - t}{12T(12T + 1)}\right) \tag{5.18}$$

The actual rebate is

$$R = B - MA(r/12,t) - \frac{(12T - t)M}{(1 + r/12)^t} \tag{5.19}$$

These loan options are applied during a construction period, where take out financing occurs. When the ultimate owner takes title, a long-term mortgage can replace the interim financing.

## Concluding Remarks

The fixed rate and payment mortgage may provide for level disbursements over a period, but the effective interest rate paid depends on a number of variables. The yield on a FRPM is not fixed, being dependent on the contract interest rate, frequency of compounding, term in years, points, and prepayment penalty.

The FRPM is not a riskless liability from the borrower standpoint. While a large portion of the interest rate risk is shifted to the lender, the FRPM is not completely riskless. Since the loan is not transferable, the borrower cannot sell a build-up of future mortgage equity if the contract interest rate is below the market interest rate. While the borrower can refinance if interest rates decline, there is a premium payable in points, as well as fees and a prepayment penalty. The borrower has the incentive to bear some of the risks of declining interest rates, paying a higher than market rate, until the expected present value of savings on refinancing exceeds the transactions costs in fees.

There is a risk of inflation affecting real interest rates. Suppose high rates of inflation are accompanied by low real rates of interest, with mortgage rates not completely adjusting for inflation.[4] Low rates of inflation are accompanied by high real rates of interest. The real burden on a borrower is affected by the rate of inflation.

The risk with the FRPM is shifted from the borrower to the lender. The lender bears interest rate risk, if mortgage assets are unmatched by deposit or other liabilities of similar maturity. Given that depositors are unlikely to purchase 30-year deposits directly, portfolio lenders bear the risk. The development of secondary markets permits the risk to be shifted elsewhere, but the allocation remains to the lender and asset holder, and away from the liability holder.

## Notes

1. On refinancing of the same property, tax regulations provide that points are to be amortized over the life of the loan, and are not to be claimed as an immediate deduction.
2. These results are derived in the appendix.
3. A purchase-money loan is one whose proceeds are used for payment on real estate, as opposed to an equity loan with proceeds used elsewhere. On refinancing, tax regulations may not permit the deductibility of points, requiring that they be amortized over the life of the loan. Where points are deductible, they must be similar to prevailing rates charged in the area.
4. A reason for this phenomenon could be the inability of individuals to qualify for loans at high interest rates, which reduces the demand. Qualification is based on nominal rather than real interest rates. Lenders cannot easily pass on higher interest costs.

# APPENDIX 5 MORTGAGE MULTIPLIER EFFECTS

The mortgage multiplier is

$$m(r,k,N) = rk^{-1}[1 - (1 + rk^{-1})^{Tk}]^{-1}$$

Let $c \equiv [1 - (1 + rk^{-1})^{Tk}]^{-1}$, positive for plausible values of the three variables. A lower bound for $k$ is 1, with annual compounding. If compounding is more frequent than annual, $k > 1$. Unless annual interest rates exceed 100 percent, $r < 1$, and $N \geqslant 1$, where $N = Tk$.

The partial derivative of the mortgage multiplier in interest rates is

$$\partial m/\partial r = k^{-1}c + rk^{-1}\,\partial c/\partial r$$

Now

$$\partial c/\partial r = -c^{-1}Tk(1 + rk^{-1})^{-(Tk+1)}$$

so

$$\partial m/\partial r = k^{-1}c - c^{-1}Tr(1 + rk^{-1})^{-(Tk+1)}$$

The first expression is positive, but the second is negative. The expression $(1 + rk^{-1})^{-(Tk+1)}$ is small, being raised to the power of the number of periods, so the second expression is smaller than the first. Consequently, $\partial m/\partial r$ decreases for increases in interest rates.

In the term of loan $T$,

$$\partial m/\partial T = rc^{-1}(1 + rk^{-1})^{-(Tk+1)} < 0$$

As the term of loan increases, and the interest rate and frequency are held constant, the mortgage multiplier decreases, as the payment is spread over a longer period.

In the frequency of compounding,

$$\begin{aligned}\partial m/\partial k &= -rk^{-2}c - rTc^{-1}(1 + rk^{-1})^{-(Tk+1)} - r^2Tc^{-1}k^{-2}(1 + rk^{-1})^{-(Tk+1)} \\ &= -rk^{-2}c - rTc^{-1}T(1 + rk^{-1})^{-(Tk+1)}(1 + rk^{-2})\end{aligned}$$

The first expression is negative, given that $c$ is positive. For the second expression, $(1 + rk^{-2})$ is positive for all positive interest rates. It remains positive if interest rates are above negative 100 percent but positive interest rates are retained. The expression $Tk(1 + rk^{-1})^{-(Tk+1)}$ is positive, for the same interest rate restriction, with both $k$ and $T$ positive. Consequently, the second expression is positive, and the mortgage multiplier is decreasing in the frequency of compounding.

# 6 INFLATION AND INTEREST RATE RISKS: VARIABLE INTEREST RATE AND PAYMENT MORTGAGES

## Introduction

For the FRPM, the payment is constant, and the borrower shifts the risk of increasing interest rates to the lender. The interest rate on the FRPM is locked in over the term. An increase in market interest rates attributable to a change in the rate of inflation reduces the real burden of borrowers holding these mortgages, and creates capital losses for the lenders.

The problems arising from increasing interest and inflation rates are more acute if lenders make the FRPM loans from short-term deposits. For a 30-year term FRPM, the lender is fully matched if there are deposits for a 30-year term paying an interest rate generating a spread to cover the operating costs. Since depositors in lending institutions are unwilling to place deposits for a 30-year term, the interest rate on deposits must be increased when interest rates and inflation rise. Otherwise, depositors withdraw their funds and disintermediation occurs.

The combination of unmatched deposits with FRPM loans, and the inability to charge market interest rates on FRPM loans causes financial difficulties for lenders. Lenders bear the risk of unanticipated interest rate and inflation shifts. The problem extends backward to the real estate industry, if the thrifts are unwilling to lend on FRPM loans, affecting construction, sales and resales. To deal with these problems, adjustable rate financing has developed, to permit more flexible allocation of the risks between borrowers, lenders, and holders of mortgage backed securities.

## Interest Rate Risk

### *The Option to Refinance*

The FRPM carries negligible interest rate risk to the borrower, but is not riskless. Risk arises from fluctuations in interest and inflation rates. An increase in interest rates reduces the market value of the mortgage so that the portfolio lender holding the mortgage faces a capital loss. For the borrower, even if market interest rates rise, the payment remains constant. If interest rates fall, the borrower has the option of refinancing at a lower interest rate.

Borrowers have the option of buying financing at lower market interest rates, at any time up to a maturity date. A put option carries the right to buy, and a call option the right to sell a security at a specific price and on a specific maturity date. An American option can be exercised at any date prior to maturity; a European option can only be exercised at maturity.

The FRPM provides a borrower with an American put option, conveying the right to sell back to the lender at the specified interest rate and the mortgage balance outstanding. If interest rates in the market exceed the contract rate, the borrower does not exercise the option. If the market interest rate is below the contract rate, the borrower may refinance depending on transactions costs. The option is in the money, covering part of the fixed costs, whenever market interest rates are lower than the rate in the contract.

More detail on options is presented in chapter 10 on mortgage securities, but the value of the option to refinance can be outlined. Let $r$ be the contract interest rate, as before, and $r_1$ be the market rate. Then if

$$\begin{aligned} r_1 &\geqslant r \quad \text{do not refinance} \\ r_1 &< r \quad \text{in the money for refinancing.} \end{aligned} \tag{6.1}$$

The existing mortgage payment is $M = m(r/k,N)B$, with $k$ the annual frequency of compounding, $N$ the number of payments, and $B$ the balance. At current date $t$, the borrower owes $b_tB$, to be refinanced.

If the borrower refinances, suppose the new term of the loan is $N - t$, until the existing loan would have expired. The new payments are

$$M_1 = m(r_1/k, N - t)b_t B$$

and the saving per payment is

$$\Delta M = M_1 - M$$

$$= [m(r_1/k, N - t)b_t - m(r/k, N)]B$$

This amount must be capitalized, and if the new market interest rate is used, the present value of the saving is $\Delta MA(r_1/k, N - t)$. The market interest rate is, however, a random variable, with probability distribution $f(r_1)$ where interest rates can vary from 0 to $\infty$. If $P$ is the price of the option, then its expected value is

$$E(P) = \int_0^r \Delta MA(r_1/k, N - t) f(r_1)\, dr_1 - G \tag{6.2}$$

where $G$ denotes the fixed costs of refinancing such as for points, lender and legal fees, appraisal, and title transfer taxes. This expected value of the option is the benefit to the borrower from being able to refinance. By comparison, noncallable debt issuers such as the federal government do not have the option to refinance. The explicit evaluation of the option price depends on the form of the density function $f(r_1)$. The lender bears the upside interest rate risk, and is not compensated by any benefit from downside interest rate risk. If there is a decline in interest rates, the lender is likely to have the loan repaid. The allocation of interest rate risk is asymmetrical.

### *Risk Trade-offs Between ARMs and FRPMs*

The calculation of the rate of return, or cost of borrowing, requires an examination of the types and degrees of risk, and their allocation between borrower, lender, and mortgage security holder. A mortgage is a risky asset for the lender and a risky liability for the borrower.

Figure 6–1 depicts mortgage choices for the borrower. The borrower is assumed to have made the choice between owning and renting in favor of owning. On the horizontal axis is indicated the mean borrowing interest

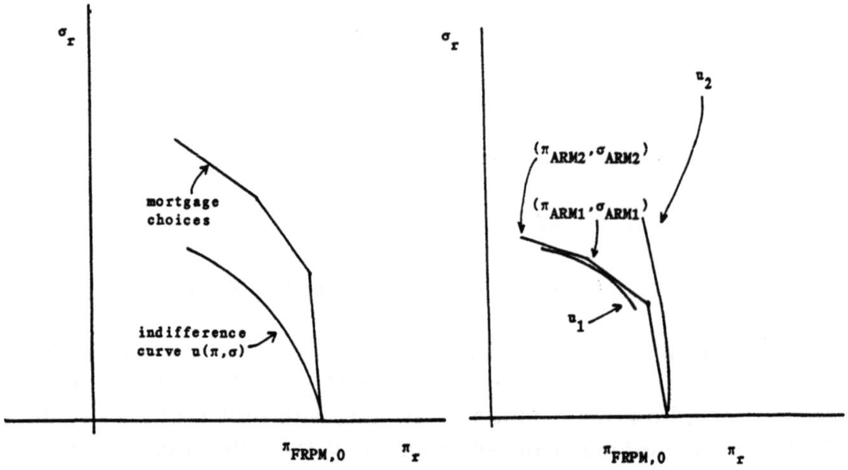


Figure 6–1. Risk-Return Trade-Offs on Mortgages

rate $\mu_r$. On the vertical axis is some measure of the risk of interest rates, through the standard deviation, $\sigma_r$. Only interest rate risk is indicated in the figure, and not inflation risk. Suppose the borrower is comparing alternative instruments available. Some have fixed interest rates; others have variable interest rates. All the FRPM interest rates lie along the horizontal axis, as there is no risk of interest rate fluctuations to the borrower.

If the borrower wants to be restricted to FRPM loans, and there are no other differences in points, penalties, or other costs, the loan closest to the origin along the horizontal axis is chosen. Among FRPM loans, this loan has the lowest contract interest rate. There is no variation in interest rates during the term, so $\sigma_r = 0$. If the borrower is willing to bear some of the interest rate risk, compensation occurs by a reduced mean interest rate. There is a negatively sloped borrowing and lending line, including some mortgages with a variable interest rate, or positive standard deviation, but a lower mean rate. Since there is no compensation by a reduced mean interest rate, there is no reason to select a mortgage with a variable interest rate.[1] The borrower has preferences between the expected borrowing cost and its risk. One level of the utility between the two is reflected by the indifference curve.

Let $u(\mu_r,\sigma_r)$ be the level of utility a borrower obtains, dependent on the expected return and risk. Higher average interest rates $\mu_r$ decrease utility; and greater variability in interest rates, through $\sigma_r$, reduces utility. Individuals are assumed to be risk-averse, with concave utility functions.[2]

For a fixed rate and payment mortgage, $\sigma_r = 0$, once the loan is in place. The subscripts ARM and FRPM denote adjustable and fixed interest rate mortgages. The utility derived from having an ARM is $u(\mu_{ARM},\sigma_{ARM})$ and that from a FRPM is $u(\mu_{FRPM},\sigma_{FRPM})$. A borrower chooses a fixed rate mortgage if $u(\mu_{FRPM},0) > u(\mu_{ARM},\sigma_{FRPM})$.

Among the FRPMs available in the market, the borrower can select that with the lowest effective interest rate, and use this rate as the expected borrowing cost $\mu_{FRPM}$. Among ARMs, both the mean and standard deviation are unknown over the term, and determining the best loan available in the market is more problematical. More variability must be compensated by lower mean interest rates. In figure 6–1a, the most favorable FRPM lies along the mean interest rate axis, for $\mu_r$, at the point $\mu_{FRPM}$,0. Various ARMs are arrayed along the risk–return trade-off line, such as $(\mu_{ARM1},\sigma_{ARM1})$ and $(\mu_{ARM2},\sigma_{ARM2})$. The trade-off line need not be straight. A level of utility is measured by $u(\mu,\sigma)$. A higher level of utility places the individual closer to the origin. In figure 6–1a the borrower chooses an ARM, since the indifference curve $u$ is tangent to the risk–return trade-off.

In figure 6–1b, the borrower is at a corner, and chooses the FRPM.[3] The trade-off between interest rate risk and return indicates that this individual is unwilling be bear any interest rate risk. It is assumed that individuals are risk-averse in these decisions on loan selection. In real estate investment, as in gambling, it is possible that individuals are risk-accepting, willing to take higher risk even if uncompensated by a higher return or lower borrowing cost. The curvature of the indifference curve is altered.

The risk–return trade-off line upwards from $\mu_{FRPM}$,0 is a set of combinations of mean and standard deviation of interest rates, or the mortgage opportunity set. The frontier delineates the constraint the borrower faces. There can be other packages offered which are not on the line, and these lie to the right of the risk–return trade-off. As the borrower is willing to accept more risk, measured by the standard deviation of the return, the mortgage interest rate offered is lower.

As the interest rate varies, the payments made on the mortgage vary. The curvature of the indifference curves depends on preferences and the willingness to trade off risk against mean interest rate. The mortgage opportunity set can shift with other factors such as the prevailing term structure of interest rates, and the secondary market for mortgages.

### Inflation Risk

The trade-offs in figure 6–1 apply only to interest rate risk. Another risk arises with inflation. For a FRPM, the real interest rate and payment, adjusted for inflation, are not constant, but variable. There is an inflation risk. With the FRPM, any positive rate of inflation reduces the real payment. For a given nominal loan-balance constant, real indebtedness declines each year, apart from the repayment of principal in the blended payments.

All mortgages face the issue of how to share this inflation risk. The fixed rate and payment mortgage has the lender bearing the risk of an increase in interest rates. The inflation risk benefits the borrower on the FRPM, in that real payments decline provided that prices are increasing. The lender can only be compensated for bearing inflation risk by increasing the fixed monthly payment. For an ARM, where the interest rate on the contract is variable, shifts in market interest rates arising from changes in inflationary expectations are partly passed on to the borrower.

### *Tilting*

Tilting is the effect of inflation on the real sequence of payments on the FRPM and its impact on nominal interest rates. In figure 6–2, the term of the mortgage, *N*, is on the horizontal axis. Consider a borrower with a FRPM. The monthly payment $M = mB$ is indicated on the vertical axis.

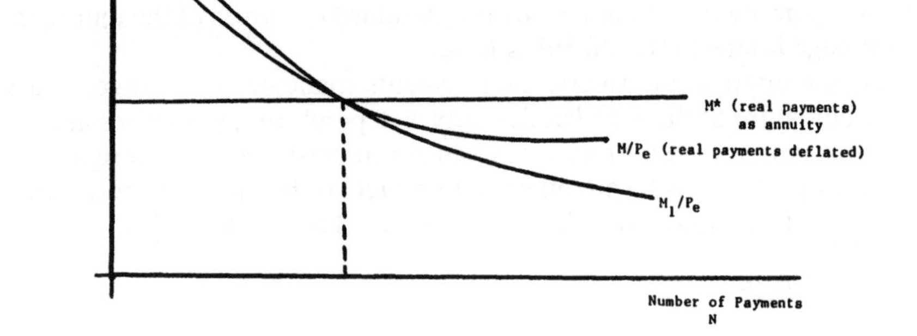


Figure 6–2. The Effect of Tilting

For a \$100,000 loan at a 12 percent annual interest rate, with $N = 30$, the monthly payment is \$1,028.61. This payment is in nominal dollars, not adjusted for changes in the price level.

If the inflation rate is zero for the entire term of the loan, the payment in real terms is constant. If the price level is not expected to be constant over the term, the real payment on a FRPM is the initial payment divided by the expected level of a price index each period. The real mortgage payment is $M_{e,t} = M/P_{e,t}$, where $P_{e,t}$ is the expected level of the price index at time $t = 1, \ldots, N$. The real mortgage payment can vary with time. If positive inflation rates are expected, then $P_{e,t}$ increases over time, and the real mortgage payment decreases. In figure 6–2, a positive inflation rate is assumed, so the real mortgage payment decreases over the term. The inflation for $P_{e,t}$ applies to a general price index, and not to price changes on the specific parcel of real estate. The borrower must make a forecast of the behavior, of some general measure, of prices, such as the Consumer Price Index. If there is no inflation, real and nominal payments are constant and equal.

For positive inflation rates, real payments under the FRPM are not constant. With inflation, the FRPM is effectively an adjustable real interest rate and payment mortgage. The present value of the real payments is

$$A_e = \sum_{t=1}^{N} \frac{M_{e,t}}{(1 + r_e)^t} \tag{6.3}$$

where $r_e$ is the effective interest rate, and time $t$ ranges up to term $N$.

The lender bears the risk of inflation. If the rate of inflation is positive, the real payment is never more than the initial payment. If the rate of inflation is negative, the real payment in the future is in excess of the initial payment. The lender on the FRPM compensates for the risk of positive inflation rates by increasing the initial payment.

The real mortgage payment equivalent to the present value $A_e$ is $M_e$ in figure 6–2. This real constant mortgage payment is less than the nominal or contract mortgage payment. If the initial $M$ is desired as the real mortgage payment by the lender, the initial payment must be increased above $M$. The constant nominal payment is $M$. The expected level of a price index of the payment period to $N$ has the sequence $P_{e1}, \ldots, P_{eN}$ over the term. The sequence of real payments is $M/P_{e1}, \ldots, M/P_{eN}$. The annuity corresponding to this real mortgage payment is $M^*$, a smaller amount than $M$, if the price index is expected to increase over the future. If interest rates increase, purely because of an increase in expected inflation rates, the constant nominal mortgage payment for a new borrower must increase to $M_1$. Since the real annuity is unchanged, the annuity $M^*$ is unaffected, but the sequence of payments is $M_1/P_{e1}, \ldots, M_1/P_{eN}$. The real payments consistent with the annuity $M^*$ are higher in the earlier periods and lower in the later periods.

The sequence of mortgage payments exhibits tilting. For the FRPM, tilting arises in that as inflation rates increase, the slope of the real payments sequence becomes more steeply negative, with a heavier burden in the early periods to maintain a constant real annuity.

Qualification for the FRPM is based on the initial nominal payments, fixed over the term. With inflation, the capability of the borrower to make this nominal payment increases over time. The qualification and underwriting standard for the FRPM is based on income at the time of originating the loan, with no allowance for increases because of inflation. As the rate of inflation rises, the initial payment on a FRPM increases, even if the real payment is constant. When there is a high rate of inflation, it becomes more difficult to qualify for a FRPM, leading to a problem of affordability.

Suppose there is an increase in the contract interest rate charged on the FRPM, arising solely from a change in inflationary expectations. The real mortgage payment is unchanged. The increase in interest rates and inflation has an effect on resource allocation. As inflation continues, there is a shift of debt burden under the FRPM toward the early payment years, increasing the difficulty of qualifying for financing. Qualifying borrowers find the initial relative prices of real estate higher than the relative long-run prices. Some borrowers may not qualify, for the underwriting standards are quoted and enforced in initial nominal terms and not on the real underlying annuity. An increase in both interest rates and inflation by similar percentage points reduces the demand for real estate because of tilting, and causes a contraction in the real estate sector, even if there is no effect on real payments.

If inflation has an effect on relative prices of reducing the return on other investments, the demand for real estate can increase with increasing inflation. Tilting requires that interest rates be adjusted to account for changes in expected inflation. If interest rates increase by more than expected inflation, the tilt shift is even steeper. As interest rates rise with increases in expected inflation, the initial debt burden on new borrowers, or tilt, increases. Existing FRPM borrowers benefit, since their payments are fixed and their real debt obligations decline.

The real payment declines over time, but is higher in earlier periods. The borrower is worse off in earlier payments, and has an incentive to reduce the demand for real estate. Since qualification for mortgages does not include a concession for tilting, the potential borrower must qualify on the initial, most unfavorable, case. The borrower pays the inflation premium initially. If there were expected deflation, the reverse would occur, and the borrower would benefit.

With fixed payment mortgages, even if income keeps pace with property prices during inflation, first-time buyers are blocked by tilting. Tilting requires more real dollars to be paid by borrowers in early years. With the FRPM, new borrowers carry the full effect of the titl tilt, which is charged as a premium by the lender to compensate for bearing the risk of positive inflation. There is a negative effect of sales, resales, and new construction.

If the risk and liquidity are included in the real return on investment, the nominal interest rate is the sum of the real return on investment and the expected rate of inflation.[4] Under the Fisher theory, the real rate of return on capital is hypothesized as being constant, so the expected rate of inflation can be inferred as the differential between the nominal interest rate and this constant return. If $E(\mu)$ is the expected rate of inflation, and $r^*$ is the real rate of return on capital including risk and liquidity, then $r = r^* + E(\mu)$, where $r$ is the nominal interest rate. The relevant real return for real estate would include an adjustment for greater risk and illiquidity.

Interest received is taxed without subtracting for inflation, so all of $r$ is reported for a taxable investor. There are nontaxable or deferred taxable investors, including insurance companies, pension funds, and retirement accounts. Other investors face positive marginal tax rates, requiring a higher nominal rate of interest to compensate them for making the investment.

The real rate of interest is the nominal rate of interest, net of taxation, less the expected rate of inflation, in an environment where tax brackets are not indexed, or

$$r^* = (1 - \lambda)r - E(\mu)$$

where $\lambda$ is the marginal tax rate of the individual. If tax brackets are indexed for inflation, the real rate of interest is

$$r^* = (1 - \lambda)[r - E(\mu)] \tag{6.4}$$

Marginal rates of tax vary between investors, from zero to the stipulated maximum rate. If the real rate of interest is constant, at $r^*$, then

$$\begin{aligned} r^* &= r - E(\mu) - r\lambda + \lambda E(\mu) \\ &= r - E(\mu) - \lambda(r - E(\mu) \end{aligned}$$

The real rate of interest is the nominal rate of interest *r*, less the expected rate of inflation $E(\mu)$, less an adjustment for taxes. Rearranging,

$$\begin{aligned}\lambda &= \frac{r - E(\mu) - r^*}{r - E(\mu)} \\ &= \frac{[1 - r^*]}{[r - E(\mu)]}\end{aligned} \tag{6.5}$$

as the critical marginal tax rate required to make the decision.

Suppose the nominal annual interest rate is 10 percent; the expected inflation rate is 4 percent; and the real rate of return, adjusted for the illiquidity and risk of real estate is 5 percent. Then

$$\lambda = 1 - 0.05/0.06 = 1 - 0.83 = 0.17$$

An investor with a greater than 17 percent marginal tax rate accepts the investment. Where the lender is unable to shift the risk to other sectors of the economy, through secondary markets, or to long-term depositors in thrifts and other institutions, the level of FRPMs is reduced.

### Adjustable Rate Mortgage (ARM)

The adjustable rate mortgage (ARM) shifts part of both the interest rate and inflation risks to the borrower. The interest rate on the mortgage is variable, and tied to a specific interest rate index. The payment is variable in most cases. If the payment is fixed, the adjustment is made in the outstanding loan balance.

Lenders typically can make adjustments at 6- or 12-month intervals. Variables in an ARM include:

*Spread or margin:* the differential between the contract rate charged, and the rate as determined by the index.

*Periodic cap* (annual or semiannual): the maximum amount that an interest rate can rise during one period.

*Total cap:* the maximum and minimum contract rate chargeable on the loan.

*Going-in Rate:* a rate used to qualify borrowers for the financing (may be below the base contract rate).

*Payment Limit:* a maximum increase in payments at any adjustment date.

If a lender applies a limit to the amount borrowed, there is potential credit rationing. Lenders must disclose the annual percentage interest rate (APR), and the payments under the worst-case scenario. The APR is the effective interest rate for the full term. Since the future interest rate is unknown, the APR is calculated assuming that the initial interest base rate, as opposed to the going-in rate, is held constant over the full term of the loan. The loans are typically assumable, if the underlying property is sold or transferred.

### *Negative Amortization*

Some ARMs contain a limit on the extent that the monthly payment on each renewal can increase. Suppose the periodic adjustment occurs after each subsequent 12 months. The new monthly payment $M_{12}$ must not exceed $(1 + \text{LIMIT})M_0$, or

$$M_{12} \leqslant (1 + \text{LIMIT})M_0. \tag{6.6}$$

Here LIMIT is the percentage rate increase limit, frequently set at 0.075 (7.5 percent) annually. The differential $M_{12} - (1 + \text{LIMIT})M_0$ for each month of the next period, here 12, accumulates, and is added to the previous balance.

By adding this differential to the loan, the outstanding balance increases. Negative amortization arises where the loan balance increases rather than decreases with successive payments. Instead of being "killed," the literal meaning of amortization, the debt burden is increasing. As negative amortization continues, in a property whose price is not increasing, the equity of the owner can be reduced or eliminated.

Negative amortization arises when an ARM provides for a fixed or restricted payment, with less restricted interest rate caps. The differential between the calculated and actual payment is added to the principal balance. The payment limit reduces the payment liability of the borrower in the short run, but at the cost of increasing indebtedness. Loans permitting negative amortization carry more risk to the ultimate holder. Default risk increases as the prospect of the elimination of equity arises. Equity in real estate changes because of two factors. The first factor is the change in property value. For a given loan balance, equity increases, reducing default risk. The second factor is the paydown of the loan balance. With negative amortization, there is a loss of equity from the paydown, since the loan balance increases. If the increase in loan balance exceeds the change in property value, equity decreases, raising the risk of default. Hence restrictions are placed on negative amortization for loans sold in the secondary market.

Once negative amortization has occurred, savings from interest rate reductions must be applied toward its elimination. For an ARM with a fixed payment, if interest rates decline, the saving in payment is applied to reducing the principal.

While secondary markets are less inclined to accept negative amortization mortgages, the criteria for sale are favorable to mortgages with ultimate interest rate caps and caps on interest rates at renewal dates, both periodic and over the life of the loan.

### *ARM Indexes*

The interest rate on an ARM depends on an index of interest rates and a margin or markup. Suppose MARGIN is the markup or margin applied by the lender. At origination, at payment date 0, the interest rate on the selected index is $I_0$. The initial interest rate charged is $r_0 = I_0 + \text{MARGIN}$. This interest rate applies until the next adjustment. If the next adjustment takes place after 12 months, the index of interest rates is $I_{12}/I_0$.

The adjusted interest rate with the index is $(I_{12}/I_0)r_0$, where $(I_{12}/I_0)$ is the index. This adjusted interest rate must fall within a limit, or cap, on the interest rate change. The adjusted interest rate is

$$r_{12} = \min\{r_0 + \text{CAP}, (I_{12}/I_0)r_0\} \qquad \text{if } I_{12} > I_0$$

$$= \max\{r_0 - \text{CAP}, (I_{12}/I_0)r_0\} \qquad \text{if } I_{12} < I_0$$

Suppose an initial level of the interest rate index is 10 percent, and MARGIN = 0.02, and CAP = 0.01. The initial interest rate $r_0$ is 0.1 + 0.02 or 0.12 (12 percent). Let the interest rate after 12 months, on adjustment, be 11 percent. Then the index is 0.11/0.1 = 1.1. The indexed interest rate is 0.132 (13.2 percent). Since $I_{12} > I_0$, the interest rate $r_{12}$ is min {0.1 + 0.01, 0.132} = min {0.11, 0.132} (11 percent).

In general, if the adjustment is done once annually, on a mortgage of term $T$ years, the interest rate at year $t$ is

$$r_t = \min\{r_0 + \text{LIFECAP}, r_{t-1} + \text{CAP}, (I_t/I_{t-1})r_{t-1}\} \quad \text{if } I_t > I_{t-1}$$
$$= \max\{r_0 - \text{LIFECAP}, r_{t-1} - \text{CAP}, (I_t/I_{t-1})r_{t-1}\} \quad \text{if } I_t \leqslant I_{t-1} \tag{6.7}$$

where LIFECAP is a lifetime cap on the total adjustment. If LIFECAP is 5 percent, the interest rate cannot vary outside of the range from 5 to 15 percent. The three most popular indexes are based on Treasury obligations, a cost of funds index for lenders in the general geographical area, and deposit interest rates at the specific lender.

Treasury obligations are United States government securities. Treasury bills are short-term securities issued in 3-, 6-, and 12-month maturities. Interest paid is the difference between the purchase price, at a discount, and par maturity value. Treasury bills are sold weekly at auction, and reflect current interest rates. Treasury notes have maturities from 1 to 10 years. They pay interest semiannually, are not callable, and are issued in denominations of $5000 for 2-year and 3-year maturities and usually of $1000 denominations for longer-term maturities. Treasury bonds have maturities of over 10 years, come in denominations of $1000, and pay interest semiannually. The term can extend to 30 years. Treasury bonds are noncallable.

A particular index used for the cost of funds is based on deposit interest rates paid by lenders in the 11th District of the Federal Home Loan Bank Board, covering California, Arizona, and Nevada. The cost of funds index lags current interest rates because of reporting delays and because the quoted rates are based on those paid at time of deposit. The least volatile interest rates are those on longer-term securities, such as Treasury notes. Since loans over a longer term are subject to more uncertainty on inflation, interest rates are higher. Loans based on shorter-term securities generally have lower interest rates, to compensate borrowers for accepting interest rate risk. The borrower is trading off thte level of interest rates against volatility.

Where the ARM is tied to Treasury securities, the index used is a constant maturities index, as published by the Federal Reserve System.[5] This constant maturities index is a theoretical construct computing the yield on Treasury securities if issued during that period, whether actually issued or not. The index provides a smoothing, because not all Treasury securities are auctioned regularly. Treasury bills are auctioned weekly, but Treasury notes and bonds are sold more infrequently.

Some ARMs use indexes based on interest rates from Treasury bills or Treasury notes. Treasury securities have more response to current overall interest rates than costs of funds. The Treasury constant maturity index is a blend of market interest rates on actively traded issues of various maturities. The index of one-year Treasury bills is one of the most widely used because of the popularity of once-annually adjusted ARMs. One-year Treasury bills are sold on a discount basis, the income determined by the discount below the face value.[6] The interest rate quoted is below the effective yield. The constant maturity index is quoted on an effective yield basis.

The Federal Home Loan Bank Board cost of funds index is calculated in several districts, to reflect what the lenders are paying to attract deposits. The most common is that published by the San Francisco Federal Home Loan Bank, because of the popularity of ARMs in California.

In comparisons of ARMs where the index is based on six month Treasury bills, one year Treasury securities and the cost of funds, the first has the lowest mean interest rate, but the highest variance, and the last has the highest mean interest rate but the lowest variance. The borrower can determine the appropriate mortgage within the set of ARMs by making the tradeoff between mean and standard deviation of borrowing cost.

### Payment

The ARM calculation of initial monthly payment is, given the determination of the initial interest rate, is

$$M_0 = m(r_0/12, 360)B \tag{6.8}$$

where $M_0$ is the monthly payment for the first period on a loan of balance $B$, and $r_0$ is the initial interest rate, on a 30 year amortization mortgage. Suppose the loan is adjusted once annually, after month 12. The loan balance after 12 months is

$$\begin{aligned} B_{12} &= [1 - A_{12}(r_0/12, 12)/A_{360}(r_0/12, 360)]B_0 \\ &= b_{12}B_0 \end{aligned} \tag{6.9}$$

from the loan balance formula, letting $B_0$ be the initial balance borrowed. Here $A_{12}$ is the future value of an annuity at interest rate $r_0$ annually, paid monthly for a term of 12 months. The future value of an annuity at the same interest rate, for the full 360 month term of the ARM is $A_{360}$.

The interest rate upon renewal is $r_{12}$. The new payment multiplier is $m(r_{12}/12, 348)$, so the monthly payments for the next twelve months, for months 12–24 under the ARM are

$$M_{12} = m(r_{12}/12, 348)B_{12}. \tag{6.10}$$

At the end of 24 months, the balance is calculated using the formula as for $B_{12}$. The loan balance at the end of 24 months is

$$\begin{aligned} B_{24} &= [1 - A_{12}(r_{12}/12, 12)/A_{348}(r_{12}/12, 348)]B_{12} \\ &= b_{24}B_{12}. \end{aligned} \tag{6.11}$$

This is the loan balance outstanding at the end of the second year.

The balance outstanding at the end of year $t$ is

$$\begin{aligned} B_{12t} = [1 - &A_{12}(r_{12(t-1)}/12, 12) \\ &\div A_{360-12(t-1)}(r_{12(t-1)}/12, 360 - 12(t - 1))]B_{12(t-1)}. \end{aligned}$$

As an example, after 36 months, $t$ in years is 3. The balance outstanding is $B_{36}$. The future value of the annuity is $A_{12}$ based on the 12 month adjustment period. The future value of the annuity to term is $A_{360-12(t-1)}$ and the term 360 − 12*2, or 336. The payment during year $t$ is

$$M_{12t} = m(r_{12(t-1)}/12, 360 - 12(t - 1))B_{12(t-1)}.$$

For this ARM, there is amortization with each payment, and the term of the loan is fixed. Other ARMs involve a fixed payment, but adjustment in the term. If the adjustment is once annually, at the first adjustment

$$m_{12}(r_{12}, N_{12}) = M/B_{12}$$

where $M = M_0$ is the constant payment for the life of the mortgage, and $r_{12}$ is as before. The number of additional payments to be made after 12 months, $N_{12}$, is solved from this equation. This feature makes the adjustment at the end of the amortization period. The present value of the saving is low to the borrower, given the long period, at a positive discount rate.

### *ARM Issues*

Several issues arise with the ARM. On risk sharing, with the FRPM, borrowers are protected on the upside on interest rates, being locked in, and can refinance if interest rates fall. The lender absorbs this interest rate risk. With the ARM, this risk is shifted back to the borrower. Not all of the risk is shifted to the borrower. The periodic cap on adjustments and the lifetime interest rate cap establish bounds for the contract interest rate.

The lender absorbs all risk of interest rate adjustments outside the relevant range. Interest rate adjustments are typically made on the basis of previous performance of the underlying index. Hence adjustments lag the movement of the index. When market interest rates are falling, the ARM interest rate falls more slowly. The flexibility feature reduces the risk to the lender or ultimate holder of the mortgage in the secondary market.

For bearing some interest rate risk, the borrower is compensated by receiving a lower initial interest rate. Because the borrower is bearing some of the interest rate risk, there is a positive probability that payments on an ARM eventually exceed those of a FRPM.

Since the initial interest rate on an ARM is lower than that on a FRPM, qualification for an ARM is easier. The interest rate is not constant, so it is not necessary that real payments decline over time, even with a positive rate of inflation. The steepness of negative slope for real payments, or tilt, is reduced or possibly eliminated. By reducing the tilt, the burden of payments on new purchasers is reduced. Buyers who are more willing to accept risk are more willing to take ARMs.

The lifetime and periodic interest rate caps set upper and lower bounds for the interest rate on the mortgage. The periodic cap places a limit on the interest rate adjustment at each renewal. The cap ranges impose calculation and programming costs on lenders. There are costs involved to the lender of administration, collection, notification, and—potentially—litigation with ARMs, that do not arise with FRPMs. The ARM, by having many variables, increases the potential for dispute and the possibility of litigation. Areas of contention are the awareness of going-in rates and negative amortization, the level of the index, and its application.

The interest rate used can vary between lenders, and may be administered or interpreted differently by lenders. Some time series of Treasury securities are published on an effective yield basis, and others only on a contract interest rate basis. Suppose the underlying index is 9 percent when the borrower takes out the loan, and 10 percent at the first renewal. The index is 10/9, or 1.111 at the renewal. With ARMs, the first interest rate is frequently subsidized as a going-in or teaser rate, to permit the borrower to qualify. The base interest rate can be 9 percent, with a going-in or teaser rate of 8 percent for the first 12 months. At first renewal, the interest rate increases to 1.111 times 9 percent, or 10 percent, a two percentage point increase.

Standards for underwriting make mortgages with negative amortization and no interest rate caps difficult to sell. Since there is heterogeneity in terms and conditions in ARMs, returns and risks are more difficult to evaluate.

### Graduated Payment Mortgage (GPM)

In the GPM, the initial interest rate is lower than the average effective interest rate over the contract. After some prespecified period, typically five years, the GPM converts to a FRPM or some other mortgage contract. The GPM is often offered by builders on new construction, as an enticement for buyers, and to permit qualification on mortgage underwriting standards. Builders attempt with GPMs to attract buyers who may not otherwise qualify because of the tilt.

On some GPMs there is a buydown, where the interest rate quoted to the buyer is held below an underlying interest rate for the mortgage. The difference in payments is made by the builder directly to the lender, with the compensation to the builder arising from a higher price for the property. Alternatively, the differential becomes a liability of the borrower, and is added to the outstanding balance after the GPM term, for example five years, and is due either as part of a balloon payment, or is included in the new financing vehicle.

Restrictions on GPMs in the secondary market make such mortgages difficult to resell, and confine their usage largely to new construction, or to where public policy has been used to assist potential owners to qualify.[7] The lender may be obliged to hold the loan as a portfolio mortgage, as opposed to selling it.

The GPM provides for increased monthly payments for some years, and then fixed payments after. It eases qualifying, and reduces the tilt for the borrower. Let $g$ be the annual graduation increase in payments and $t$ be the number of years of graduation, frequently 5 years.

The sinking fund rate for the GPM is defined by

$$x = \left[\frac{(1 + g)}{c(r/12, 12)}\right] - 1 \tag{6.12}$$

where $c = (1 + r/12)^{12}$ is the compound present value of 1 at annual interest rate $r$ and monthly payments. The numerator is the future value of payment, after gross-up at rate $g$. The mortgage payment multiplier for the GPM is

$$m_{\text{GPM}} = 1/A_{\text{GPM}} \tag{6.13}$$

as for the fixed rate and payment mortgage, where $A_{\text{GPM}}$ is the annuity factor for the GPM. This annuity factor is the sum of two components. The first component is the present value of the incremented payments up to year $t$, when the graduated payments are completed. This present value is the product of a monthly sinking fund factor $s(x,t)$ over the $t$ years, at rate $x$, defined above, and the annuity $A(r/12, 12)$.

The second component is the present value of the annuity after the graduation has been completed, from year $t$ to year $T$. At year $t$, the graduated payment has been increased by $(1 + g)^t$, and is held constant at this rate. The number of payments is $N = Tk$, with $k$ the frequency of compounding. The annuity is $A(r/12,N - t)$. This is multiplied by $(1 + g)^t/c(r/12,t)$. The numerator is the grossed up multiplier. The denominator is the present value of one dollar $t$ years hence, compounded monthly.

So

$$A_{\text{GPM}} = A(r/12, 12)s(x/12,t) + \frac{(1 + g)^t A(r/12,N - t)}{c(r/12,t)}$$

and the monthly payment is

$$M_{\text{GPM}}(t) = B/A_{\text{GPM}}$$

The annual payment each month is

$$M_{\text{GPM}}(t) = (1 + g)^t B/A_{\text{GPM}}$$

with $t = 0$ in the first year.

As an example, consider

$$T = 30 \qquad g = 0.075$$
$$r = 0.1 \text{ annually} \qquad k = 12$$
$$t = 60 \qquad N = Tk = 360$$

which are common parameters. Then

$$x = \frac{(1+g)}{c(r/12, 12)} - 1 = \frac{1.075}{1.104713} - 1 = -0.0268966$$

and negative values for $x$ are possible. The sinking fund factor is

$$s(x,t) = \frac{(1+x)^5 - 1}{x} = \frac{(1-0.0268966)^5 - 1}{-0.0268966} = 4.738172$$

Also

$$A(r/12, N-t) = A(0.1/12, 300) = 110.047230$$

$$c(r/12, t) = c(0.1/12, 60) = 1.64309$$

$$A(r/12, 12) = A(0.1/12, 12) = 11.374508$$

and

$$A_{GPM} = 11.374508 \times 4.738172 + (1.075)^5 \times \frac{110.047230}{1.645309} = 149.917064$$

$$m_{GPM} = 0.006670$$

Multiplying this by the balance, for a 50,000-dollar loan produces 333.50 dollars. Then the graduated payments are increased by 7.5 percent for the beginning of years 2 through 6.

### *GPM Issues*

The payments with the GPM are below those of the fixed payments mortgage in the early years, since they are increasing, and those of the latter are constant. The nominal payments on the GPM are increasing. Provided that the rate of inflation is below the rate of increase in GPM payment, there is an increasing real sequence of payments. The FRPM has a decreasing real sequence of payments with positive inflation rates.

The initial payments are lower than under the FRPM. The difference between the interest owing, using the contract interest rate, and the GPM payment is added to the initial loan balance, implying negative amortization. In the example, for a regular FRPM with a 10 percent rate, compounded monthly, and $B$ = \$50,000, the payment is \$438.97 monthly. The GPM payment is \$333.50 monthly, so \$105.47 per month must be added to the loan balance.

The inherent negative amortization of the GPM increases lender risk by increasing the probability of default. On a loan with a high loan-to-value ratio, the possibility of negative net equity arises. On selling, if transactions costs are added, equity can disappear. Public programs involving GPMs in the residential sector frequently require that the borrower-owner be restricted from selling during the graduation period. If points are charged, the calculation is as for the FRPM. The borrower receives $(1 - p)B$, raising the effective cost of borrowing. Lower cash flow during the initial period arises from the reduced payments, so a higher interest rate than on a regular ARM is required to compensate.

### *Buydowns*

The buydown method is used in new residential construction, and in public programs aimed at subsidizing homeownership. The builder makes a payment to a lender to reduce the payments. As an example, a municipality floats a bond issue, tax free to the holder. These funds are used either to finance housing construction directly or to finance mortgages.

The buyer wants to buy a house for $125,000 with a 10 percent down payment and a mortgage of $112,500. The mortgage is for a 30-year term. Suppose market mortgage rates are 14.25 percent. The monthly payment is

$$M = m(r,N)B$$

$$= m(0.1425/12,\ 12 \times 30) \times 112{,}500$$

If underwriting standards are such that a borrower is not permitted to spend more than 33 percent of total gross income on housing payments for principal, interest, and taxes, the buyer needs $58,000 of annual income.

Under a buydown, the initial interest rate is subsidized downward to permit the buyer to qualify. If the subsidized rate is 10.25 percent at the same terms, the buyer requires $44,000 of annual income instead of $58,000, permitting easier qualification.

### **Renegotiable Rate Mortgage (RRM), Rollover, or Canadian Mortgage**

The renegotiable rate mortgage (RRM), or rollover mortgage is the typical real estate loan offered in Canada. The reason for its prevalence in

Canada is legislation under the Canada Interest Act of 1968 prohibiting lenders from offering an interest rate locked in for longer than five years on residential real estate loans. The loans are amortized over longer periods, usually either 25 or 30 years, but the loan is rolled over as a balloon payment after a period not exceeding five years. The prevailing current market interest rate is charged at the renewal date.

The RRM is effectively a renegotiable loan with the property as collateral. There is a difference between the term, the number of years on the loan, and the amortization period. The interest rate is fixed for the term, but amortized over 25 to 30 years. Typically, there are no points, with options for prepayment. The calculation of payment is similar to that for the ARM.

The borrower bears some of the interest rate risk, shifted from the lender, since the interest rate is adjusted periodically. The entire loan is renegotiated. If there is no cap on the adjustments, there can be large changes in loan interest rates, since negative amortization is typically not permitted.

The RRM in Canada involves no interest rate caps and large fluctuations in payments; extensions are provided to households who would not be able to satisfy qualification and underwriting standards as new borrowers. Suppose the initial interest rate on the RRM is $r_0$, and renewal occurs only once every 12 months. The renewal interest rate $r_{12}$ is not generated by an index, nor by a formula with a cap. The payment at renewal is

$$M_{12} = m(r_{12}/12, 349)B_{12}$$

analogously as for the ARM, with the interest rate $r_{12}$ having no restriction. The British variant involves renegotiation at market interest rates, frequently once annual, but the payment remains constant and the number of payments is adjusted upward or downward.

## Flexible Payment Mortgage (FPM) and Seller Financing

The FPM is a loan where payment in initial periods is for interest only, with no amortization of the loan. The reduction in payment, as compared with the FRPM is not substantial, since early payments are largely interest, with little principal repayment. The FPM is sometimes used in seller financing to reduce the complication of calculation. Seller financing is used as a last resort, and frequently applies in depressed markets. The seller offers to carry the loan at market or below market rates. A common case is 10 percent down, 80 percent lender financing, and a 10 percent second by the seller. Assumable loans are more difficult to find given the nontransferability of most FRPM financing. A typical term is for 5–7 years, with a full or balloon payment. Buyers with a larger down payment can obtain better terms. Nothing-down strategists offer to have the seller take back financing. This strategy can be unsuccessful, especially if the seller has a real estate broker, because there is no up-front cash to pay the brokerage commission.

Seller financing mortgages can be treated as an installment sale for tax purposes, delaying capital gains tax. These loans can be sold for cash on the secondary market. The Federal National Mortgage Association (Fannie Mae) has a program under which seller financed loans are purchased from individual lenders. If not structured to Fannie Mae terms, they are nonstandard paper; and Fannie Mae will not buy them. Other buyers are loan brokers, but a large discount is taken on nonstandard paper. Some thrifts will package seller financed loans for sale in the secondary market. The seller sells at a higher price to compensate, and there is greater risk of default.

### Shared Appreciation Mortgage (SAM), Price-Level Adjusted Mortgage (PLAM)

For the shared appreciation mortgage (SAM), the lender takes an equity position, reducing the interest rate payable. A SAM does not involve alternative payment calculation, but presents a mechanism for allocating equity between borrower and lender. Any mortgage form, such as a FRPM, ARM, GPM, or RRM can be used as a shared appreciation mortgage. Upon sale, the lender is entitled to share in the capital gains if any.

The lender is illiquid, as it is difficult to enforce sale; and the equity is locked in the property. For a depository institution, with interest payments required on deposits, there is a problem of matching cash flow. When-to-sell timing is not controlled by the lender.

In the price-level adjusted mortgage (PLAM), with inflation, the mortgage balance is altered by a measure of inflation. This occurs where there are high rates of inflation.

The mortgage balance at time $t$ is

$$B_t = (1 + P_t)B$$

where $P_t$ is the level of a price index. The PLAM increases risks for both borrower and lender, although the relative price distortion from inflation is reduced. The payments fluctuate, because the loan balance is adjusted to retain the same real indebtedness. The adjustment $P_t$ is based on a general price index, such as the Consumer Price Index, and not on the value of the property. If general inflation exceeds the inflation rate on the property, equity can decline or be eliminated, increasing the risk of default. PLAMs are used infrequently because of risks in calculation and potential default.

## Equity Unlocking Financing

### *Equity Loan (EL)*

Financial mechanisms exist for unlocking the equity arising in real estate. Equity loans are used in the residential sector under the term *home equity loan* (*HEL*). The property owner with long-term tenure, a declining loan balance under the FRPM, and possibly increasing prices of real estate, has a buildup of equity. This equity can be realized by selling the property. Otherwise the owner is property rich and cash poor.

One method for unlocking equity is to take out a second or higher mortgage against the property. The lender on this mortgage stands behind the lender on the first mortgage. In the event of foreclosure, all claims on the first mortgagge must be paid prior to any on the second. Both variable and fixed interest rate financing is applicable.

A home equity loan in the residential sector is supplied by lenders to permit borrowing for any purpose. An open line of credit is supplied by the lender, and payments are made by writing checks against the lender, or by drawing against a credit card. The line of credit is secured by the equity of the owner in the property.

The lender charges points on the loan at origination, for the entire amount of the line of credit, even if all is not borrowed immediately. There is typically a minimum transaction size, but the borrower has the flexibility of taking out many small loans. The interest rate is tied to an index, as for an ARM. The interest rate $r_t$ on the open line of credit for the home equity loan (HEL) is

$$r_t = (I_t/I_0)r_0$$

where $I_0$ is the initial index, $I_t$ is the index at time $t$, and $r_0$ is the initial base interest rate on the index. At the beginning, teaser rates can be charged. In each period, the lender can charge fees, $f_t$ per dollar borrowed. Unlike with the ARM, there is no upward cap in typical interest rates $r_t$, so interest rate risk is transferred to the borrower.

The effective borrowing cost is obtainable from the sources and uses of cash statement.

**Sources and Uses of Cash, Home Equity Loan Borrower, Term of Loan**

| ***Cash Disbursements*** | | ***Cash Receipts*** | |
|---|---|---|---|
| Date of origination | | Date of origination | |
| Points-full credit line | $pF$ | Loan balance | 1 |
| Fees, commissions | $C$ | | |
| During payment period | | | |
| Interest rate, time $t$ | $r_t$ | | |
| Fees, time $t$ | $f_t$ | | |
| Present value, at effective borrowing cost | | | |
| $r_e$ | $\sum_{t=1}^{N} (r_t + f_t)/(1 + r_e)$ | | |
| Loan repayment, present value | | | |
| | $1/(1 + r_e)^N$ | | |
| Present value, cash disbursements | | Present value, cash receipts | 1 |
| $pF + C + \sum_{t=1}^{N} (r_t + f_t)/(1 + r_e) + 1/(1 + r_e)$ | | | |

At origination, the borrower receives one dollar from the lender. From each dollar, points and fees are deducted. During the life of the loan, interest payments and fees are made. At the term, the dollar is repaid. Borrowing occurs continuously, and the borrowing cost varies depending on the date. Borrowing occurs continuously; $F$ is the total line of credit; and $C$ is the total initial cost. In actual calculation, there are series of different loans, and the initial cost $pF + C$ is amortized over a series of borrowings. There is no amortization, unlike with a conventional mortgage.

Excluding the fixed cost, the marginal effective cost of borrowing the dollar is, solved from

$$\sum_{t=1}^{N}\left(\frac{r_t + f_t}{1 + r_e}\right) + \frac{1}{(1 + r_e)^N} = 1$$

as $r_e$. If all the fixed cost is charged against the first dollar, the effective borrowing cost is solved from

$$pF + C\sum_{t=1}^{N}\left(\frac{r_t + f_t}{1 + r_e}\right) + \frac{1}{(1+ r_e)^N} = 1$$

These are upper and lower bounds on the effective cost for the initial drawing.

The HEL has some advantages. Since the loan is secured, by the equity of the owner, the interest rate is lower than on an unsecured loan. The interest paid, and possibly some fees, can have favorable tax implications, if or owner-occupied mortgage interest is deductible, and interest paid on other consumer debt is not, in calculating taxable income. The loan permits a borrower access to varying amounts of funds, permitting drawings for short-term emergencies, or to purchase items available only instantaneously. Capital market imperfections and rigidities in obtaining funds are removed.

The costs of the loan are the encumbrance of the equity. Equity is frequently illiquid, while the debt is liquid. If the owner is not generating sufficient cash elsewhere to service the debt, a cash flow problem arises. The lack of a bound on the interest rate implies that there is risk in the loans, and that the owner is increasing the leverage on the property, further increasing the financing risk.

### *Reverse Annuity Mortgage (RAM)*

The purpose of a reverse annuity mortgage is to unlock the equity held by an owner without having to sell the property. Sale of the property involves transactions costs for brokerage and other fees, and possible capital gains taxes. The owner can face favorable financing and property taxes in the current location that are not duplicated elsewhere. The RAM involves a nonresident, such as a child or lender, providing funds through an annuity. The principal portion of the annuity payment is applied as an increasing mortgage lien against the property.

The parent and child share ownership in one variant. The parent sells some of the equity to the child, who finances the purchase by taking out a mortgage, and making the payment to the parent. For both parent and child, interest and property taxes are deductible against other income. Rent need not be charged against the parent; if it is, then depreciation expenses are claimable. The parent, with the sale proceeds, buys an annuity contract from a supplier such as an insurance company.

In another variant, the resident makes a contract directly with the financial institution. The institution takes a lien against the property. Upon death or other circumstance, the property is sold and part of the proceeds are used to pay off the obligation. The funds are used by the resident to buy an annuity.

Suppose $B$ is borrowed against equity. A monthly annuity is received, such that, with interest, the total debt after date $N$ is $B$. Using the sinking fund formula, the monthly receipt to sink $B$ is

$$M = s(r/12,N)B$$

the monthly income of the borrower from the lender.

**RAM Issues.** The lender, either the child or the financial institution, is providing liquidity for illiquid real estate investments, thus increasing the efficiency of real estate markets. Owners can remain in their property for longer than otherwise, and people are not as land rich and cash poor.

The amount loaned on a RAM is typically small, since the potential to service debt is low. The lender receives no cash flow during the investment period, and the only return is on the equity in the property.

There are tax implications. Interest payments are deductible, if interest on a second residence can be charged against other income. Since there is no rental income, depreciation expenses cannot be claimed. If the lender is an institution, the interest payable by the resident to the lender may not be deductible until the end of the term. The reason is that the owner is not borrowing a lump sum, but an additional amount each month.

This situation can be alleviated by borrowing the principal immediately. The interest received by the owner from the annuity is taxable under all circumstances, so the arrangement can have unfavorable tax implications. By receiving an annuity, the parent defers capital gains taxation, since the principal is being obtained slowly, instead of as a lump sum.[8]

There are estate implications. If the lender has advanced funds periodically, the balance owing can be subject to dispute. There are costs of probate and sale, which may have to be borne by the co-owner child or the lender. As an owner, the child can be liable for other claims against the estate.

A subsidiary agreement is required, which can lead to contentious and potentially litigious problems. A written subsidiary agreement is usually necessary to address issues arising subsequent to the placement of the RAM. The parents may seek some protection on rent increases, if rent is payable to the lender (child). Where the lender is advancing funds cumulatively, without an initial mortgage, a limit in dollars or term can be required.

As a consequence of these problems, RAMs are not widely used. Some programs advance funds from nonprofit agencies for such mortgages, but the beneficiaries are relatively few. The intergenerational option remains for children willing to assist parents in unlocking equity and obtaining tax benefits. With the RAM, the parents are able to remain in their property, which can have sentimental value and convenience, while not remaining cash poor.

### *Shared Equity Mortgage (SEM)*

The shared equity mortgage (SEM) attacks the affordability problem by having the parents and children sign on the loan. Parents help children to purchase real estate, but usually through the provision of a down payment—that is, a loan not recorded as a lien against the property. The parents obtain no tax benefit from such an investment.

The SEM can describe any ownership arrangement where more than one person has an ownership interest in the property and mortgage. The parents, nonresidents, or landlords, have high borrowing capability and a relatively high marginal tax rate. The children, residents, or tenants, have low borrowing capability and a relatively low marginal tax rate.

The total income of parents and children is used to qualify for the loan. On individual tax returns, as owners, the children deduct the interest and property taxes on their portion of the mortgage. They cannot deduct all the interest payments, but because of the relatively low tax bracket, the deduction is worth less.

For the remaining portion of the property not owned, rent is paid to the parents. The rent charged must be at fair market value. The rent is not deductible for the children, and is taxable income for the parents. Either one or two mortgages can be drawn up, but the usual arrangement is a single mortgage with all the parties liable. In the initial years, the investment is likely to produce losses for the parents. Revenue is rental income, and expenses are for depreciation, interest, maintenance and repairs, and property tax shares. With the initial losses, a tax refund can be obtained. Accounting losses are created. These are not necessarily losses on cash flow, but depend on the share of depreciation in total expense. These family backed mortgages involve a sale and leaseback transaction. The parents, co-owners of the real estate, buy the property with the children, and then lease their portion to the children.[9]

Tax deductions offset the parents' cash outlay. Since the rent increases and the expenses are relatively constant the child can eventually buy out the parents' interest. This interest can be conveyed as a gift for tax purposes. Table 6–1 compares the SEM with the regular fixed rate and payment mortgage.

**SEM Issues.** There are fees and transactions costs not applying to other mortgage arrangements. In case of marital breakdown, it must be specified as to how the proceeds are to be distributed. Tenancy in common is the most likely method to hold title, but the shares must be spelled out in an agreement.

Both the SEM and the RAM have a feature that is potentially applicable to other real estate finance problems. Two problems in real estate are the locked-in aspect of real estate equity, and the restricted bundling of tax shelter and income investments as a package. The RAM attempts to unlock real estate equity, and the SEM decouples the tax shelter and investment characteristics of real estate, supplying each to a party appropriately willing to pay.

## Concluding Remarks

Under the FRPM, the risks of interest rate and inflation are borne in the short run by the lender. This risk allocation does not imply that the borrower never bears any risk with the FRPM. For inflation risk, the implication is that a premium must be charged, in the basic interest rate, to compensate FRPM lenders for the risk. Since incumbents cannot be charged the premium, the cost is borne by new buyers, which raises interest rates, payments, and the difficulty of qualifying for mortgages.

Adjustable rate mortgages, in their variants, provide alternative methods for qualification in property purchases. The alternatives involve sharing risk on interest rates, inflation, and between generations of the same family.

**Table 6-1. Comparison of SEM FRPM with Regular FRPM**

| | | |
|---|---|---|
| *Assumptions* | | |
| Increase in property value (annual) | | 0.06 |
| Rent increase (annual) | | 0.06 |
| Deemed fair market rent, as proportion of market value | | 0.06 |
| Portion owned by parents | | 0.5 |
| Portion owned by children | | 0.5 |
| Initial purchase price (dollars) | | 100,000 |
| Structure portion depreciable | | 60,000 |
| Depreciation rate (straight line) | | 1/30 |
| Land portion nondepreciable | | 40,000 |
| Loan assumptions (FRPM) | | |
| Term (years) | | 30 |
| Number of payments | | 360 |
| Interest rate | | 0.1 |
| Balance initial | | 80,000 |
| Tax assumptions | | |
| Marginal tax rate—parent | | 0.30 |
| Marginal tax rate—child | | 0.15 |
| | *Shared Equity* | *Full Ownership* |
| *Child/resident* | | |
| Mortgage interest | 4,000 | 8,000 |
| Rent payment | 3,000 | — |
| Taxes | 900 | 1,800 |
| Before-tax cash outlay | 7,900 | 9,800 |
| Tax saving | (735) | (1,470) |
| After-tax cash outlay | 7,165 | 8,330 |
| *Parent/investor* | *Year 1* | *Year 5* |
| Rent | 3,000 | 3,377 |
| Mortgage interest | (4,000) | (4,000) |
| Depreciation | (2,000) | (2,000) |
| Taxable income (loss) | (3,000) | (2,623) |
| Tax saving | 900 | 787 |
| After-tax cash flow | (100) | 164 |

## Notes

1. There can be market conditions where, because of the slope of the term structure and the restricted secondary market for ARMs, the interest rates on FRPMs are similar to those of ARMs.

2. The function can exhibit concavity properties without being differentiable. If the utility function is twice differentiable, then concavity implies diminishing marginal utility, or that $\partial u/\partial \mu$ decreases in $\mu$, and $\partial u/\partial \sigma$ decreases in $\sigma$, implying that $\partial^2 u/\partial \mu^2 < 0$ and $\partial^2 u/\partial \sigma^2 < 0$.

3. If the utility level is $u(\mu,\sigma)$, and the trade-off between risk and return is linear, then where the borrower chooses as ARM, the slope of the indifference curve, the marginal rate of substitution between risk and return is equal to the slope of the trade-off line.

The total derivative of the utility function is $du = (\partial u/\partial \mu)\, du + (\partial u/\partial \sigma)\, d\sigma = 0$ if utility is constant along an indifference curve. Hence $d\sigma/d\mu = -(\partial u/\partial \mu)/(\partial u/\partial \sigma)$ is the constant, and let this be $-\omega$. Where

$$(\partial u/\partial \mu)/(\partial u/\sigma) = \omega \qquad \text{(ARM chosen)}$$

$$(\partial u/\partial \mu)/(\partial u/\sigma) > \omega \qquad \text{(FRPM chosen)}$$

The slope of the indifference curve exceeds that of the trade-off line, and the borrower is in a corner. A large percentage of households are observed at the corner, selecting the FRPM.

4. See Fisher [1930]. The relationship, even if supported in earlier years, appears to break down in the 1970s, where real interest rates become negative, or low and positive. In the 1980s, real interest rates become high and positive. For the negative real interest rates, explanations include (1) a decrease in the marginal productivity of capital caused by increasing energy prices [Wilcox 1983]; (Energy and capital are assumed to be complements); (2) an increase in the effective marginal tax rates of individuals, caused by inflationary increases in an unindexed tax regime, without necesarily accompanying real wage increases, termed bracket creep; and (3) a decrease in the marginal productivity of capital caused by regulations increasing cost but not output, such as environmental and building code regulations. If inflationary expectations were for low rates, there would have been large errors in calculations for the 1970s. The high real interest rates of the 1980s could arise from sluggish inflationary expectations, and an increase in the marginal productivity of capital, given changes in taxes and regulatory treatment and decreases in energy prices.

5. The weekly or monthly Treasury constant maturity indexes are obtained from the Board of Governors of the Federal Reserve System, Publication Services, MS 138, Washington, DC. The weekly index, publication H15, and the monthly index, publication G13, are published each Monday.

6. Treasury securities are frequently sold at a discount. A discounted short-term Treasury bill with annual interest rate $r$ is sold at a price $1 - r$, where all the interest is paid through the discount. The effective yield on an annual basis is $r/(1 - r)$, which exceeds $r$. Some Treasury bill and note interest-rate series are published on a contract basis for $r$, as opposed to an effective yield basis, $r/(1 - r)$.

7. Mortgage loans to assist those whose current income is below some threshold are examples in the residential sector. Some households have high potential income and low current assets, to make a down payment. Public programs entail a contribution to the down payment or initial payments as a buydown.

8. Capital gains can be deferred by not being realized through sale, while capital losses can be recognized immediately through sale.

# III REAL ESTATE INVESTMENT: HOLDING PHYSICAL ASSETS AND PROPERTIES

# 7 ACTIVE INVESTMENT IN REAL ESTATE: *Residential Owner Occupancy*

## Introduction

Underwriting standards govern the decision as to how lenders determine who is permitted to borrow funds. There are various lender and borrower risks. Comparison of alternative financing options, and whether refinancing should be contemplated, are examined.

The investment decision for holding residential property is developed. The strategy is derived for the owner occupier and for the investor who typically owns more than one property. The strategy has general implications for leverage, risk, and other aspects of real estate investment, including both owner occupied and rental property.

This chapter focuses on owner occupancy. The only major issue excluded in owner-occupied active real estate is depreciation. The owner occupier must make decisions of financing and loan packages, on timing when to sell, and on calculating the effective rate of return to holding real estate. If tax laws permit the deduction or shielding of interest payments on one or more than one property, then investment decisions are required on the timing of sale, optimizing with respect to regulations.

## Underwriting Standards

Lenders that advance financing are searching to minimize two types of risk in credit scoring. The property and neighborhood can vary in characteristics. The borrowers vary in liquidity and characteristics. Consequently, the screening of borrowers relies on the development of rules of thumb to distinguish high-quality borrowers and properties. There can be asymmetrical information in the loan market, with the borrowers knowing more about themselves than they reveal in loan applications. There is a large error term in any prediction as to the probability of default, with the borrowers being unable to predict the risk of job loss or personal dislocation. The rules of thumb are based on standards set by buyers of mortgages in the secondary market.

### *The Borrower*

Under underwriting standards for purchases of residential property, the borrower is permitted to apply total income from earnings of family members, such as both spouses.[1] Income from nonlabor sources such as interest, dividends, and investment cash flow excluding depreciation can be included, adjusted by a probability. The lender on a loan application can obtain a credit check, to determine the borrower's credit rating (from 0 to 9), and to obtain employment and compensation verification, together with prospects for future employment. The lender has the right to verify sources of interest and dividend income.

Underwriting standards are established by purchasers in the secondary market. When lenders apply these standards to borrowers, they assure themselves of liquidity for the mortgages, by facility of sale to the secondary market.

Underwriting standards include restrictions on low down payments and high loan-to-value ratio mortgages. There are two criteria. The total expense on the property cannot exceed a given percentage of total monthly income of the borrower. The total monthly expense on the property, plus all other debt service costs, cannot exceed another percentage of total monthly income. Such standards are established for sale into the secondary market by the Federal National Mortgage Association and the Federal Home Loan Mortgage Corporation.

As a specific policy for debt service ratios, a borrower with $\upsilon > 0.9$, or less than 10 percent down, can be restricted to spending no more than 25 percent of gross monthly income on the property—for interest, principal, taxes, and insurance—and 33 percent on the property and other installment debt. A borrower with $v > 0.8$, or less than 20 percent down, can face debt service ratios of 33 and 38 percent respectively. Tighter standards on those with low-equity ratios reduces the risk of default.

Other imposed underwriting standards include restrictions on purchases of adjustable rate mortgages in the secondary market, unless there is an ultimate and periodic cap on the adjustable interest rate. Graduated payment mortgages, where payments are increased over an initial period, are restricted in resale. Such restrictions affect buydowns offered by builders, which frequently come with such mortgages.

External contributions to the down payment of the borrower are limited. External sources include the seller, builder, or real estate agent. A particular underwriting limit on external contributions is to 3 percent of the sale price or appraised value, whichever is lower. No external contributions are permitted on ARMs with less than 10 percent down, or buydowns on any ARMs. Monitoring and enforcement of restrictions on external contributions is difficult. External contributions in a transaction can be made by a seller, broker, or developer; restrictions by lenders or the secondary market can be circumvented.

Transactions in real estate frequently entail equity contributions by several partners. Arrangements include contributions by relatives or friends. Under tightened underwriting standards, a coborrower is placed in a position of legal liability against the debts of the property. A coborrower, such as a relative, can be required to take title, and to occupy the property if down payments by the borrower and coborrower combined are less than 10 percent of the loan amount. A borrower can be required to contribute 5 percent down if any outside funds have been applied toward the down payment. Enforcement of this provision is difficult. Other provisions imposed by lenders include restrictions on loans to investors who do not plan occupancy, on refinancings, or on second homes.

Underwriting standards exist to reduce the risk of default and to increase the marketability of the mortgages. There are various underwriting or default risks for the lender. Employment stability is difficult to measure. There is an additional problem if the borrower is self-employed. Income streams are difficult to verify. Two years of previous income tax returns are required for completion of a file. Younger borrowers, or borrowers who have not previously used credit, may have little or no credit history. evidence on savings and investment are obtained, but income from such assets cannot be predicted with accuracy, other than in low-risk and low-return cash equivalents. The lender is prohibited from using personal characteristics such as age, sex, or race in the determination of qualification.

The borrower faces various financing considerations. The debt-equity ratio must be determined. If contract interest rates increase with amount borrowed, borrowers face a rising supply price of funds. Higher interest rates must be paid on all dollars borrowed. Points and shorter maturities increase the effective interest rate paid. On a loan of balance $B$, and points $p$, the borrower receives $(1-p)B$, and pays the periodic payment $m(r/k,N)B$, where $r$ is the contract interest rate and $k$ is the frequency of compounding.

### *The Property*

The property must qualify with underwriting standards and this requires an appraisal. Appraisals are subject to the various difficulties discussed in chapter 3. The market approach, as applied with three comparables, is subject to statistical unreliability. Adjustments for quality and characteristics are required. All transactions used should be at arm's length. The cost approach to appraisal involves using the sum of the lot plus the depreciated value of replacement of the structure. Since a depreciation rate must be selected, errors arise in estimating the value of an older property, the cost approach is more suitable for new construction. The package of documents indicating total income and property and credit characteristics of the borrower, income and investment verification of the borrower, and the property appraisal are used to sell the mortgage in the secondary market.

### *Closing*

On approval, the lender issues a loan commitment. The lender can require an escrow account be opened for the prepayment of property taxes. Property taxes are deductible from ordinary income in computing taxable income of an owner occupier, and always deductible for an investor. If regulations state that the owner must pay the taxes directly to obtain credit for the deduction, an escrow account can cause problems.

Private mortgage insurance, to protect the lender against default, is required if the borrower has less than a particular percentage of equity in the property, for example, 20 percent. Hazard insurance for flood and earthquake can be required by the lender, depending on the location. Flood insurance is provided through a federal government program, administered by the Federal Emergency Management Administration

(FEMA). Earthquake insurance in areas at risk, such as parts of California, can be required. In California, insurers are obliged to offer earthquake insurance as part of the homeowner insurance package, which normally covers fire and comprehensive damage.

Some lenders require a declining-term life insurance policy be taken out, to protect the mortgage against default due to death. Title insurance fees and legal fees are costs at closing, as are the real estate and brokerage commission. These costs are negotiable between buyer and seller.

Legislation covers settlement and closing costs on residential real estate transactions. Legislation applies under the Real Estate Settlement and Procedures Act (RESPA) whereby kickbacks are prohibited. Payments of commission on sale of property can generally be made only to licensed real estate practitioners, including mortgage brokers and moving companies. No referral fees are chargeable to the individual, over any predetermined fees. The annual percentage rate (APR) on the loan must be disclosed. The APR as calculated is over a 30-year term. If the borrower plans to remain on the property for a shorter time, the effective APR is higher.

The calculation of the APR is based on mortgage multipliers. As before, for loan balance $B$, the mortgage payment over $N = Tk$ periods, where $T$ is the term in years and $k$ is the frequency of compounding per year at interest rate $r$, is

$$M = m(r/k,N)B$$

so

$$M = m(r_e/k,N)(1 - p)B = m(r/k,N)B$$

implying that

$$m(r_e/k,N) = \frac{m(r/k,N)}{1 - p}$$

The mortgage multiplier $m(r/k,N)$ and points $p$ are known, so the right-hand side is fixed. The left-hand side is known except for $r_e$, which is solved by iteration. Select an annual interest rate $r_e$, and substitute in the left-hand side formula. If the left side exceeds the right side, reduce the interest rate, and $m_e$ declines. If the left side is below the right side, increase the interest rate. The APR, or effective interest rate, is the interest rate on a no-points loan if held to term.

For a FRPM with a 30-year term, monthly compounding, 12 percent interest rate, and 2 points,

$$\left[\frac{r_e/12}{1-(1+r_e/12)^{-360}}\right] = \left[\frac{0.12/12}{1-(1+0.12/12)^{-360}}\right] \Big/ (1-0.02)$$
$$= \frac{0.01}{1-(1.01)^{-360}} \Big/ 0.98 \tag{7.1}$$

and $r_e$ can be solved.

## Residential Real Estate Holding Decisions

### *Tax Preference Items*

For the borrower, investment in residential housing, as an owner occupier, provides a tax shelter. Capital gains taxes can be deferred, if the sale proceeds of one principal residence are rolled over into another principal residence within a specific period. On principal residences, there is an exemption from taxation for capital gains up to a limit of $125,000 once per married couple or individual on the sale of a principal residence, if the seller is aged over 55.

There is no tax on the imputed rental income of owner occupiers. The owner occupier is acting as a landlord paying rent to himself. This rent is not counted as taxable income. Were the owner not occupying, rent would be paid to another landlord, who would report this as taxable income.

There is a tax shield, with mortgage interest and property taxes deductible against other income. There are preferential property tax rates in some jurisdictions, and limits on property tax levels and increases in others. The tax shield provides an incentive to use debt as opposed to equity financing, depending on the opportunity cost after tax of equity for the owner.

### *Single-Period Holding*

There are tax incentives favoring owner occupancy as opposed to renting. Tax regulations provide an incentive to use debt financing on residential property. Let $V$ be the price of the property and $a$ the rate of return to holding real estate. This rate of return can be the economic rate, including capital gains and imputed income, or the opportunity cost of investing $V$ in an asset with risk equivalent to that on physical property.

Consider the owner occupier as viewing the residential property as an investment. The project counts as revenue the imputed rental income and potential capital gains, or total revenue $aV$. The mortgage balance at purchase is $B$, so equity is $E = V - B$.[2]

The economic income statement of the owner occupier were there no taxes, would be

**Economic Income Statement, Owner Occupier, During Period *t***

Gross revenue
- Imputed rental income
- Plus: Accrued capital gains during period (not necessarily realized)

Less: Operating expenses (cash, not tax shielded)
- Maintenance
- Utilities

Less: Noncash expenses
- Economic depreciation

Less: Tax-shielded expenses
- Interest expense
- Property taxes

Equals: Net income

Tax regulations affect the rate of return on owner occupied investment. Suppose the tax regime has the following characteristics. Imputed rental income of owner occupiers is not taxed, and capital gains can be deferred or be subject to a large ultimate exemption. The gross rate of return is nontaxable. Depreciation and maintenance expenses are not deductible for the homeowner. While no portion of principal residence income is taxed, mortgage interest and property taxes are deductible.

The tax-purposes income statement of the owner occupier differs from the economic income statement. All of the same items are included, except that imputed rental income and accrued capital gains (those arising during the current period) are reported as zero, since they are not counted as part of taxable income. Maintenance and utility expenses are not reported, nor are noncash expenses, since they are not deductible expenses. The only expenses reported in this business, of an owner occupied engaged in providing shelter services, are those of interest and property taxes. For tax purposes, the property management business shows a loss, which is deductible against other expenses.

For the financial analysis of the owner occupier, the gross revenue variable $a$ is defined to include from the economic income statement the imputed rental income and accrued capital gains, less maintenance expenses, utilities, and economic depreciation. For the owner occupier, these expenses are treated similarly, and depreciation cannot be claimed as an expense.

Gross revenue, less operating, nonshielded expenses and economic depreciation, is $aV$, where $V$ is the value of the property. The loan balance is $B$, and interest paid is $r$. There are property taxes at the rate $\lambda$ levied on the market value of the property, or $\lambda V$, and interest payments on the mortgage $rB$.

Were there no taxation, that is, if the investor faced a zero income tax rate, other than for property taxes, the income statement of the owner occupier cum investor produces net variable profit per period of

$$aV - \lambda V - rB = Y = r_e E \tag{7.2}$$

where $Y$ is financial income. The equity of the owner is $E$, and $r_e$ is the rate of return on equity.

Dividing by $V$,

$$a - \lambda - rv = y = r_e(1 - v) \tag{7.3}$$

Here $v = B/V$ is the loan-to-value ratio, and $1 - v = E/V$ is the equity-to-value ratio. The rate of return on equity is

$$r_e = (a - \lambda - rv)/(1 - v) \tag{7.4}$$

If $a$, the net revenue, is 10 percent, or 0.1, and the property tax rate is 0.01, with interest rate $r = 0.08$, then $r_e = (0.09 - 0.08v)/(1 - v)$. The return on equity depends on $v$, the loan-to-value ratio, the leverage the owner occupier has in the property. The leverage multiplier is $1/(1 - v)$. Suppose the owner occupier has a loan-to-value ratio of 0.8, or an 80 percent mortgage. Then the leverage multiplier is $1/(1 - 0.8)$, or 5. The rate of return is $(0.09 - 0.064) \times 5$, or 13 percent. If the owner occupier increases the loan-to-value ratio to 0.9, by placing a smaller down payment, the leverage multiplier becomes $1/(1 - 0.9)$, or 10. The rate of return is $(0.09 - 0.072) \times 10$, or 18 percent. Increased leverage increases the rate of return on equity, provided the numerator is positive.

### *Leverage and Risk*

Leverage entails risk for the investor in real estate. The rate of return on equity expected is $r_e = (a - \lambda - rv)/(1 - v)$. In the calculation, the loan-to-value ratio $v$, determining the leverage, is fixed at the beginning of the period, and is not a random variable. The interest rate $r$ is fixed, for FRPM financing, and $\lambda$, the property tax rate, can be viewed as parameters, with no variation.

The only variable subject to randomness is the gross return $a$, dependent on expected inflation in real estate and market conditions. If $\sigma(a)$ is the standard deviation of the gross return, and $\sigma(r_e)$ is the standard deviation of the return on equity, then

$$\sigma^2(r_e) = \left(\frac{1}{1 - v}\right)^2 \sigma^2(a)$$

and if $L = 1/(1 - v)$ is the leverage multiplier, then

$$L = \frac{\sigma(r_e)}{\sigma(a)} = \frac{1}{1 - v} \qquad (7.5)$$

The leverage multiplier is the inverse of the equity ratio. When $v = 0$, the real estate is purchased with all cash, so $1 - v = 1$, and $\sigma(r_e)/\sigma(a) = 1$. The risk of the return on equity, as measured by the standard deviation, is the same as the risk of the gross income, for a completely unleveraged purchase.

At the other polar extreme, when real estate is purchased with nothing down, $v = 1$, so $L = \infty$, and the ratio of the risk on the rate of return, relative to the risk on gross income, is also infinite. Hence, increased leverage raises the relative risk of the investment, in effective rate of return as opposed to gross income.

### *Tax Effects*

This one-period analysis does not include tax effects. The income statement for tax purposes of the owner occupier is, if mortgage interest and property taxes are deductible,

**Tax Purposes Income Statement, Owner Occupier, During Period *t***

Gross Revenue
Imputed rental income
Plus: Accrued capital gains during period (not necessarily realized)
Equals: Total gross revenue

Less: Operating expenses (cash, not tax shielded)
Maintenance
Utilities

Less: Noncash expenses
Economic depreciation
Equals: Excluded income and expenses for tax purposes $aV = 0$

Less: Tax-shielded expenses
Interest expense $rB$
Property taxes $\lambda V$
Equals: Net income $-rB - \lambda V$

The owner occupier reports a loss for tax purposes of $rB + \lambda V$. If the marginal rate of personal income taxation is $\tau$, the amount $\tau(rB + \lambda V)$, is receovered in taxes otherwise payable. The economic income statement of the owner occupier is

**Economic Income Statement, Owner Occupier, During Period *t***

Net income (operations)
Imputed rental income
Plus: Accrued capital gains
Less: Maintenance
Less: Utilities
Less: Economic depreciation (noncash)
Equals: Net income nonshielded $aV$

Less: Shielded expenses
Mortgage interest $rB$
Property taxes $\lambda V$
Plus: Tax-shielded recovery
Mortgage interest $\tau rB$
Property taxes $\tau\lambda V$
Equals: Net income from owner occupancy $aV - (1 - \tau)(rB + \tau V)$

Net income, for an owner occupier with a positive marginal tax rate, is

$$Y = aV - (1 - \tau)(rB + \lambda V) = r_e E$$

and dividing by the value of the property

$$y = a - (1 - \tau)rv + \lambda) = r_e(1 - v) \tag{7.6}$$

with the effective expected rate of return on equity

$$r_e = [a - (1 - \tau)(rv + \lambda)]/(1 - v) \tag{7.7}$$

In the above circumstance, if the marginal rate of taxation of the owner occupier is 0.25, the rate of return is 22.2 percent:

$$\frac{0.1 - 0.75 \times (0.064 + 0.01)}{1 - 0.8} = (0.1 - 0.0555) \times 5 = 0.0445 \times 5$$

The presence of taxation deductions increases the rate of return. The risk of the investment remains determined by $\sigma(r_e) = L\sigma(a)$, if the tax rate can be viewed as a parameter with no variance. Increased leverage in $L$ increases the risk of the investment, as indicated by $\sigma(r_e)$.

Suppose the property tax rate is fixed, but the income tax rate is unknown, because the tax rate is determined by other income. Then

$$r_e = La - L(1 - \tau)(rv + \lambda) \tag{7.8}$$

The two random terms are $La$ and $-Lrv\tau$. So

$$\sigma^2(r_e) = L^2[\sigma^2(a) + r^2v^2\sigma^2(\tau) - 2arvX(a,\tau)] \tag{7.9}$$

where $X(a,\tau)$ is the covariance between gross income and the tax rate. As gross income increases, one would expect the tax rate to increase, so $X(a,\tau)$ is positive.

The effective rate of return $r_e$ is increasing in the net income $a$. A one percentage point increase in the rate of appreciation increases the rate of return by the leverage multiplier $1/(1 - v)$. A one percentage point increase in the interest rate reduces the rate of return by $(1 - \tau)v/(1 - v)$. A one percentage increase in the property tax rate reduces the rate of return by $(1 - \tau)/(1 - v)$. The reduction is less than if the tax rate is zero, because these expenses are shielded. An increase in the marginal tax rate $\tau$ increases the rate or return $r_e$ by $(rv + \tau)/(1 - v)$. The numerator is the shielded expense, and this amount is leveraged. Correspondingly, a reduction in marginal tax rates reduces the effective rate of return.

Real estate investments are directed toward those facing the highest marginal tax rate. Select a predetermined rate of return, for real estate or assets of comparable risk and liquidity as $r_e$, and find the threshold marginal tax rate required. Then

$$r_e(1 - v) = a - (1 - \tau)(rv + \lambda)$$

$$r_e(1 - v) - a - rv - \lambda = \tau(rv + \lambda)$$

$$\tau^* = \frac{r_e(1 - v) - a - (rv + \lambda)}{rv + \lambda} \qquad (7.10)$$

This relation establishes the threshold marginal tax rate. If a person has a marginal tax rate $\tau > \tau^*$, then the investment can be undertaken, assuming attitudes toward risk are the same over groups. If $\tau < \tau^*$, then the investor does not undertake the investment.

Leverage increases the risk of the investment. This occurs for any real estate project, and not only owner occupancy. If net income is positive, or $a > (1 - \tau)(rv + \lambda)$, then a higher loan-to-value ratio produces a higher rate of return, with an explosive characteristic. The return is infinite if the investor puts nothing down, or where $v = 1$. Where $v = 1$, the denominator is zero, and the leverage multiplier is infinite. Provided net income is positive, the rate of return on investment is infinite. The prospect of such returns accounts for the popularity of nothing-down seminars.

At the same time, nothing down increases the real estate leverage risk substantially. If $a < (1 - \tau(rv + \lambda)$, then the return becomes negative infinity. The return is a knife edge, being very large either positive or negative depending on the net income.

The response to the loan-to-value ratio is

$$\partial r_e/\partial v = \{-(1 - v)(1 - \tau)r + [a - (1 - \tau)(rv + \lambda)]\}/(1 - v)^2 \qquad (7.11)$$

The denominator $(1 - v)^2$ is positive, so increased leverage increases the rate of return if

$$a > (1 - \tau)(r + \lambda)$$

It is not sufficient that the net income, after nonshielded expenses, exceeds operating costs. The return has to exceed the expenses with $v = 1$, or where cash disbursements are highest. If the net income is below $(1 - \tau)(r + \lambda)$, the increased leverage reduces the rate of return.

Neglected are any other possible tax credits, attitudes toward risk, interest subsidies, or tax benefits from ownership as opposed to renting.[3] The owner occupier has the alternative of renting. If the market rent is the same as the imputed rent, there is an incentive to own, particularly as the marginal tax rate rises. In areas with high rates of owner occupancy, the prices of properties relative to rents can reflect the tax benefits, which are capitalized into prices; only those with greater than a threshold marginal tax rate find it attractive to own.

### *Multiple-Period Holding*

The above is a one-period analysis and calculation. Real estate is a long-lived asset. If there were no transactions costs of purchase and sale, and all variables had the same pattern over time, the single-period calculation above would suffice. The optimal holding period cannot be determined from a single-period calculation.

Over one period, the net income is $y = a - (1 - \tau)(rv + \lambda)$ per unit value of the property. Even if all the components of net income were constant over time, and $y$ could be viewed as an annuity, there are holding and transactions costs. It is convenient to use $y$ as the net income per unit value of the property. The $y$ has the interpretation of a price; the value $V$ is a quantity. Suppose there are no transactions, closing, or brokerage costs. The owner occupier seeks to determine the optimal holdin gperiod, or when to sell. At the date of purchase, a down payment is paid out. Per one dollar of value, the down payment is $(1 - v)$, which is cash disbursed. The investment is made with once-annual compounding frequency. Cash received is net income. The owner occupier's statement for the sources and uses of cash is

| Date | |
|---|---|
| Initial purchase | $-(1 - v)$ |
| Ownership (net income) | $y$ |

The cash flow statement, equating cash in and cash out, for the period up to $t$ is

$$(1 - v) = yA(r_e, t)$$

with $A = [1 - (1 + r_e)^{-t}]/r_e$. If $y$ is an infinite annuity, and the owner never sells

$$A(r_e,t) = (1 - v)/y$$

Now $y$ is expressed in percentage terms, as is the equity ratio $1 - v$. The rate of return $r_e$ solving this equation is the return to owner occupancy given holding period $t$. Alternatively, the owner can have a target rate of return for $r_e$, and seeks to determine the holding length to attain the return. Either is soluble from the equation.

At purchase date, the owner investor faces transactions costs for points and other fees. Let these costs be $p$, since points account for the bulk of thte direct costs, though time in search is part of the cost. At sale date, there are transactions costs of prepayment penalties, if applicable, and brokerage commissions. Let the prepayment penalty be $q$, applied to the loan balance, and let $n$ represent the real estate brokerage commission rate and other transaction fees.

At date of sale, the owner pays a prepayment penalty on the loan, of $C$ periods of interest. If $r$ is the interest rate, $k$ the frequency of compounding, and $t$ the sale date,

$$q_t = (r/k) \sum_{i=1}^{C} b_{t+i} \tag{7.12}$$

plus a brokerage commission $n$. The owner receives $(1 - n)$ upon date of sale, as a percentage of the value of the property.

The cash out for the borrower includes the initial equity $E = V - B$. Dividing by $V$, $1 - v = E/V$ is the equity contributed per dollar of value of the property. The borrower also pays points, in initial cash out of $pB$, or $pv$ on a per dollar basis. Total cash originally contributed at purchase is $(1 - v) + pv$, per dollar of property.

Let the effective rate of return be a real rate of return, net of expected real estate inflation. So th expected gains in price of the property, less depreciation, are netted out in the discount rate $r_e$. The income from ownership $yV$ is then imputed rent less interest expense, property taxes, and other operating expenses, plus the tax shield add-back for interest and property taxes. So $y$ is defined as above, as $a - (1 - \tau)(rv + \lambda)$, except that capital gains are excluded. The capital value is $yA(r_e,t)$ over $t$ years, per dollar of initial value.

After year $t$, suppose sale is contemplated. The prepayment penalty $q_t$ is based on the loan $B$, or $q_tB$, or $q_tv$ per dollar of property. Real estate commissions are levied at rate $n$, so for each dollar, $(1 - n - q_t v)$ is received. Cash in for the owner occupier includes the net income present value from ownership $yA(r_e,t)$ and the present value of the receipts at sale, or $(1 - n - q_t v)/(1 + r_e)^t$.

Equating cash in and cash out on a present-value basis

$$(1 - v) + pv = yA(r_e,t) + \frac{1 - n - q_t v}{(1 + r_e)^t} \qquad (7.13)$$

Cash out is for the down payment, per dollar value of the property $v$, and for points on the loan. Cash in is for the net income while an owner, and the present value of the proceeds upon sale. The value of the property is held constant, and $r_e$ is the real rate of return to holding real estate in owner occupancy.

There is a different rate of return for each time period $t$. The left side of the equation, cash out, is constant, as it occurs at date of purchase. Alternatively, at prospective date of sale, the equation can be expressed in future-value terms

$$[(1 - v) + pv](1 + r_e)^t = yA_t(r_e,t) + (1 - n - q_t v) \qquad (7.14)$$

If $y$ is not constant, then it must be redefined as a function of $t$ as $a_t - (1 - \tau)(rv + \lambda)$, where $a_t$ is the imputed rent less operating expenses as a percentage of the property value. Rents do not have to be projected to grow, as the effective rate of return $r_e$ is measured net of inflation. If $y$ is not constant, but equal to $y_t$, then the present value is $\Sigma_{s=1}^{t} y_s/(1 + r_e)^s$. Since there is no tax depreciation effect, inflation less economic depreciation is included in the discount rate, and $(1 - \tau)(rv + \lambda)$ can be viewed as constant, it is convenient to treat $y$ as an annuity for owner occupiers.

At date of sale, the initial expenditures are indexed forward by the holding rate of return. The annual income per dollar value of the property is capitalized by the future value of an annuity. At date of sale, for each one dollar of sale value gross, $n$ cents are paid in real estate brokerage and other fees, and $q_t v$ is paid in penalties on the mortgage. The prepayment penalty is $q_t$, and $v$ the initial loan-to-value ratio.

The rate of return to owner occupancy provides a strategy on when to sell, given projections on the future. Under a specific scenario for the variables, the rate of return is determined as a function of the points $p$, the loan-to-value ratio $v$, the contract mortgage rate $r$, real estate commission $n$, months of prepayment penalty $C$, and all the operating variables in the annual net income $y$.

The rate of return $r_e$ is a function of the holding period $t$. With front-end and back-end costs, a short-term holding period is unlikely to be profitable, unless there are substantial capital gains in $a$. The owner occupant also faces the prospect of finding alternative shelter should sale occur.

The effect of various variables on rate of return to the owner occupier investor can be tabulated:

| *Increase in Variable* | *Effect on* $r_e$ |
|---|---|
| Points $p$ | Decrease |
| Net income $y$ | Increase |
| Capital gains—increase $a$ | Increase |
| Imputed rental income—increase $a$ | Increase |
| Maintenance expense—decrease $a$ | Decrease |
| Utility expense—decrease $a$ | Decrease |
| Marginal tax rate | Increase |
| Contract interest rate $r$ | Decrease |
| Property tax rate $\lambda$ | Decrease |
| Months of prepayment penalty $C$ | Decrease |
| Real estate commission $n$ | Decrease |

A number of simulations can be played on the basic equation, for changes in the optimal holding strategy. If $r_e$ is set at some target interest rate, the optimal holding period can be determined. The effective rate of return $r_e$ is the return to owner occupancy. A measure of the total return in dollars is the product of $r_e$ and the property value, or $r_e V$, the net income from ownership. The rate of return is not constrained to be positive.

The income statement, for economic and tax purposes of the real estate owner occupier has been developed. The balance sheet is also relevant. Here, each year the paydown of mortgage debt increases the equity in the project. The return on capital has been expressed in real terms. The inflation on the real estate is on a net basis, after economic depreciation has been subtracted.[4]

The asset and liability position of the owner occupant can be indicated by the balance sheet

**Balance Sheet, Owner Occupant, Date $t$**
(nominal, not inflation adjusted, dollars)

| Assets | | Liabilities and Owner Equity | |
|---|---|---|---|
| Real estate | $V_t = V(1+g)^t$ | Mortgage balance | $B_t = b_t B$ |
| | | **Owner Equity** | |
| | | Capital contributed | $V - B + pB$ |
| | | Additions in nominal equity | |
| | | Mortgage paydown | $B - B_t$ $= B(1 - b_t)$ |
| | | Capital gains | $V_t - V$ |

The mortgage balance is held constant in nominal terms, so in real terms the mortgage debt for a FRPM declines. There are no additions during the holding period. When the property is initially purchased for $V$, the value of land is $L$, and the value of structures is $S$, so $V = L + S$. For tax purposes, on realization, capital gains taxes are levied on the nominal differential between $V_t$ and $V$. If the tax regime is indexed for inflation, part of this problem is corrected. The mortgage balance is not indexed for inflation, part of this problem is corrected. The mortgage balance is not indexed for inflation, except in the price level adjusted mortgage (PLAM), so the asset and liability sides of the financial statements are asymmetrical. In inflationary periods, real liabilities decline. The owner derives equity from the mortgage paydown, and from capital gains.

Equity can also be accumulated if interest rates are higher in the market than on the contract. This creates mortgage equity. Suppose the contract mortgage provides for payments $M = m(r/k,N)B$. At time $t$, there are $N - t$ periods to go. If alternative financing were to be purchased in the market, the cost, at market interest rate $r_1 > r$, is $M_1 = m(r_1/k,N)B$. Using the opportunity cost of funds $r_1$, assuming no other costs such as points, the present value of the mortgage equity is

$$(M_1 - M)A(r_1,N - t)$$

the differential between market mortgage payments and current payments, over time to go, capitalized. Mortgage equity is added to the asset side of the balance sheet, and to owner equity on the right side of the balance sheet.

The balance sheet, revised to include mortgage equity is

**Balance Sheet, Owner Occupier**
(nominal, not inflation adjusted, dollars)

| *Assets* | | *Liabilities and Owner Equity* | |
|---|---|---|---|
| Real estate | $V_t = V(1 + g)^t$ | Mortgage balance | $B_t = b_t B$ |
| Mortgage equity $(M_1 - M)A(r_1,N - t)$ | | *Owner Equity* | |
| | | Capital contributed | $V - B + pB$ |
| | | Additions in nominal equity | |
| | | Mortgage paydown | $B - B_t = B(1 - b_t)$ |
| | | Capital gains | $V_t - V$ |
| | | Mortgage equity | $(M_1 - M)A(r_1,N - t)$ |

Mortgage equity has not been included in the calculation of the effective rate of return, but it can be included in a straightforward manner. The balance sheet of the owner occupier, for accounting purposes, with all assets valued at historical cost is

**Balance Sheet, Owner Occupant, Date *t***
(nominal, not inflation adjusted, dollars)

| **Assets** | | **Liabilities and Owner Equity** | |
|---|---|---|---|
| Real estate | $V$ | Mortgage balance | $B_t = b_t B$ |
| (no depreciation claimable) | | Capital contributed | $V - B + pB$ |
| | | Additions in nominal equity | |
| | | Mortgage paydown | $B - B_t = B(1 - b_t)$ |

Only the mortgage paydown is adding to owner equity on the balance sheet.

## Financial Strategies with Changing Interest Rates

With both long- and short-term interest rates fluctuating, there are alternative financial strategies for real estate investing. If interest rates have declined below those when the mortgage was taken out, refinancing is a possibility, particularly for borrowers on FRPM loans, but also for those with adjustable rate financing. If interest rates have increased subsequent to the date of the mortgage, the objective of a buyer is to assume, or take over, the financing. Where such assumption is not possible, there are other alternatives including wraparound financing. Wraparound financing entails the seller retaining the original loan, typically with below-market interest rates, and making the payments on it. The seller then writes a new loan with the buyer, to cover all the financing.

### *Comparing Mortgages*

A strategy is required to choose between alternative financing packages at initial purchase, or wehre there are no costs of refinancing. Let subscripts 1 and 2 describe two fixed rate and payment mortgages. The interest rate on the first is $r_1$, with loan balance $B_1$ and points $p_1$. The alternative mortgage has the same term $N$, but a different interest rate, loan balance, and points. The borrower wishes to compare the two FRPM packages. The differential between the two loan payments is

$$\Delta M = m(r_1/k,N)B_1 - m(r_2/k,N)B_2 \tag{7.15}$$

assuming the same frequency of compounding. For most FRPM packages, there is monthly compounding, and $T$ is either 15 or 30 years.

The differential between the net receipts on the loan is

$$\Delta B = (1 - p_1)B_1 - (1 - p_2)B_2 \tag{7.16}$$

received at the time of closing. Suppose the balance $\Delta B = B_1 - B_2$ is positive, that is, the proceeds on the first loan exceed those on the second. The differential in loan receipts of the borrower, $\Delta B$, is equated to the differential in mortgage payments, $\Delta M$, times an annuity factor converting the payments into a capital sum. The effective rate of interest $r_e$ from this annuity is the threshold to choose one mortgage over the other, or

$$\Delta MA(r_e/k,N) = \Delta B \tag{7.17}$$

and the effective interest rate is a solution. The right-hand side is constant, and the effective interest rate is adjusted to solve the equation iteratively. Choose an initial $r_e$, and substitute it in the annuity formula. If the product with the change in mortgage payments exceeds the change in loan receipts, increase $r_e$, to reduce the present value of the annuity $A$. If the product is below the change in loan receipts, reduce $r_e$, which increases the present value of the annuity. When the two sides are arbitrarily close, or

$$|\Delta MA(r_e/k,N) - \Delta B| < \xi$$

where $\xi$ is some small number, and $||$ denotes the absolute value, the effective interest rate is solved. As the effective rate of interest is increased, the present value of the annuity falls, reducing the left-hand side. The higher the effective interest rate, the less attractive is mortgage 1 relative to mortgage 2. The loan balance need not be the same in both mortgages. Lenders can have different underwriting standards on the balance to be provided.

### *Refinancing*

For the borrower already making payments on a mortgage, a strategy is required on when to refinance. The borrower is choosing between an existing FRPM or taking out another.

The direct costs of refinancing are for a prepayment penalty (if applicable), the points on the new loan, and fixed costs of title search, fees, and recording. There are indirect costs of time in search, in filling out loan applications, and in obtaining the relevant documentation. These costs are neglected in the calculation, but can be significant in the refinancing decision.

The balloon payment is the sum of prepayment penalties and the loan balance outstanding. The prepayment penalty is $q_t$, and the loan balance per dollar of original loan is $b_t$. There are points chargeable on the new loan. Points on the old loan have already been absorbed; they are a sunk cost and do no affect the refinancing decision. The points are, for the alternative loan balance $p_1B_1$, an initial capital cost of the refinancing. Loan fees for title search, fees, and recording are $Z$. The total capital costs, at the time of refinancing $t$, are $q_tB + p_1B_1 + Z$. Prepayment penalties apply on the old loan, for a total of $q_tB$, and points on the new loan, for $p_1B_1$. All occur immediately, and no discounting is required. The date of refinancing affects the prepayment penalty, but not necessarily the points or loan fees. This total represents the costs of refinancing.

The benefit of refinancing is the saving on the payments, from undertaking the new mortgage. The contract interest rate $r_1$ on the new mortgage is lower than the contract rate $r$ on the existing mortgage, otherwise refinancing is unlikely to take place. The existing payment is $M = m(r/k,N)B$. The new payment is $M_1 = m(r_1/k,N)B_1$. The difference is $M_1 - M$, on a per $k$ basis, or per month if $k = 12$. Remaining on the original mortgage are $N - t$ payments. The difference in mortgage payments over this period is converted to a present value. The present value is $A(r_e/k, N - t)(M_1 - M)$, where $r_e$ is the effective annual rate of interest for carrying out the refinancing transaction. Equating benefits and costs of the transaction,

$$A(r_e/k, N - t)(M_1 - M) = q_t B + p_1 B_1 + Z \qquad (7.18)$$

As for the comparison of the two mortgages at initial purchase, the right-hand side is a constant. The effective rate of interest $r_e$ solves the equation. As $r_e$ increases, $A$ decreases, and the left-hand side decreases. The higher the $r_e$, the greater is the rate of return to the borrower from carrying out the refinancing transaction. A larger differential between the two mortgage payments requires a higher interest rate to reduce the present value of the annuity, or a higher rate of return from refinancing.

The $r_e$ is selected iteratively, as before. The equation can be rewritten

$$|A(r_e/k, N - t)(M_1 - M) - q_t B - p_1 B_1 - Z| < \xi \qquad (7.19)$$

where $\xi$ is an arbitrary small number. Choose an initial $r_e$. If it is too small, $A$ is large, and the benefits exceed the cost, so increase $r_e$. If $r_e$ is too high, and the costs exceed the benefits, reduce $r_e$.

There are other considerations in refinancing, apart from personal search costs. The borrower may face a budget or borrowing constraint, or there can be capital market constraints preventing new borrowing. No tax considerations are included. The tax treatment of the costs, for the individual owner investor, can differ. Interest on mortgages may be deductible against other income, but not the points for a refinancing.

### *Effective Borrowing Cost*

The effective borrowing cost on a mortgage is a function of the rate of interest, points, fees, and other prepayment penalties. While the annual percentage rate (APR) disclosure calculates the borrowing cost to term o fthe loan, what is required is the cost for each length of holding.

The present value of an annuity is $A = 1/(1 + r/k)^N$, where $r$ is the interest rate, $k$ is the frequency of compounding, and $N = Tk$, where $T$ is the term. The mortgage multiplier is $m = 1/A$. For monthly payments, an interest rate of 12 percent and a 30-year term, the annuity is 97.21833, with a mortgage multiplier of 0.0103.

Suppose there were a 15-year mortgage with a monthly interest rate of

11 percent. The mortgage multiplier is 0.0114, which is lower than that for the previous mortgage. The monthly payments are greater, because the principal is being paid off more rapidly.

The loan balance is expressed net of points, that is, $(1 - p)B$. For a loan with two points, $0.98B$ is received for each $B$ dollars borrowed, but the payments are made on the full $B$. Suppose the borrower has been occupying the property for five years, and wants to know whether refinancing is appropriate. Interest rates have declined since the loan was originally extended. Suppose the original loan was for 30 years at a 12 percent interest rate.

The monthly payment is $M = mB$, where $m$ is calculated as $m(0.12/12, 360)$, $m = (r/k)/[1 - 1/(1 + r/k)^N]$, the mortgage multiplier. The effective interest rate paid up to the time of refinancing, $r_e$, is to be determined from the calculation. The annuity based on $r_e$ is at five years

$$\begin{aligned} A_e &= [1 - (1 + r_e/k)^{-t}]/(r_e/k) \\ &= [1 - (1 + r_e/12)^{-60}]/(r_e/12) \end{aligned} \tag{7.20}$$

where $t$ is the date of refinancing and $k$ is the annual frequency of compounding. For the example, $k = 12$ and $t = 60$. Here $A_e$ is the annuity arising from monthly payments over the 60 periods. The present value of the total payments of mortgage interest and principal made is $mBA(r_e/k,t)$, the product of the effective annuity and the periodic payment. The variables $k$, frequency of compounding, $r$, contract interest rate, and $N$, the term, are fixed once the mortgage is in place, and are exogenous. The variable $t$ is selectable by the investor, and $r_e$ is the effective rate of interest at refinancing date $t$.

The balloon payment to the lender is the loan balance $b_t$ plus the prepayment penalty $q_t$, discounted to the present by the effective interest rate. The present value of one dollar $t$ periods hence, discounted at annual interest rate $r_e$ is $1/(1 + r_e/k)^t$. The present value of the balloon payment is

$$D = \frac{b_t + q_t}{(1 + r_e/k)^t} \tag{7.21}$$

The effective borrowing cost is solved by equating cash flow in and out. The cash flow in for the borrower is the net loan proceeds at date of origination, $(1 - p)$ per dollar of loan. The cash flow out is the capital value of the mortgage payment. The payment per dollar of loan is

$m(r_e/k,N)$, and the present value of payments at the date of refinancing is $m(r/k,N)A(r_e/k,t)$. The present value of the balloon payment is $D$. Equating cash flow in and out,

$$(1 - p) = m(r/k,N)A(r_e/k,t) + D$$

or

$$mA(r_e,t) + D - (1 - p) = 0 \qquad (7.22)$$

The interest rate $r_e$ can be solved iteratively, given $t$, as all other parameters are fixed once the loan is in place. Choose an initial effective interest rate $r_e$. If the left side expression is positive, increase $r_e$, reducing present values. The $r_e$ is obtained when

$$|(mA + D - (1 - p))| < \xi \qquad (7.23)$$

where $\xi$ is an arbitrarily small number.

The procedure can be applied to comparing alternative FRPM financing options when the parameters for points, prepayment penalties, interest rates, and term vary across lenders. What is produced is the effective interest rate on borrowing, as a function of the holding period.

### *Retaining Existing Financing*

Several financing strategies are available when market interest rates on a real estate purchase are higher than the contract rate on th existing mortgage. One alternative, provided the mortgage is transferable, involves assuming the existing mortgage and paying cash for the remainder of the purchase price. A second is to assume the existing mortgage and take out a second mortgage. A third is to take out a new loan. If the loan is not assumable, there are other alternatives. One involves a wraparound loan. Where the owner had a mortgage with interst rates below market rates, mortgage equity is created. This equity represents the differential between the market payments and the contract payments capitalized over the remaining term of the mortgage.

### *Assumable Financing*

Consider the situation where the financing is assumable. The existing mortgage is for an initial amount $B$. When the investor is buying the property with the loan, the balance is $b_tB$. The purchase price of the property is $V$, so if the mortgage is assumable, $V - b_tB$ is required in addition to the original balance.[5] It is assumed that there are no other costs in taking over the loan, though in practice there may be legal, administrative, and title registration fees.

The alternative of taking out a second mortgage is examined, for loan balance $B_2$, with interest rate $r_2$. The interest rate on a second mortgage is usually greater than that on a first mortgage under the same conditions, because the first mortgage has a prior claim in lien. Upon default, the entire amount owing on the first mortgage is payable prior to any claim on the second mortgage. The second mortgage is thus a more risky instrument. New mortgages have interest rates in excess of that on the existing first loan. The alternative is to take out a new loan for the entire amount required, in the amount $B_1$. The payment on the existing financing is $m(r/k,N)B$, and that on a proposed second mortgage is $m(r_2/k,N-t)B_2$. The new mortgage has a term $N - t$ in periods. The target interest rate on a new loan $r_e$ is solved by

$$m(r_e/k,N-t)B_1 = m(r/k,N)B + m(r_2/k,N-t)B_2 \qquad (7.24)$$

If the interest rate is below $r_e$ on the new loan, it is preferable to take out this financing. The interest rates $r$ and $r_2$ are known, so the right-hand side is fixed. The effective interest rate $r_e$ solves the equation. The solution to $r_e$ is the borrowing cost. As $r_e$ increases, the existing mortgage is preferable. Points on the mortgages for $B_2$ and $B_1$ are not included. The loan $B_2$ is a second mortgage to the existing first. The loan $B_1$ is a new financing.

Including all costs, a new loan involves the payment of points, $p_1B_1$, a prepayment penalty on the existing first mortgage—assuming the buyer bears this cost in the purchase price—of $Q_t = q_tB$, and loan fees $Z$. Interest payments arise on the balance $B_1$. The alternative requires loan fees and points to be paid on the second mortgage. The overall comparison is

$$m(r_e/k,N-t)B_1 + p_1B_1 + Q_t + Z_1 = m(r/k,N)B + m(r_2/k,N-t)B_2$$
$$+ p_2B_2 + Z_2$$

where $r_e$ is the effective interest rate, solved by iteration. If the contract interest rate on the new financing is less than $r_e$, refinancing is preferred.

### *Nonassumable Financing—Wraparound Loans*

Where the borrower is not permitted to assume the existing financing, the above calculation is inappropriate. The borrower is restricted to taking out a new loan. An alternative is a wraparound loan, also known as an all-inclusive loan, all-inclusive mortgage, or all-inclusive deed of trust in jurisdictions where these replace mortgages. A wraparound loan can be applied when the property has an existing mortgage with an interest rate below prevailing market rates. A wraparound loan combines the existing loan into a new package. Wraparound financing is not common on residential or owner-occupied properties, but is common for investment properties.

The wraparound loan unlocks the mortgage equity. Lender 1 extends a new mortgage, and, under some variants, makes the payments on the existing mortgage. Alternatively, the previous borrower continues making the payments on the existing loan. The previous borrower receives, net of points, the difference between the two loans. There remains the possibility that the original lender will not cooperate, by demanding payment.

Let loan 1 denominate the wraparound, with balance $B_1$, interest rate $r_1$, for number of payments $N$, with $p_1$ points taken. On the new loan, for a larger balance than the previous loan, payments are $M_1 = m(r_1/k,N)B_1$. On the existing loan, not paid off at date $t$, the payments are $M = m(r/k,N)B$. For the number of periods $N - t$, the net additional mortgage payment is $M_1 - M$. If it is possible to secure wraparound financing to match exactly the maturity date on the existing loan, the term is $N - t$.

The new borrower is financing the difference between the wraparound loan balance $B_1$ and the balance on the existing loan $b_tB$. This new amount is contributed by the seller (the provider of the wraparound), to the buyer (the new borrower). If points are deducted, then $(1 - p_1)B_1 - b_tB$ is advanced to the buyer.

The cash flow statement for the seller (holder of the existing financing) is

**Cash Flow Out**

| | |
|---|---|
| At sale | |
| Advance of funds to complete wraparound | $(1 - p_1)B_1 - b_tB$ |
| During tenure of new borrower | |
| Present value of payments on existing loan | $m(r/k,N)BA(r_e/k,N - t)$ |

**Cash Flow In**

| | |
|---|---|
| During tenure of new borrower | |
| Present value of payments on wraparound loan | $m(r_e/k,N - t)B_1$ |

In typical application, the seller provides the advance to fund the differential between the wraparound and existing financing from the equity in the property. The buyer is willing to bid a given price and provide equity, in exchange for being provided with financing via the wraparound loan.

Equating the present values of cash flow in and out, where $r_e$ is the target interest rate to be charged on the wraparound

$$m(r_e/k,N - t)B_1 = m(r/k,N)BA(r_e/k,N - t) + (1 - p_1)B_1 - b_tB \tag{7.25}$$

where $b_t$ is the loan balance on the existing loan at sale date $t$. If the term on the wraparound does not match exactly, the seller faces the prospect of collecting for an alternative period. Suppose the wraparound is for $N_1 > N - t$. Then the left-hand side becomes $m(r_e/k,N_1)B_1$, and $r_e$ is calculated similarly. Also, there can be several subsequent sales and wraparounds. In the sale of income property, there are frequently several wraparound loans, as the equity is channeled into effectively providing financing.

Instead of extending a second mortgage, the wraparound loan maintains the initial financing. Second mortgages can carry relatively high interest rates, and the lender assumes a greater risk. A risk for the original borrower arises, since the existing mortgage must be paid. If payments on the wraparound are delinquent, the original borrower may face difficulties, since a different party manages the property. As with the refinancing, there are some other considerations. Credit rationing, for example, prevents the borrowing of desired amounts and limits the set of borrowing opportunities.

## Concluding Remarks

Real estate investment is where entrepreneurial talent abounds. Various methods for investing and financing residential property have been discussed. Financial statements for investment and tax or accounting purposes have been developed to enable the investor to plan a strategy. When interest rates are below existing contract rates, a refinancing option can be exercised. The effective rate of return to refinancing is obtainable. For cases where interest rates are above contract rates and the financing is assumable, alternative strategies are developed.

Lenders are reluctant to provide transferable mortgage equity for owners, where the borrower is paying below-market interest rates. There remains an asymmetry. The owner holding a property with below-market interest rate financing has an incentive not to transact, if the mortgage equity is not transferable. If the mortgage equity becomes large and transferable, financial transactions evolve to unlock this equity and increase its liquidity.

## Notes

1. Contributions from extended-family members, such as parents, are frequently important in the residential purchase decision. The SEM of chapter 6 permits family members to obtain tax and other benefits from real estate investment by purchasing but being nonresidents of the property.

2. Increases in equity from the paydown of the mortgage are neglected in this analysis.

3. It is assumed that the individual or filer is above the zero bracket, or the threshold level of deductions necessary for itemization of deductions, to provide a benefit. If the filer is below the zero bracket in total itemizable deductions, there is no tax benefit, and the original $r_e$ applies.

4. Economic depreciation rates on structures for investment purposes have been estimated by Hulten and Wykoff [1981], and used in the development of service lives for tax purposes by the Treasury [Bradford et al. 1984].

5. Assumable mortgages arise for most financing other than the FRPM. Some FRPM mortgages can be assumable, provided the initial terms specify or the lender permits. The lender has the option of exercising a due-on-sale clause if the original document provides, implying that the financing is not assumable.

# 8 ACTIVE REAL ESTATE INVESTMENTS: HOLDING STRATEGY

## Introduction

Chapter 7 investigated the acquisition and holding decision for active, owner-occupied real estate. In addition to the issues surrounding owner occupancy, investment real estate involves actual rental revenues and tenant management, as opposed to imputed rent. Depreciation expense is included in the economic calculation of returns to investment, owner occupied or not. If tax laws permit accelerated depreciation at a rate greater than the economic depreciation rate, real estate provides an additional source of cash. Accelerated depreciation either reduces tax payable or, typically in early years of an investment, creates or increases tax losses, generating a source of cash from tax refunds. The rate of return depends on tax policy, including the permitted depreciation schedule, asset life over which depreciation expense is claimable, marginal tax rates, and the extent to which losses on real estate investments are deductible against other income.

This chapter determines a real estate holding strategy. The strategy is derived in a series of accounting statements, integrated with a spreadsheet, to examine the income statement, balance sheet, cash flow, and rate of return after tax. With this strategy, the investor determines the optimal holding period. For a given holding period, the effective rate of return is obtained. The effective rate of return for the holding period is dependent on income and expenses, and tax variables exogenous to the investor. If any of these latter variables changes, the investor examines, with simulation or 'what if' analysis, the effect on the investment.

The earlier analysis of nondepreciable property is extended to cover depreciable property. In including depreciation, there is a difference between alternative methods of expensing real estate investments. Typical methods create a differential between tax and economic depreciation rates. In usual accounting statements, the basis, or cost, on which depreciation is calculated is not increased to allow for the effect of inflation.

A high rate of inflation, coupled with depreciation expense constant in nominal dollars of the date of purchase, provides an insufficient reserve to replace a depreciating asset. One solution is to permit the basis to be adjusted periodically for price changes. For falling real estate prices, a writedown of the asset can be taken and included as an expense, reducing taxable income. A problem arises in selecting an appropriate index applicable to investment real estate, or in appraisal. Another solution, that adopted in tax laws, is to permit higher depreciation rates, increasing the expense and reserve. Such a procedure is not neutral with respect to the rate of inflation. Low rates of inflation can imply an overallowance for depreciation expense.

Physical real estate investments are illiquid. The target rate of return required to undertake a real estate investment should include adjustments for illiquidity. If the real estate investment is active, requiring more from the investor than a down payment and the absorption of losses, an imputation for management time is required. Active real estate investments are considered, where the player takes a role in purchasing, financing, and managing the property. Passive real estate investments are subject to similar calculations but do not entail investor management.

## Single-Period Investment Returns

Leverage and risk remain issues with investment real estate. With the investor being a landlord, time potentially spendable on other matters is assigned to tenant disputes, learning about structural problems, and other stimulating aspects of property management. Even where these matters are delegated, the investor faces costs for hiring, and cannot be completely a distant observer. Additional risk arises, as compared with owner occupancy, because in the latter case, the risk of payment is known.

In investment real estate, actual rental income is part of income for both economic and tax purposes. The costs of vacancy, allowances and concessions, and collection fees are subtracted to generate net rental income. Accrued capital gains are included in economic income, but not in income for tax purposes. Maintenance and utility expenses are deductible under both tax and economic income statements. Depreciation expense is treated differently for tax and economic income statements.

The tax income statement for the real estate investor is

**Tax Income Statement, Investment Real Estate, During Period *t***

Gross Revenue
  Gross rental income
  Less: Vacancy, allowances, and collection fees
  Equals: Net rental income
Less: Operating expenses
    Maintenance
    Utilities
    Property taxes
Less: Interest expenses
Less: Noncash expenses
    Depreciation expense permitted for tax purposes
Equals: Net income for tax purposes (loss)

Times: Marginal income tax rate, investor
Equals: Tax payable (refund)

The economic income statement of the real estate investor is

**Economic Income Statement, Investment Real Estate, During Period *t***

Gross Revenue
  Gross rental income
  Less: Vacancy, allowances, and collection fees
  Equals: Net rental income

  Plus: Accrued capital gains during period
  (not necessarily realized)
  Equals: Total gross revenue

Less: Operating expenses
Maintenance
Utilities
Property taxes
Equals: Operating income

Less: Interest expenses
Less: Noncash expenses
Economic depreciation
Equals: Income after direct and noncash expenses

Less: Tax payable (add refund) from tax income statement
Equals: Net economic income

A complete definition of net income would subtract as a noncash expense the imputed price of the management time and any other contributions of the owner. No subtraction is made here. For the investment return and holding strategy, since capital gains are treated differently from rental income, they are separately distinguished.

To focus the analysis, rental income is defined net of maintenance and utilities, as variable $a$. In underwriting standards for investment real estate loans, an interest-coverage ratio is used, of rental income divided by interest expense. For the interest-coverage ratio, rental income alone would be included in $a$. Capital gains accrued but not realized during the current period are $h$. Depreciation rates for tax purposes are $\delta_t, t = 1, \ldots, T$, where $T$ is the length of holding, and economic depreciation rates are $d_t$. Interest expense on the loan $B$, at interest rate $r$, is $rB$ in the first period. The rate of property taxation is $\lambda$.

The tax income statement is

Net revenue $aV$
Less: Depreciation (for tax purposes) $-\delta_t S$
Less: Interest $-rB$
Less: Property taxes $-\lambda V$
Equals: Income for tax purposes $aV - \delta_t S - rB - \lambda V$

Depreciation arises on the improvements and structure alone, with $S$ the value of structure. The income for tax purposes is

$$Y_{\mathrm{TAX}} = aV - \delta_t S - rB - \lambda V$$

and dividing by the value of the property $V$,

$$y_{\mathrm{TAX}} = a - \delta_t u - rv - \lambda \tag{8.1}$$

where $u = S/V$ is the structure-to-value ratio, and $v = B/V$ the loan-to-value ratio.

The income for tax purposes, if positive, attracts tax at the rate $\tau$, which can be a function of $y_{\mathrm{TAX}}$. The tax payable is $\tau y_{\mathrm{TAX}}$, and if $y_{\mathrm{TAX}}$ is negative, a refund $\tau y_{\mathrm{TAX}}$ is received. Whether positive or negative, $\tau y_{\mathrm{TAX}}$ is included with the economic income statement.

The economic income statement, corrected for the tax benefits on a cash flow basis, or corrected for income statement adjustments, is

| | | |
|---|---|---|
| Net revenue | | $aV$ |
| Plus: | Accrued capital gains | $hV$ |
| Less: | Interest | $-rB$ |
| Less: | Property taxes | $-\lambda V$ |
| Less: | Income tax payments (tax recovery if negative) | $-\tau y_{\mathrm{TAX}}$ |
| Equals: | Economic cash flow | |
| Less: | Depreciation (economic purposes) | $-d_t S$ |
| Equals: | Net income on current account (income statement) | |

$$(a + h)V - rB - \lambda V - \tau Y_{\mathrm{TAX}} - d_t S$$

Net income is $(a + h)V - rB - \lambda V - \tau Y_{\mathrm{TAX}} - d_t S$. Rental income net of operating expenses is $aV$. From rental income is subtracted interest expense $rB$, property taxes $\lambda V$, and the tax payment $\tau Y_{\mathrm{TAX}}$. The last item is typically negative, or a refund if accelerated depreciation is permitted for tax purposes. Net income per unit dollar value of the property is obtained by dividing by the value $V$. Capital gains accrued but not realized during the period are included in economic income. Capital gains taxes are paid only upon realization, through sale or other transfer, so the taxes can be deferred.

The balance sheet for tax or accounting purposes of the real estate investor measures assets and liabilities at historical cost. If depreciation provisions apply to the package of land and improvements or structure together, separate accounts on the structure and land in the property value $V$ need not be maintained. If depreciation applies only to improvements, separate balances for land and improvements are required. It is assumed that depreciation applies only to improvements and separate balance must be maintained. The balance sheet for tax purposes is

**Balance Sheet, Real Estate Investor, Date $t$, Tax Purposes**
(nominal, not inflation adjusted dollars)

**Assets**
Real estate
Land LAND
Improvements
Initial balance $S$
Less: Accumulated tax depreciation $S \Sigma_{i=1}^{t} \delta_i$
Equals: Undepreciated balance
$S(1 - \Sigma_{i=1}^{t} \delta_i)$

**Total Assets**
$\text{LAND} + S(1 - \Sigma_{i=1}^{t} \delta_i)$

**Liabilities and Owner Equity**
Mortgage outstanding $B_t = b_t B$

**Owner Equity**
$\text{LAND} + S(1 - \Sigma_{i=1}^{t} \delta_i) - B_t$

**Total Liabilities and Owner Equity**
$\text{LAND} + S(1 - \Sigma_{i=1}^{t} \delta_i)$

It is assumed that there are no additions or improvements to the structure. Additions are counted at nominal cost in the year added, at historical cost. Depreciation expense for tax purposes is taken on the previous undepreciated balance, plus additions during the current period. There can be more than one mortgage. Total owner equity at historical cost is the land, with value LAND, plus the undepreciated structure, less the loan balance $B_t$, or

$$\text{LAND} + S\left(1 - \sum_{i=1}^{t} \delta_i\right) - B_t$$

Suppose the property is sold for price $V$. The book value, as per the tax and accounting balance sheet, is at historical cost, with the basis being the original purchase price not adjusted for inflation. Selling costs for real estate brokerage commissions are $n$, so the net price received is $(1 - n)V$. The capital gain for tax purposes is the selling price net of commission, less the book value on the tax balance sheet, less the loan balance outstanding. If the capital gain for tax purposes is $\text{CAPGAIN}_{\text{TAX}}$, then

$$\text{CAPGAIN}_{\text{TAX}} = (1 - n)V - \text{LAND} - S\left(1 - \sum_{i=1}^{t} \delta_i\right) - b_t B \qquad (8.2)$$

The selling price net of commission is $(1 - n)V$. The historical cost (initial purchase price) of the land is LAND. The undepreciated balance of the structure is $S(1 - \Sigma_{i=1}^{t} \delta_i)$. The claimed depreciation expense for tax purposes is added to the selling price for the computation of capital gains taxes. The capital gains are subject to taxes, and so the tax payable is $\alpha CAPGAIN_{TAX}$, where $\alpha$ is the tax rate on capital gains, which can vary with the amount of capital gains. If capital gains are taxed as ordinary income, $\alpha = \tau$, where $\tau$ is the marginal tax rate of the investor. The amount of tax is $\alpha CAPGAIN_{TAX}$.

The capital gains tax does not arise unless the property is sold. If there is tax depreciation in excess of economic depreciation, even with a low or zero rate of property appreciation, a sale can generate a capital gains for tax purposes. Accelerated depreciation increases the amount of capital gains. Transferring ordinary income to capital gains results in a tax saving if capital gains are taxed at a preferential rate. Such a transfer can result in a tax saving even if capital gains are taxed as ordinary income. The reason is that capital gains taxation can be deferred until realization, while ordinary income is taxed as currently earned.

The economic balance sheet, applying whether or not the property is sold is

**Balance Sheet, Real Estate Investor, Date *t*, Economic Purposes**
(inflation adjusted dollars)

| **Assets** | | **Liabilities and Owner Equity** | |
|---|---|---|---|
| Real estate | | Mortgage outstanding | $B_t = b_t B$ |
| Land | $L_t$ | | |
| Improvements (net of accumulated economic depreciation) | $S_t$ | **Total Liabilities** | $B_t$ |
| | | **Owner Equity** | $L_t + S_t - B_t$ |
| **Total Assets** | $L_t + S_t$ | **Total Liabilities and Owner Equity** | $L_t + S_t$ |

Land and improvements are measured at current market prices, net of depreciation. Owner equity at date $t$ is $L_t + S_t - B_t$. Owner equity is the market value of the land, less the market value of the improvements, less the loan balance, measured at historical cost, since the loan does not change with the price level. The exception is if the loan is a price-level adjusted mortgage (PLAM). The analogous economic balance sheet for the previous period produces owner equity $L_{t-1} + S_{t-1} - B_{t-1}$. The accrued but not necessarily realized capital gain during period $t$ is

$$\text{CAPGAIN} = L_t - L_{t-1} + S_t - S_{t-1}$$
$$= V_t - V_{t-1}$$

or the change in market value of the property.

The change in loan value through paydown $B_t - B_{t-1}$, does not constitute income directly, but is a residual increase in equity. Cash has been paid out to reduce the loan balance, and owner equity is increased. Assets in cash have been reduced, but, since owner equity is increased the transaction does not increase income. The accrued capital gain is added to the net income of the project, so the complete income statement, including the contribution from the balance sheet is

$$Y_t = aV_t - rB_t - \lambda V_t - \tau Y_{\text{TAX}} + H_t$$

where $H_t = V_t - V_{t-1}$ is the dollar change in market value of the property and the economic depreciation $d_tS$, typically unmeasureable, is included with the market valuations at successive dates. Dividing by current market value $V_t$,

$$\begin{aligned} y &= a - rv - \lambda - \tau y_{\text{TAX}} + h \\ &= (1 - \tau)(a - rv - \lambda) + \tau\delta u + h \end{aligned} \tag{8.3}$$

where $h$ is the percentage change in market value between successive balance-sheet dates. This accrued but not realized capital gains rate $h$ is measured net of economic depreciation. A market appraisal at date $t$ takes into account the economic depreciation occurring since the date $t - 1$ balance sheet.

Net income per dollar of property value during a given period is the sum of three components. The first, $(1 - \tau)(a - rv - \lambda)$, is the net operating income after tax. Net after-tax income is rental revenue $a$, less interest payments $rv$, less property taxes $\lambda$, times the net income per dollar after taxes are paid $(1 - \tau)$. The term $(a - rv - \lambda)$ is the before-tax cash flow (BTCF) from the property, excluding the effect of depreciation. Maintenance and utilities are subtracted from the gross rent received. The second is the cash recovery from the tax-depreciation provision, $\tau\delta u$. This term is the product of the tax rate $\tau$, the rate of depreciation for tax purposes $\delta$, and the structure-to-value ratio on the initial basis $u$. The third is capital gains. Capital gains, in appreciation of the property, less economic depreciation, are reflected in $w$. All components of $y$ are in percentage terms. The real estate investor has three sources of income. These are, respectively, net cash flow from operating income, cash flow from tax-depreciation provisions, and net capital gains after economic depreciation. The second term is always positive; the other two terms need not be positive.

If there is one period of holding, no transactions costs of purchase or sale, and no capital gains taxes, the income $y$ represents the return on equity of the investor. Since $v$ is the loan-to-value ratio, $(1 - v)$ is the equity-to-value ratio. The total return per dollar of property value is $r_e E/V = r_e(1 - v)$, where $r_e$ is the effective rate of return. Then

$$r_e(1 - v) = (1 - \tau)(a - rv - \lambda) + \tau\delta u + h = y$$

and the return on equity is

$$r_e = [(1 - \tau)(a - rv - \lambda) + \tau\delta u + h]/(1 - v) \qquad (8.4)$$

### Threshold Marginal Tax Rates (MTRs)

The threshold marginal tax rate required to undertake the investment is obtained by rearranging the return on equity equation. Select a predetermined rate of return, for real estate or assets of comparable risk and liquidity, as $r_e$, and find the threshold marginal tax rate required. Then

$$r_e(1 - v) = a - rv - \lambda - \tau(a - rv - \lambda - \delta u) + h$$

$$r_e(1 - v) - a + rv + \lambda - h = \tau(\delta u + rv + \lambda - a)$$

$$\tau^* = \frac{a + h - r_e(1 - v) - rv - \lambda}{a - \delta u - rv - \lambda} = y_{EC}/y_{\mathrm{TAX}} \qquad (8.5)$$

establishes the threshold marginal tax rate at which an investor would consider the investment. If an investor has a MTR greater than $\tau^*$, the investment is undertaken, and if the MTR is less than $\tau^*$, it is not carried out.

The threshold MTR $\tau^*$ is the ratio of two definitions of income, $y_{EC}/y_{\mathrm{TAX}}$, consistent with the two sets of financial accounts being maintained.

Economic income, $y_{EC}$, is the income arising from all sources outside tax regulations. Since it excludes tax-recovery sources of income, but includes the opportunity cost of the equity of the investor, economic income can be negative. If $y_{EC}$ is negative, the tax laws subsidize the investment. In practice, the actual rent received may capitalize and reflect tax laws, and so the distinction between economic and tax income is less complete.

The threshold MTR is the ratio of economic income to tax income, per dollar of value. Economic income is rental income net of operating expenses and capital gains, less the opportunity cost of equity, interest expense, and property taxes. Tax income is rental income net of operating expenses, less tax depreciation, interest, and property taxes. The opportunity cost of funds depends on investor attitude to risk and return, and need not be equal to the mortgage interest rate.

In the example, economic income is

**Economic Income $y_{EC}$**

| | | | |
|---|---|---|---|
| Net operating income | $a$ | | 0.11 |
| Plus: Capital gains less economic depreciation | $h$ | | +0 |
| Less: Opportunity cost of equity investment | $r_e(1 - v) = 0.154 \times 0.2$ | | −0.0308 |
| Less: Interest expense | $rv = 0.1 \times 0.8$ | | −0.08 |
| Less: Property tax | $\lambda$ | | −0.01 |
| Equals: Economic income | $y_{EC}$ | | = −0.0108 |

Income for tax purposes is

**Income for Tax Purposes $y_{TAX}$**

| | | |
|---|---|---|
| Net operating income | $a$ | 0.11 |
| Less: Tax depreciation | $\delta u = 0.05 \times 1$ | −0.05 |
| Less: Interest payment | $rv = 0.1 \times 0.8$ | −0.08 |
| Less: Property taxes | $\lambda$ | −0.01 |
| Equals: Income for tax purposes | $y_{TAX}$ | = −0.03 |

The threshold marginal tax rate is

$$\tau^* = y_{EC}/y_{TAX}$$

$$= 0.0108/0.03 = 0.36$$

An investor requires a marginal tax rate of at least 36 percent to contemplate the investment. If no MTR is as high as 36 percent, the returns must shift until the investment becomes feasible. If the rent, as a percentage of value, falls to 10 percent, from 11 percent, the threshold MTR rises to 47 percent. If the rent ratio rises to 12 percent, the threshold MTR falls to almost zero.

The impact of a tax reform need not be substantial, as a 9 percent increase in rent—from a rent-to-value ratio of 0.11 to 0.12—would switch investment from feasible for none, if the two MTRs were 35 percent, to feasible for almost all. A smaller increase would make the investment feasible for some. Of course, a tax reform can change many parameters simultaneously, so a greater effect on rent is possible.

The price $V$ paid for the property can capitalize the tax benefits from depreciation. If the owner paid an initially higher price, the rate of return $r_e$ does not increase above that for comparable risks in investment. All benefits can be capitalized into the price of land. A given tax policy need not increase the supply of real estate, if the benefits are capitalized by increasing the price of property and not the marginal rate of return.

## Risk

### *Sources of Risk*

Lenders do not only use prices, through interest rates and other components of the cost of funds, to allocate funds among borrowers. There can be allocation by quantity, that is, credit rationing. Credit rationing can take the form of limits on the amount borrowed, restrictions on the loan-to-value ratio and other types of debt service requirements. During periods of low interest rates, when there is an excess demand for funds at existing prices, lenders choose to allocate funds to regular customers. The investor may not be able to obtain the desired leverage on a project.

The rate of economic depreciation must be estimated. The tax depreciation rate is typically higher. Improvements are subject to depreciation. The rate of return after tax must be net of economic depreciation, or the projected appreciation (capital gains) must be on a net basis after depreciation has been subtracted.

Inflation cannot accurately be predicted in advance, and there is no guarantee of a positive rate. Long-term studies of the rate of inflation, as a general price index, shows almost stable prices over centuries. Real estate investments are packaged and calculated showing an increase in rents and prices over time, with a positive inflation rate. The inflation rate need not be positive, let alone a given projection.

### *Risk–Return Trade-off*

Physical real estate is relatively risky and illiquid, as compared with other assets. Investments such as Treasury bonds are less risky than physical real estate. The least risky are certificates of deposit (CDs) and cash, where there is no risk of capital loss. The acceptance of greater risk requires a higher rate of return to compensate.

Physical real estate, either actively or passively managed, poses risks. Time passes before a transaction is consummated; there are costs of search for buyers and sellers, and costs of brokerage, legal, title, escrow, taxes, and fees. There are differentials in information and prices on apparently homogeneous properties. These differentials, with asymmetric information between buyer and seller, create returns to search and to knowledge of specific real estate markets.

Real estate investments are lumpy, in that physical asset purchases are large, cannot be bought in one dollar units usually, and hence cannot be easily diversified. Real estate investments are long term and the assets are long lived, increasing the risk. The future is unknown; and real estate returns depend on estimates of the future course of inflation generally, for real estate in a specific location, and for a particular property. Legislative and tax policy is uncertain; and the benefits do not necessarily accrue to the investor, if they are capitalized in higher land prices.

Real estate markets are highly technical and thin, and there are appraisal and valuation difficulties. Construction quality is difficult to measure for the untrained. In many cases it is not directly observable, for example, in areas such as the foundation. Demand, tastes, and preferences are uncertain.

In an uncertain environment, the expected rate of return on investments can be calculated. Suppose $y(i)$ is the income dependent on the state of the world $w$, which can occur with probability $q(i)$. Then the expected return, where there is a discrete number of possibilities $I$ is

$$E(y) = \sum_{i=1}^{I} y(i)q(i)$$

The variance of the return is

$$\sigma^2(y) = \sum_{i=1}^{I} q(i)[y - E(y)]^2$$

and the standard deviation is the square root of this. The coefficient of variation, that is, the standard deviation divided by the mean, $V(y)^{0.5}/E(y)$, can be used to compare two distributions.

### Leverage

Regarding risk, with $L = 1/(1 - \upsilon)$ being the leverage, the rate of return on equity is $r_e = L[(1 - \tau)(a - r\upsilon - \lambda) + \tau\delta u + h]$. The return depends on the marginal tax rate (MTR) $\tau$, the net rental income $a$, interest rate $r$, loan-to-value ratio $\upsilon$, property tax rate $\lambda$, depreciation rate permitted for tax purposes $\delta$, structure-to-value ratio $u$, and capital gains $h$.

If the investor has a tenant with a long-term lease, a reliable, or seasoned, payment history, and a FRPM loan, and expected tax policy to be unchanged, then the only risk is on expected capital gains. The standard deviation of the return is $\sigma(r_e) = L\sigma(h)$, where $\sigma(h)$ is the standard deviation of capital gains. When $L = 1$, or the investor has $\upsilon = 0$ or buys with all cash, the risk on the return is the same as on the capital gains. As $L > 1$ and increases, the risk increases with leverage.

Rent and tax policy are subject to risks, complicating the overall risk structure. The risk depends on the interactions between the various variables. The return on equity is adjusted by the leverage term. If net income plus tax depreciation recovery, plus net capital gains is positive, then increased leverage increases the rate of return. Increased leverage contributes to increased risk.

If $a$, the net revenue is 11 percent, or 0.11, and the property tax rate is 0.01, with interest rate $r = 0.08$, then $a - r\upsilon - \lambda$, the net income before tax, is $0.10 - 0.08\upsilon$. The return on equity depends on $\upsilon$, the loan-to-value ratio, or the leverage the investor has in the property. Net income is multiplied by $(1 - \tau)L$, the product of the net income per dollar received after tax and the leverage multiplier $L = 1/(1 - \upsilon)$. If the property has a loan-to-value ratio of 80 percent, or 0.8, and the marginal and average tax rates are 20 percent, or 0.2, then the multiplier is 0.8/0.2, or 4. If the investor faces a zero marginal tax rate, the multiplier is 5. Increased taxes reduce the effect of leverage. The effect of net income on the rate of return is $0.10 - 0.08 \times 0.8 \times 4$, or 0.114. A return of 11.4 percent is obtained.

The recovery of depreciation expense for tax purposes is $\tau\delta u$. If the tax depreciation rate is 0.05, and applies to the entire property, then $u = 1$. The property can be a condominium, with no land ownership, or land value cannot be separated from structure. The tax recovery is 0.01, or $0.05 \times 0.2 \times 1$. Multiplied by leverage $L = 1/(1 - \upsilon) = 4$, the contribution to the return on equity is 0.04. If capital gains are equal to the economic depreciation rate, then $h = 0$. The rate of return on equity is 15.4 percent.

The rate of return $r_e$ increases when net income $a$ increases. A one point increase in the rent as a percentage of the property value increases the rate of return by $(1 - \tau)/(1 - \upsilon)$. A one percentage point increase in the interest rate reduces the rate of return by $(1 - \tau)\upsilon/(1 - \upsilon)$. The more leveraged the investor, the greater the decrease in the rate of return. A one percentage point increase in the property tax rate reduces the rate of return by $(1 - \tau)/(1 - \upsilon)$. A one point increase in the marginal tax rate reduces the net operating rental income by $(a - r\upsilon - \tau)$. The tax change increases the depreciation recovery by $\delta u$, the product of the tax depreciation rate and the depreciable portion.

Leverage increases the risk of the investment. If net rental income plus depreciation recovery and accrued capital gains are positive, then a high loan-to-value ratio produces a higher rate of return, with an explosive characteristic. The return is infinite if the investor puts nothing down, or where $\upsilon = 1$. Where $\upsilon = 1$, the denominator of $L = 1/(1 - \upsilon)$ is zero, and the leverage multiplier $L$ is infinite. Provided net income is positive, the rate of return on investment is infinite. The leveraged investor benefits from depreciation for tax purposes in excess of economic rates. The depreciation component $\tau\delta u$ is multiplied by $1/(1 - \upsilon)$, so that the explosive aspect of the leverage applies to the depreciation expense.

When $\upsilon = 0$, the investor makes an all-cash purchase, and $L = 1/(1 - \upsilon) = 1$. Such an investment reduces risk and increases net income. An all-cash investment is typically made by nontaxable or deferred taxable entities such as pension funds, insurance companies, or individuals investing in tax-deferred form such as through individual pension accounts. The rate of return is $r_e = L[(1 - \tau)(a - r\upsilon - \lambda) + \tau\delta u + h)]$. Hence $\sigma(r_e) = L\sigma(\text{RETURN})$, where $\sigma$ indicates a standard deviation, where $\text{RETURN} = (1 - \tau)(a - r\upsilon - \lambda) + \tau\delta u + h)$. Whenever $L$ is reduced, risk is reduced. If there is an all-cash purchase, $\upsilon = 0$, and

$$r_e = (1 - \tau)(a - \lambda) + \tau\delta u + h \qquad (8.6)$$

An investor retains the tax advantages of the accelerated depreciation. The absence of interest expense increases the net rental income, but some of this income is offset by the shielded depreciation term. Capital gains also accrue. If the investor is in a zero tax bracket, the depreciation conveys no additional benefit, and

$$r_e = a - rv - \tau + h$$

Figure 8-1 shows the effect of leverage on the rate of return on equity. On the vertical axis is the rate of return of equity, $r_e$. On the horizontal axis is leverage, $v$. For nothing down, $v = 1$, and for an all-cash purchase, $v = 0$. In the simplest case, with no depreciation and the investor facing no taxes on the gross revenue, the criterion for leverage being beneficial is that gross revenue exceeds costs. Interest at rate $r$ is deductible, so this case faces the owner-occupier. The marginal tax rate is $\tau$. The property tax rate $\lambda$ is zero. Interest is deductible, and all income is shielded, as for an owner-occupier. If revenue exceeds cost, and $a - r(1 - \tau)v > 0$, as the leverage increases, the rate of return explodes, tending to positive infinity as $v$ tends to unity. If $a - r(1 - \tau)v$ is negative, the rate of return on equity tends to negative infinity as $v$ tends to unity. Increased leverage increases the risk of the real estate investment.

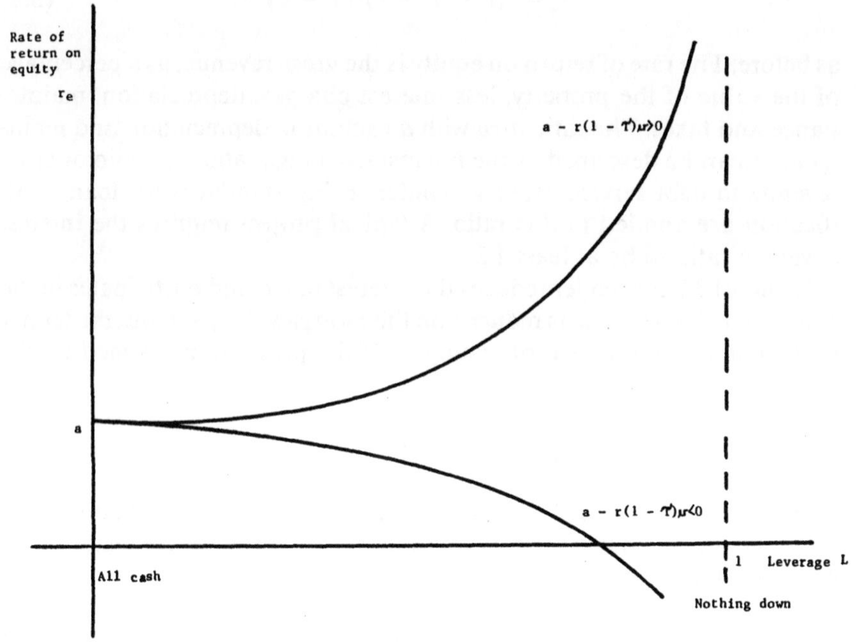


Figure 8-1. Effect of Leverage on Return on Equity

### *Investor–Lender Risk Sharing: Equity Participation Mortgage (EPM)*

One method for sharing the risk of a project is through an equity participation mortgage (EPM), an analogue of the shared appreciation mortgage (SAM). Suppose the net income from a project is

$$Y = aV - rB - \tau V = r_e E$$

where $aV$ is rental income net of economic depreciation and maintenance revenue, $rB$ is interest expense, and $\tau$ is the rate of property taxation, with $V$ the value. The income $Y$ is before taxes, and other tax considerations are neglected. The return on equity is $r_e$.

Dividing both sides by the property value $V$,

$$y = a - rv - \tau = r_e(1 - v) \tag{8.7}$$

and if $v = B/V$ is the loan-to-value ratio,

$$r_e = (a - rv - \tau)/(1 - v) \tag{8.8}$$

as before. The rate of return on equity is the gross revenue, as a percentage of the value of the property, less interest charges, depreciation, maintenance and taxes. The ratio $a/rv$ with $a$ excluding depreciation and maintenance can be described as the interest-coverage ratio, the ratio of gross revenue to debt service expense. Underwriting standards for loan qualification are applied to this ratio. A typical project requires the interest coverage ratio to be at least 1.2.

In the EPM, the lender reduces the interest rate $r$, and participates in the equity. The interest rate is reduced on the mortgage to $r_1 < r$, but the lender participates in the return on equity $r_e$. If the proportion claimed by the lender is $x$, then

$$r_e = (1 - x)(a - r_1 v - \tau)/(1 - v) \tag{8.9}$$

where $x$ is the "portion" retained by the lender for participation in the EPM. There are no taxes in this solution. Where taxes are applicable, they would be levied prior to the portion for the lender.

The borrower makes a trade-off between interest costs, reduced with certainty, and a reduced but uncertain profit. If there are losses, the borrower shares them with the lender. The risk of the borrower is reduced, and partly shifted to the lender. Hold the observed rate of return on equity constant, and change the share $x$ and the EPM interest rate $r_1$, holding the remaining variables constant. Then

$$0 = -(a - r_1 v - \tau)\,dx - (1 - x)v\,dr_1$$

or

$$(a - r_1 v - \tau)\,dx = -(1 - x)v\,dr_1 \tag{8.10}$$

where $dx$ is a small change in the lender share $x$, and $dr_1$ is a small change in the reduced interest rate. Then

$$dx/dr_1 = -(1 - x)v/(a - r_1 v - \tau) < 0 \tag{8.11}$$

As the interest rate in $r_1$ increases, the share the lender requires declines, provided the rate of return is positive. The condition for $dx/dr_1$ indicates the trade-off the lender is willing to make between interest rate concessions and profit share.

There are other risk factors in the EPM. Taxes and tax legislation can change, affecting the rate of return for both participants. There is refinancing risk for the lender, if the borrower decides to leave the project. The lender must rely on the management skill and real estate acumen of the borrower, and the market conditions facing the project.

## Multiple-Period Investment

### *Cash-on-Cash Returns*

The above is a one-period analysis, to determine the direction of the response of the rate of return. Real estate is a long-lived asset, and a holding strategy is required. Such a holding strategy involves several periods of calculation.

On purchase, there are transactions costs for points, financing fees, and taxes. On sale, there are transactions costs for brokerage commissions and other costs. A sale is a realization, triggering a liability for capital gains taxes. If there were no transactions costs of purchase and slae, and all variables had the same pattern over time, the single-period calculation would suffice. In general, these conditions do not occur and the optimal holding period cannot be determined from a single-period calculation.

Over one period, net income per dollar of property value is

$$y = (1 - \tau)(a - rv - \lambda) + \tau\delta u + h$$

Even if all the components of net income were constant over time, and $y$ could be viewed as an annuity, there are holding and transactions costs. The income $y$ is a price or return per dollar of value $V$. Suppose there are no transactions, closing, or brokerage costs. The investor has the objective of determining the optimal holding period.

On a cash-flow basis, the real estate investor has three types of calculation, at purchase, during ownership, and at sale. At purchase, transactions costs are paid out. During ownership, returns are received. At sale, cash is paid out for brokerage fees, loan prepayment, and capital gains taxes. At the date of purchase, a down payment is paid out. The cash flow statement, in these three periods is

**Sources and Uses of Cash, Investment Property, Sale Date *t***
(in present-value terms, as of date of purchase)

| **Uses of Cash (Net Disbursements)** | **Sources of Cash (Net Receipts)** |
|---|---|
| Date of Purchase<br>Initial purchase<br>Down payment<br>$(1 - v)V$<br>Points paid (an closing costs) $pB$ | Period of Ownership (undiscounted)<br>Income during ownership, period (cash flow, excluding capital gains) $y_{\text{CASH}}$<br>$= (1 - \tau)(a - rv - \lambda) + \tau\delta u$ |
| Date of Sale (undiscounted)<br>Brokerage fees (and other closing costs) $nV$<br>Prepayment penalty $q_tB$<br>Loan balance outstanding $b_tB$<br>Capital gains taxes<br>$\alpha\text{CAPGAIN}_{\text{TAX}}$ | Date of Sale (undiscounted)<br>Sales price $V_t$ |
| *Total cash out* | *Total cash in* |

The cash accounts are constructed with $y_{\text{CASH}}$ being cash flow each period, and the capital gains being taken at date of sale. The investor continues to accrue the capital gains. The prepayment penalty is

$$q_t = (r/k) \sum_{i=1}^{C} b_{t+i}$$

The optimal holding strategy of the real estate investor involves equating the present value of total cash out with total cash in. At date of purchase, for price $V$, cash out is the down payment $(1 - v)V$ plus points $pB$ and other closing costs. Suppose income during ownership occurs as an annuity. Then income, as a percentage of the property value, is constant.[1] The present value of the income, compounded at the same frequency per year as the mortgage, is $y_{\text{CASH}}A(r_e/k,t)$, where $r_e$ is the effective rate of return on the investment.

### Sell Strategy

At sale, the amount subject to capital gains taxes is the net sales revenue $(1 - n)V_t$, less the undepreciated basis on the initial value taken. If $D_t = \Sigma_{i=1}^{t} \delta_i$ is the proportion of the initial price depreciated for tax purposes, then $D_tV$ is subject to taxes on recapture.

Depreciation up to the straight-line rate can be taxed as capital gains if a preferential tax rate is available. Here, it is assumed that all depreciation is taxed at rate $\alpha$. If $\alpha = \tau$, capital gains are taxed as ordinary income. The undepreciated balance outstanding, or current basis, is $(1 - D_t)V$. This balance is the value of land plus undepreciated value of the structure,

$$(1 - D_t)V = \text{LAND} = S\left(1 - \sum_{i=1}^{t} \delta_i\right)$$

is the purchase price. No improvements or additions are assumed. If included, they are counted at historical cost in the year provided. Let prepayment penalties be deductible in calculating net capital gains. The proceeds subject to capital gains tax are

$$\text{CAPGAIN}_{\text{TAX},t} = (1 - n)V_t - (1 - D_t)V - q_tB$$

The amount CAPGAIN is subject to capital gains taxes at the rate $\alpha$. Capital gains tax is levied on the net sales revenue, less the initial purchase price $V$, plus the depreciation recapture $D_tV$, less the prepayment penalty. Net sales revenue is

$$\begin{aligned}\text{REVENUE}_t &= (1 - n)V_t - (q_t + b_t)B - \alpha\text{CAPGAIN}_{\text{TAX},t} \\ &= (1 - \alpha)[(1 - n)V_t - q_tB] + \alpha(1 - D_t)V - b_tB\end{aligned} \qquad (8.12)$$

The net sales revenue should the investor decide to sell in period $t$ includes the current sale price after commission, $(1 - n)V_t$. Subtracted are the prepayment penalty $q_tB$, the repayment of the outstanding balance $b_tB$, and capital gains taxes. Net revenue upon sale is discounted to the date of purchase by $1/(1 + r_e/k)^t$, where frequency of compounding is at annual rate $k$. Equating cash in with cash out for the investor is

$$(1 - v)V + pB = y_{\text{CASH}}\text{VA}(r_e/k,t) + \frac{\text{REVENUE}_t}{(1 + r_e/k)^t} \tag{8.13}$$

which provides the holding strategy. The $r_e$ solving this equation determines the rate of return to holding the real estate for $t$ periods. Dividing by initial price $V$,

$$(1 - v) + pv = y_{\text{CASH}}A(r_e/k,t) + \frac{w_t}{(1 + r_e/k)^t} \tag{8.14}$$

where $w_t$ is revenue at sale per dollar of initial purchase. Then

$$w_t = \frac{\text{REVENUE}_t}{V} = (1 - \alpha)\left[\frac{(1 - n)V_t}{V - q_tv}\right] + \alpha(1 - D_t)v - b_tv \tag{8.15}$$

The amounts are expressed in present-value terms for convenience. They can be expressed in future-value terms as of date of sale, but the results, and effective rate of return, are the same. At date of sale, for each dollar of sale value gross (the 1), $n$ cents are paid in real estate brokerage and other fees, and $q_tv$ is paid in penalties on the mortgage.

Cash out per dollar for the investor is the sum of the down payment $(1 - v)$ and the points paid on the loan $pv$. Cash in is the present value of the cash flow net $y_{\text{CASH}}A(r_e/k,t)$, plus the after-tax recovery at sale. The recovery at sale is the sale price, less the loan balance and prepayment, subject to capital gains tax, less capital gains tax. The effective rate of return $r_e$ solves the equation, and is a function of holding period $t$.

The cash flow per time period is unlikely to be constant over time. The advantage of real estate investments is frequently in having early losses offset by income later in the holding period. If the series of cash flows per period is $y_{\text{CASH},t}$, then the effective rate of return solves

$$(1 - v) + pv = \frac{\sum_{i=1}^{t} y_{\text{CASH},t}}{(1 + r_e/k)^i} + \frac{w_t}{(1 + r_e)^t} \tag{8.16}$$

The real estate investor has some target rate of return. If the effective rate of return $r_e$ is in excess of that target, the investor holds. When the return falls below, the investor sells.

The frequency of compounding in most circumstances is once annually. If the interest in $y_{\text{CASH},t}$ is calculated annually, then

$$(1 - v) + pv = \frac{\sum_{i=1}^{t} y_{\text{CASH},t}}{(1 + r_e)^i} + \frac{w_t}{(1 + r_e)^t} \tag{8.17}$$

with $t$ defined in years. There is potentially a different rate of return for each time period $t$. The left side of the equation, cash out, is constant, as it occurs at date of purchase. Alternatively, at prospective date of sale $t$, the equation is expressed in future value terms

$$[(1 - v) + pv](1 + r_e)^t = \sum_{i=1}^{t} y_{\text{CASH},t}(1 + r_e)^i + w_t \tag{8.18}$$

From date of purchase, the initial expenditures are indexed forward by the holding rate of return $r_e$. The annual income per dollar value of the property is capitalized by the future value of an annuity.

The rate of return to the investor provides a strategy on when to sell. The rate of return is a function of the points $p$, the loan-to-value ratio $v$, the contract mortgage rate $r$, real estate commission $n$, months of prepayment penalty $C$, and all the operating variables in the annual net income.

The rate of return $r_e$ is a function of the holding period $t$. With front-end and back-end costs, the rate of return is unlikely to be constant over time. The effect of various variables on the effective rate of return $r_e$ is

| *Increase in Variable* | *Effect on $r_e$* |
|---|---|
| Points $p$ | Decrease |
| Net income $y$ | Increase |
| Capital gains—increase $V_t$ | Increase |
| Rental income—increase $a$ | Increase |
| Maintenance expense—decrease $a$ | Decrease |
| Utility expense—decrease $a$ | Decrease |
| Marginal tax rate $\tau$ | Indeterminate |
| Contract interest rate $r$ | Decrease |
| Property tax rate $\lambda$ | Decrease |
| Months of prepayment penalty $C$ | Decrease |
| Real estate commission $n$ | Decrease |
| Tax depreciation $\delta_t$ | Increase |

If $r_e$ is a target interest rate, the optimal holding period can be determined. The rate of return is a price for the services provided by the property to the investor per period. Spreadsheet analysis with "what if" scenarios can be played for any policy changes. There are various risks in the ownership of investment real estate. For residential property, there is the prospect of regulation and rent control.

### *Hold Strategy*

The rate of return can be calculated at time $t$ for a hold. Rent receipts are net of vacancy and collection costs. Net cash flow is

$$Y_{\text{CASH}} = (1 - \tau)(aV - rB - \lambda V) + \tau\delta V \tag{8.19}$$

Net cash flow $Y_{\text{CASH}}$ is the sum of receipts from rent $aV$, less operating expenses, less interest payments $rB$ and property taxes $\lambda V$. The tax refund is the tax depreciation rate $\delta$ times the marginal tax rate $\tau$ and the value of property, if the depreciation applies to the entire purchase price, that is, if $u = 1$. The structure may not be distinguishable from the land, or the calculation of the depreciation adjusted to include a zero land depreciation rate. Dividing by the initial value of the property

$$y_{\text{CASH}} = (1 - \tau)(a - rv - \lambda) + \tau\delta \tag{8.20}$$

If the property is held, accrued capital gains or losses are taken into current income at rate $h$. So

$$y = h + y_{\text{CASH}} = h + (1 - \tau)(a - rv - \lambda) + \tau\delta \tag{8.21}$$

The investor does not incur capital gains taxes or brokerage fees.

**Cash Flow, Active Investor, Hold Strategy**
(per dollar of property purchased)

| **Uses of Cash** | | **Sources of Cash** | |
|---|---|---|---|
| **Cash out (Disbursements)** | | **Cash in (Receipts)** | |
| Purchase date | | Purchase date | |
| Purchase price | 1 | Loan receipts | $v$ |
| Points | $pv$ | | |
| | | Period of ownership (undiscounted) | |
| | | Net income per period | $y$ |
| Total cash out | | Total cash in | |

Capital gains on an accrued basis are counted as income. Income $y$ need not be positive every period. The effective rate of return on a hold at time $t$ equates the present values of cash in and cash out

$$1 - v + pv = \frac{\sum_{i=1}^{t} y_i}{(1 + r_e)^i} \tag{8.22}$$

The return can also be computed excluding capital gains $h$. The investor may not be able to consume the accrued capital gains. The return for a hold can be compared with the return for a sell. The rate of return on a hold can exceed that for a sell because of the transactions costs at sale. The rate of return on a hold can fall below a sell if the income declines. A criterion for holding can be if

$$r_e \text{(hold)} > r_e \text{(sell)} \qquad \text{hold}$$

$$r_e \text{(hold)} < r_e \text{(sell)} \qquad \text{sell}$$

at time $t$, though such depends on the other investments available to the limited partner.

## Depreciation

### *Depreciation for Tax Purposes*

Investment real estate decisions depend on the depreciation schedule adopted. For investment real estate, various depreciation schedules have been applied, dependent on when the property was first put into service. Figure 8-2 shows three alternative forms of depreciation rates. On the vertical axis is the depreciation rate permitted for tax purposes, $\delta_t$. On the horizontal axis is the number of payments, $N$. For the straight-line form, the depreciation expense is constant at $1/T$, where $T$ is the number of years permitted for expensing the asset. For the geometric form, the expense is greater in the early years than for straight line, if the depreciation is taken on a declining balance. Any accelerated form, such as permitting a rate of 175 percent of straight line in the early years, or permitting higher depreciation rates in early years, produces a potential schedule resembling ACRS in figure 8-2.

On January 1, 1981, with the passage of the Tax Equity and Fiscal Responsibility Act (TEFRA), the length of period for depreciation on real estate is 15 years. For assets placed into service after this date, and up to

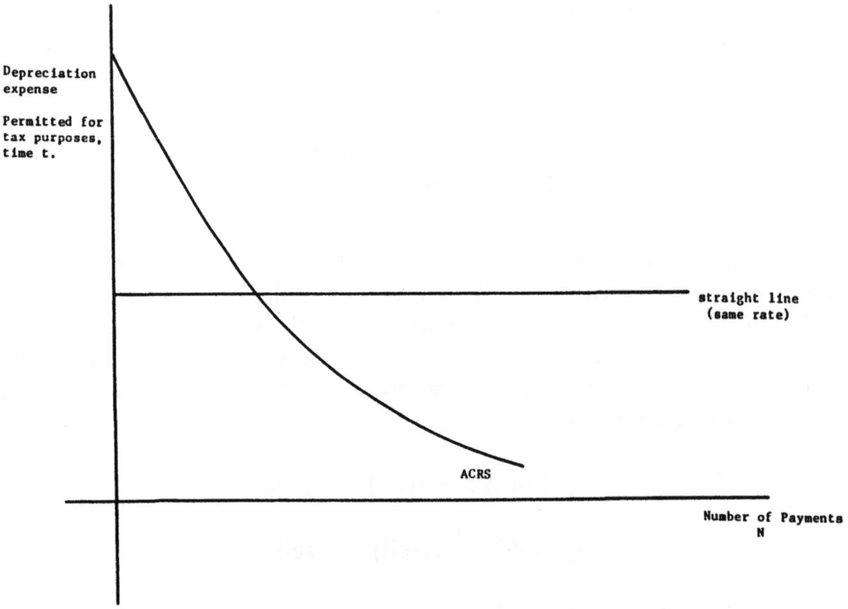


Figure 8-2. Tax and Economic Depriciation

March 18, 1984, the length of depreciation period is 18 years, and there have been further increases.[2] The trend has been toward lengthening the depreciation period. The effect has been to restore the length of write-off period approximately to that prior to 1981. The period 1981–1986, and particularly 1981–1984 contains atypically high tax depreciation rates on real estate. Between 1981 and 1986, the holder of investment real estate has the option of using the accelerated cost recovery system (ACRS) depreciation schedule, or straight-line (SL) rates. Since 1986, under the Tax Reform Act, the length of depreciation period is 27.5 years on residential, and 31.5 years on nonresidential property, and only straight line procedures are permitted. In either case, the rate of depreciation as permitted on the tax schedule is likely to exceed the economic depreciation rate in early years. If economic depreciation rates are 3 percent annually, a straight-line method would provide a period for write-off of 33.3 years. On SL depreciation, the annual rate is

$$D_{SL} = 1/T$$

where $D_{SL}$ is the straight-line depreciation rate and $T$ is the useful life permitted. For a 27.5-year life, the annual depreciation rate is 3.636 percent and for 31.5 year life, the annual rate is 3.175 percent. The ACRS schedule provides for a higher rate of depreciation in earlier years than does SL.

Any accelerated depreciation schedule permits a greater than straight-line rate in early years, and a lower than straight-line rate in later years. Let an accelerated depreciation schedule, such as a 175 percent declining balance rate, provide for a schedule $\delta_t$, $t = 1, \ldots, T$. The depreciation is claimed on the initial basis usually historical cost at purchase, and the basis is not indexed for price changes. Suppose there is no depreciation claimable on the land, and the structure, with initial purchase price $S$, is depreciable. There are no additions. If present, additions are treated similarly for tax purposes to the initial purchase.

The depreciation expense permitted in period $t$ is $\delta_t S$. In the first year, assuming placement in service in January, the depreciation expense is $\delta_1 S$. The sequence of depreciation expenses is $\delta_1 S, \ldots, \delta_T S$. If the investor has a discount rate $R$ on investments, assumed constant over time, the present value of the depreciation expense is

$$PV_{ACC} = S \sum_{t=1}^{T} \delta_t/(1 + R)^t \qquad (8.23)$$

where $PV_{ACC}$, is the present value under an accelerated schedule. The initial balance $S$ is unchanged. Tax depreciation rates are those permitted by fiscal regulations. In such regulations, a serviceable average life is determined. For real estate, the service life for tax purposes has ranged between 15 (in 1981) and 35 years. The tax code then specifies a depreciation rate to be used. Suppose the tax laws permit the improvement component of real estate to be depreciated in $T$ years, the life for tax purposes. If the tax laws permit straight-line (SL) depreciation, the annual depreciation rate is

$$\delta_{SL} = 1/T$$

If the tax laws permit real estate to be depreciated over 30 years, $T = 30$, then the annual depreciation rate permitted in $\delta_{SL} = 1/30 = 0.0333$. The tax laws can also permit a more rapid claim of depreciation expense over the tax life in early years. Depreciation rates greater than $\delta_{SL}$ in early years provide a greater saving. The schedule would be $\delta_{ACC,t}$. The annual differential between the two schedules is $\delta_{ACC,t} - \delta_{SL,t}$, though the straight-line rate is constant and not dependent on $t$. The present value of the depreciation deduction differential, is where depreciation expense is assumed claimed at the end of the period, and $R$ is the discount rate used by the investor:

$$\mathbf{D}_{\text{ACC,SL}} = \frac{\delta_{\text{ACC},1} - \delta_{\text{SL},1}}{1+R} + \frac{\delta_{\text{ACC},2} - \delta_{\text{SL},2}}{(1+R)^2} + \cdots + \frac{\delta_{\text{ACC},L} - \delta_{\text{SL},L}}{(1+R)^L}$$
$$= \sum_{t=1}^{L} \left( \frac{\delta_{\text{ACC},t} - \delta_{\text{SL},t}}{(1+R)^t} \right) \qquad (8.24)$$

The two sets of depreciation rates sum to unity, or

$$\sum_{t=1}^{L} \delta_{\text{ACC},t} = 1 \qquad \text{and} \qquad \sum_{t=1}^{L} \delta_{\text{SL},t} = 1$$

If the present value is positive, accelerated depreciation provides a benefit.

The basis is not indexed for inflation. The basis, or historical cost, of the original asset, is that used for the claiming of depreciation. With inflation, the depreciation provisions are insufficient to replace the asset. The discount rate $R$ includes the effect of inflation and a real rate of return to capital. Since the depreciation charges are not indexed, and $R$ is a nominal interest rate, higher inflation, as reflected in interest rates, reduces the present value of depreciation expenses. Suppose the owner of a depreciating asset selects a straight-line rate. The present value of the depreciation expense, with $V$ being the historical cost basis of the asset being depreciated is

$$\sum_{t=1}^{L} \left( \frac{\delta_{\text{SL}} V}{(1+R)^t} \right)$$

Now $V$ is constant, since the basis is not indexed for inflation, and the depreciation rate is constant. So the depreciation expense in dollars is $\delta_{\text{SL}} V$, an annuity, and the present value is

$$\delta_{\text{SL}} V A(R,T)$$

where $A(R,N)$ is an annuity at interest rate $R$ and term $T$ in years. If the value of the asset were increased for inflation, the real rate of interest could be used. In periods of rapid price change, the failure to increase the historical cost basis provides an insufficient reserve to replace the depreciating asset. One solution is to increase the historical cost basis by the amounts of price changes, so that the nominal depreciation expense increases.

### *Economic Depreciation*

Economic depreciation rates are required to determine the actual decay of the improvements, for calculation of the rate of return. Further, the asset lives used in the tax code require estimates of economically useful service. Two methods are typically used to estimate rates of economic depreciation. When aggregate data are available, the perpetual inventory approach is used. For a time series, suppose data are known on investment, $I_t$, $t = 1, \ldots, T$, preferably measured in real terms, deflated by a price index. The capital stock for the beginning of the next period is the sum of current investment $I_t$ and the undepreciated capital stock available in the current period:

$$K_{t+1} = I_t + (1 - \delta)K_t$$

where $\delta$ is the rate of economic depreciation, constant in this specification. The perpetual inventory method is used to calculate aggregate capital stocks of structures and other capital in the national accounts. The next-period capital stock is

$$K_{t+1} = I_t + (1 - \delta)I_{t-1} + (1 - \delta)^2 K_{t-2}$$

$$= \sum_{j=0}^{J-1} (1 - \delta)^j I_{t-j} + (1 - \delta)^J K_{t-J}$$

summing over $J$ years.

Suppose by a survey, or by insurance value, the total value of the physical real estate capital stock $K_{t+1}$ at the current time is known, as is also the stock at time $K_{t-J}$, the initial or benchmark year. If the first year with balance sheet or other capital data is 1930 and $t + 1 = 1980$, then $t - J =$ 1930, so $t + 1 - (t - J) = 1980 - 1930 = 50$, and $J = 49$. The investment series is known. Then $\delta$ is estimated as the depreciation rate that best fits the data. The perpetual inventory method requires capital stocks for the years 1930 and 1980 to be known.

Another solution is to estimate the economic depreciation rate by having a survey estimate of the average service life $L$. A geometric depreciation rate specification produces the rate $\delta = 2/L$, or a straight-line estimate as $1/L$.

For individual properties, economic depreciation is estimated by a hedonic procedure. The value of the property, $V$, is a function of both age and other characteristics, $X$, that is, $V = F(X, \text{AGE})$, where AGE denotes the age of the structure and $X$ the characteristics other than age. The depreciation rate is the change in price with age, or $\delta = \partial V/\partial \text{AGE}$. In applied work, a hedonic regression as in appraisal is performed, such as

$$V = \sum_{i=1}^{M} \beta_i X_i + \beta_{\text{AGE}} \text{AGE}$$

This specification assumes that the variables in $X$ do not affect age.

Economic depreciation rates are used to provide information on the appropriate tax depreciation rates. Land either does not depreciate, or does so in a variable pattern but cannot be separated from the improvements. The perpetual inventory method assumes that depreciation is constant and is not dependent on the maintenance policy of the owner. The hedonic procedure usually assumes that all characteristics depreciate at the same rate, but a roof can decay more or less rapidly than a foundation.

## Investment Issues

### *Specific Risks*

Physical real estate investments are risky and generally illiquid. Real estate investments involve risk with the performance of the local and general economy, changes in tax and regulatory policy, and the future. Certain tax policies, such as the investment tax credit, have applied temporarily.[3]

There is a problem of capitalization. It is possible that all benefits have been capitalized into the price of land by an efficient real estate market. The only return to the investor, purchasing the property at an initial price capitalizing these returns, is compensation for the additional risk. In such an efficient real estate market, there is no room for excess profits.

Nothing-down strategies are advocated as methods of increasing the return, at the cost of increased risk.[4] The increased leverage multiplier implies increased risk. Methods for putting nothing down include property trades; supplying the down payment in kind, with goods rather than cash;

taking signature loans; applying the balance to charge cards; borrowing from friends and relatives; or convincing the seller to take back the equity in financing.[5]

As marginal tax rates are reduced, the benefit of the tax shield for real estate is reduced. As depreciation write-off periods are increased, and schedules are changed from accelerated to straight line, the return on equity for existing owners declines. If the market is efficient, and the observed real estate return merely compensates for the attributes of such investment, the asset prices fall until the return is restored. New entrants can be unaffected, with the windfall loss borne by existing owners. If land markets capitalize the tax policy, the existing landholders suffer a capital loss, but new investors ultimately obtain the underlying rates of return on real estate assets.

The formulas derived assume that tax benefits are permanent. This assumption is not appropriate, given the prospect of policy change. Some adjustment for the probability of the continued existence of given tax benefits is required. The benefits of the tax program depend on tax capitalization. The effective rate of return is not necessarily increased because of tax changes for all investors. An unexpected tax policy change, more favorable to the effective rate of return, can be immediately capitalized by increasing the asset prices of existing properties. A one-time windfall capital gain accrues to current investors, who had made their decisions based on previous tax policy. Since the stock of existing property cannot be increased in the short run, the price of current properties rises, and the effective rate of return for new investors need not be any different than before.

### *Investment Tactics*

There are other possibilities for obtaining the down payment, as opposed to signature loans. An individual can borrow from a pension plan or profit sharing plan, if so permitted. The employee contribution to such funds can be withdrawn, and the employer portion borrowed against. Up to $50,000 can be borrowed from a plan. Interest is paid back to the plan, which holds the investment as an asset. Since mortgage interest is deductible in computing taxable income, and the interest received is not taxed currently, a tax saving arises. In pension or other plans that are self-directed and permit such investments, a source of funds for a down payment arises. Some plans permit withdrawals for such purposes as purchase of a residence.

Another possibility is to cash in certain retirement investments.[6] A tax penalty can be paid on withdrawal, and a tax liability arises for the amount withdrawn. There may be no other sources of liquidity for real estate purchase. Some lenders will lend with a pension account at the institution as collateral, so withdrawal and its tax and penalty payments, are not incurred. A typical secured loan can be borrowed at two percentage points over the interest rate earned on the deposited funds. An individual with $10,000 in an account earning 10 percent could pay 12 percent for a secured loan, and receive the $10,000 toward a down payment. The alternative is to withdraw the funds and pay a tax and penalty.

One check of a real estate investment is to determine whether initial cash flow is positive, or rental income less expenses except depreciation is positive. If positive, the property is potentially a source of cash, to be exploited, or milked (a "cash cow"), in earning income. If initial cash flow is negative, with no prospects for recovery, the property can be an "alligator," eating cash. All else equal, positive cash flow is beneficial. Yet positive cash flow frequently arises in deteriorating or deteriorated neighborhoods where there is no short-run prospect of capital gains; and negative cash flow arises where the prices have been bid up in the expectation of capital gains. The return to real estate is the sum of net income, tax benefits, and capital gains, as opposed to only one component. One could follow a Graham strategy of the stock market in real estate purchases. The Graham theory advised purchasing stocks where the current price-to-net-earnings ratio is low, and selling when this ratio has reached a target threshold.

Appraisal and valuation are required of each purchase. One possibility is to verify the appraisal with a licensed contractor and then determine the amount of repair required to upgrade the property. On the purchase offer, some advise low-balling, that is, putting in bids well below the asking price, and having the negotiations and counter offers take several iterations. Escape clauses can be added to the offer to purchase or sell. Informed agents on both sides of the transaction would not permit such activities, but real estate markets remain inefficient, particularly in the one-on-one bargaining that often arises.

Nothing-down strategies entail maximizing the leverage and, consequently, the risk. The source of the down payment varies between advocates of the strategy. Sources include trading other real estate, physical assets such as automobiles, obtaining signature loans elsewhere, or attempting to persuade the seller to take back the equity as a second or higher-order mortgage. Since no cash changes hands, there is nothing to pay the broker, so real estate agents are frequently opposed to such transactions. One strategy involves buying a second or higher mortgage at a discount of face value for cash, and using the higher face value as a down payment. The seller is offered the higher mortgage at face value as a down payment. This approach requires that there be an uninformed seller. Other approaches involve finding "must sell" cases where there is marital breakdown. The seller must typically have a large equity in the property.

On the other side of the market, high returns are offered to investors in real estate mortgages. Frequently, these mortgages are high order, standing in claim only after the full satisfaction of other debts. Having a fifth mortgage as an asset can entail a large discount for risk. A prudent response to an investor willing to take the risk is to perform a title search, if the mortgage is secured by the property, to determine the number and magnitude of liens outstanding. Such a search can be performed by the individual at the local county property records office.

## Tax Rules

### *Direct (Income) Taxation*

Aspects of the tax code for both individuals and corporations affect the return to holding real estate. One provision affecting the return is the extent to which losses on real estate investments are deductible against other income. Even where the tax and economic depreciation rates are equal, provided part of the return is in deferrable capital gains, there are early-year losses. For corporations, real estate losses are deductible to an unlimited extent, and there does not appear to be policy change to affect this situation. For individuals, restrictions can be placed on the deductibility of real estate losses.[7] Such restrictions reduce the effective rate of return to holding real estate.

Another provision of tax policy is in the rate of depreciation permitted. Any rate of depreciation in excess of the economic rate provides an initial loss, which if deductible against other income, increases the short-run cash flow of a real estate project. Straight-line depreciation, at a constant rate over a tax life shorter than economic life, provides an increased expense. Restriction on accelerated depreciation provisions reduces the rate of return for incumbent holders. The same conclusions apply to both individuals and corporations.

Property taxes on real estate can be deductible for owner occupiers in calculating taxable income. Taxation of capital gains at rates below those of ordinary income have an effect on investment decisions on assets that depreciate slowly or not at all. In real estate, as compared with other investments, a large proportion of the return is composed of capital gains. Tax laws permit shifting of ordinary income to capital gains, implying a reduction or deferral of taxation.

Debt issues of local governments, municipal bonds, pay interest free of federal income tax and income tax (if applicable) in the state of issue for resident bondholders, to both individuals and corporations. Municipal bonds have been used to finance residential and nonresidential construction. The tax-free status of municipal bond interest implies that yields on such securities are lower than on United States Treasury obligations for similar maturities and on mortgages. By passing on the lower interest rates to borrowers, a subsidy is created. Under typical programs, municipal bonds are issued to finance construction of single-family houses for first-time buyers. Income and purchase price limits are set.

Reduction of marginal tax rates on individuals and corporations reduces the tax-shield benefits of deductions, as well as the return on real estate investments. In evaluating the effects of tax reform, current and proposed legislation are compared and the appropriate marginal tax rate is based on charging against income the deductions to be eliminated first.

Suppose a tax filer has an income before various deductions of \$31,000, and the tax table provides:

| | |
|---|---|
| taxable income \$10–19,999 | MTR 20 percent |
| taxable income \$20–39,999 | MTR 30 percent |
| taxable income \$40,000 or over | MTR 40 percent |

A deduction for mortgage interest is permitted, and the filer has such interest of \$8,000. There are \$5,000 in other deductions. Tax rule changes reduce the marginal rate on all taxable income over \$20,000 to 30 percent, and removes the \$5,000 deduction.

In calculating the effective marginal tax rate applying to the mortgage interest prior to tax reform, the deductions lost by the reform are the first items to be charged against income, reducing taxable income to \$26,000. Then \$6,000 of mortgage interest is deducted at a 30 percent rate, and \$2,000 at a 20 percent rate. The average MTR facing mortgage interest is 27.5 percent, and the average tax shield is (1 − MTR) or 0.725.

After the tax reform, if the income is the same, all mortgage interest is deducted at 30 percent, since the other deductions are no longer permitted. The tax-shield is 70 percent of income. Mortgage interest deductions are more valuable after the tax reform than before. Filers face a higher or lower benefit from the mortgage interest deduction after a tax reform. If a tax reform removes other deductions and tax shelters, but leaves deductions for residential real estate of owner occupiers intact, it is possible for the tax-shield saving to increase on such property subsequent to a tax reform.

Another aspect of reduction in marginal tax rates affects individuals. If federal marginal tax rates are reduced, and state and local taxes are deductible in computing taxable income, the effective rates of state and local taxes are increased. If the highest marginal federal income tax rate is 50 percent, and is reduced to 30 percent, a person in a 10 percent state income tax bracket faces a 55 percent total marginal tax rate prior to the change, and a 37 percent rate afterward. Any limit on the deductibility of mortgage interest against other income reduces the effective rate of return on equity for existing holders. Lower marginal tax rates reduce the value of tax shield, all else equal.

### *Indirect (Property) Taxation*

Taxation on property has been traditionally levied by local governments to support schools and other local public goods. Separate property tax rates can be levied on land, and on improvements. Let a property have market price $V$, composed of $V_L$ in land value, and $V_I$ in improvement value. The municipality sets the assessment of land and improvements for tax purposes. The assessed value for tax purposes is $A_L$ for land and $A_I$ for improvements. The ratio of assessed land value to market value is $A_L/V_L$, with a corresponding improvement assessment ratio $A_I/V_I$. Alternative methods of setting assessments include using full market value, whereupon $A_L$ and $A_I$ are respectively equal to $V_L$ and $V_I$.

The property tax rate is set as a mill rate, providing for the payment of a certain number of dollars per mill, or thousand dollars, of assessed value for property tax purposes. The property tax bill is the product of the mill rate and the assessment for tax purposes. The effective property tax rate is the ratio of the property tax bill to the value of the property.

Tax revolts against property taxes have been sparked by increases in assessed values with increases in real estate prices, while the cash income of property owners either fails to keep pace with these price increases, or owners have low consumption levels of local public goods, notably schools. Two such revolts are Proposition 13 in California, and Proposition 2½ in Massachusetts, passed by a state-wide ballot initiative. Under Proposition 13 in California, passed in November 1978 and enshrined as part of the state constitution, the full cash value, or assessment basis, is the assessed value as of the 1975–1976 taxation year, for existing owners. For subsequent-to-Proposition-13 owners, the full cash value is the price actually paid, subject to adjustments for concessionary financing. All provisions apply to residential, commercial, and industrial property.

The maximum property tax rate, ad valorem, as a percentage of the full cash value, is 1 percent, although debt obligations prior to Proposition 13 for municipalities and the unfunded pension liabilities of municipal employees are added to the tax rate. The maximum annual increase in assessment (full cash value) is limited to 2 percent. The effect is a substantial reduction in property tax bills, for owners as of November 1978.

Prices of real estate, notably residential property, increased substantially, indicating that the benefits of Proposition 13 were at least partially capitalized into prices.[8] Existing owners receive a windfall gains, both through a reduction in property taxes payable each year and in perpetuity, and through the higher market values of property. If the benefits are capitalized in higher values, new buyers receive no savings. Prices are higher, since the revolt reduces the supply of existing property. An entry tax is imposed on new buyers. A distortion arises in real estate markets. This phenomenon is acute for commercial and industrial property, where turnover rates are lower than for residential property. The notion of horizontal equity, where owners of properties with similar market value pay the same taxes, becomes inapplicable.

The benefits of Proposition 13 are generally not portable to other properties. The exception is for single family homes owned by those aged over 55. Under Proposition 60, in California the assessment can be transferred to a new house. Existing owners within the state have an incentive not to be mobile, with benefits tied to current location. The consequence is a lower level of real estate transactions than otherwise would be the case, less job and industrial mobility, and greater inefficiency in goods markets tied to real estate markets.[9] Tax revolts, apart from reducing the effective tax rate shift the overall tax burden away from old to new owners. Tax revolts, where incumbents are protected by special provisions, reduce the turnover and availability of property, as owners have a greater incentive to stay than to move. Since commercial and industrial turnover rates are lower than those in the residential sector, there is an increased relative subsidy to long-time commercial enterprises.

## Relocation

The real estate investor, in a commercial or industrial context in particular, can be a tenant. The real estate market contains a distribution of rents and purchase prices. With this distribution, there is a possibility of a return to searching for property, and of changing location. In changing location, moving costs must be paid, including any payoff on the current lease. Business is affected directly, through lost customer sales; reprinting letterheads, stationery, and business cards; and new business listings. There are costs of disconnecting and reconnecting utilities, and cost differences arise in utility rates between the old and new locations.

The renting firm can lose its current investment in tenant improvements (TIs) installed in the existing shell or unoccupied office space. The tenant is provided an allowance for TIs as a subtraction from the rent. The TIs depend on the type of business, but include improvements to the building. The firm is faced with TIs in the new location, so the rental comparisons require inclusion of the net rents exclusive of TIs. Some firms have capital equipment particularly expensive to move, including computer hardware, confidential hard copy data and files, that render them locked into the existing location.

Relocation costs include commuting, for employees. Some firms choose a location convenient for employee commuting, and others shift the costs of commuting to employees. There is a trade-off in overall costs of location, for employees, customers, and direct rental costs. A lower cost of rent is offset by higher commuting costs—in time, transportation expenses, and lost output and sales for customers and employees. Firms pay higher rents to concentrate operations in one location in order to take advantages of economies of scale and interaction. Firms use an employee commuting cost gradient as well as a rent gradient in their cost minimization decision on location.

Another location factor is proximity to transportation outlets such as the airport, rail links, and port facilities. Executives who travel need to minimize the costs of dislocation. Brokerage commissions paid to outside real estate firms, either on the sell or buy side can be involved. Some firms expend resources on an internal real estate department, and there are marginal costs of relocation expended in such a department.

## Strategy

The typical real estate investment is predicated on the following three considerations:

1. Total revenue increases at a rate greater than total expenses. If interest payments are based on a FRPM, and depreciation expense is constant, a large percentage of expenses is constant. Positive revenue growth implies that revenue increases faster than expenses. Total expenses can be large in the initial period, particularly if the FRPM has an increased in-

terest rate to compensate for the tilt effect. Even if revenue increases, cash flow and net income after depreciation can be negative for a long period. Revenue increases can be lower than projected in a noninflationary environment.

2. As revenue increases, a constant cap rate or times gross obtains, implying that the asset price of the property increases. Equity increases both from capital gains and the paydown of the loan. If the times gross decreases, the expected capital gains need not materialize.

3. The tax environment can change. Tax benefits in real estate include tax depreciation rate schedules more rapid than economic depreciation rates, favorable tax treatment of capital gains, the ability to deduct losses from real estate losses against other income on an unlimited basis, and the tax rates. Capital gains can be deferred, and capital losses realized.

An optimal holding period on real estate is derived. The effective rate of return after tax is obtained as a function of the holding period. Where the effective rate of return exceeds the target return of the investor, the holding of the real estate continues. When the effective rate of return falls below a threshold rate, the property is sold. The strategy is divided into five segments, to correspond to accounting measures, and generally accepted accounting practice (GAAP). There is an income statement, or profit and loss statement, a balance sheet, a cash flow statement or cash flow triangle, and a rate of return on equity after tax.

The strategy is formed for an individual investor, that is, an investor facing personal income tax, so passive investment in limited partnerships can be included. For corporate holding of real estate, the strategy is similar, except that the parameters differ. In real estate, there are various rules of thumb, such as "one should hold for five years, and then sell." The strategy model derives an optimal holding period, dependent on a series of parameters, as an alternative to rules of thumb.

The strategy determines the price an investor should pay for a project, given a target rate of return and holding period. Alternatively, the asking price for a seller, and the price a buyer is willing to pay, is obtainable, given a predetermined rate of return. For the seller, an asking price can be calculated providing a projected rate of return to the buyer. Pro forma financial statements are constructed. Any changes in the parameters can be adjusted.

Upon sale or other realization depreciation claimed for tax purposes is recaptured. Accelerated depreciation involves any schedule with greater than straight-line rates in early years. The effect of accelerated depreciation is to reduce income or generate losses for tax purposes. The present value of the depreciation deduction saving is positive. On recapture, depreciation expenses are taxable as ordinary income, assuming that no differential tax rates between capital gains and income exist. Even if all depreciation expense is recovered as ordinary income, the expense is on a historical cost basis on the initial investment. As the property is held longer, the present value of the recapture declines.

The optimal holding period for real estate, while not uniform at five years, is likely to be longer than one year. The motivating force is the transactions cost of purchase and disposal. As the holding period increases, there is a longer time to amortize the fixed transactions cost of purchase, for points, fees and taxes, and sale, for brokerage fees and closing costs. Depreciation benefits are exhausted, and the rate of return declines. The rate of return profile has an inverted U shape. The degree of curvature depends on tax policies and other projections.

## Concluding Remarks

Active real estate investments involve individual decision making. By being an active investor, the fees and commissions paid to others for investment selection and advice, brokerage, financing, and property management can be avoided as direct costs, though they may remain as indirect costs of supervisory time.

Some rules of thumb have been developed for active real estate investment, but these are merely guidelines. The active real estate investor usually starts buying first in familiar neighborhoods, to reduce the transactions and management costs. With changing technology, remote management is more feasible. If the active real estate investor is buying condominium units, it is preferable to have a large number of owner-occupied units in the building. Yet this argument assumes that the market has not adequately priced the ratio of tenants to owners. At the beginning of a condominium project, there is a large percentage of tenants, while the developer retains possession. Even a relatively inefficient market would contain a discount for early condominium buyers.

Another rule of thumb is that apartments are better investments than single-family houses. They are cheaper to buy and easier to rent. All else equal, an apartment is generally cheaper to buy than a house. With the more favorable affordability comes increased competition. The tenant can benefit from the competition through reduced rents.

The inefficiency of the real estate market lies more in heterogeneity of properties and lack of information of buyers, than in unexploited opportunities in aggregate selection, such as rental housing generally, selfstorage warehouses, or time vacation units. Rules of thumb, while possibly avoiding some pitfalls, are not likely to produce rates of return above those prevailing in real estate as a whole. By deleting some opportunities, the rules of thumb may actually produce below-average rates of return. In any calculation of the rate of return, the opportunity cost of the time and any resources of the owner must be included. Sweat equity arises, but is possibly compensated at below the minimum wage.

## Notes

1. Mortgages on investment property are frequently of the FRPM type, with declining nominal interest payments. With SL depreciation, expenses other than for maintenance are largely fixed.

2. The period was increased to 19 years effective May 8, 1985, and then to a range varying between 27.5 to 31 years, effective January 1, 1987. The depreciation schedules are published in the Internal Revenue Service, Publication 436.

3. The investment tax credit (ITC) has been applied for various periods in a policy-on, policy-off manner. As applied, the ITC does not pertain to structures and real estate, though some improvements can qualify, such as appliances and energy conservation devices. ITCs are subtractions from taxes actually paid at a given percentage rate. If the ITC is 10 percent, that proportion of the purchase price is deductible from the taxes otherwise payable. Since the ITC is directed at equipment, policy off, when it is removed—all else equal—increases the structures-equipment ratio within the capital stock, and is favorable for the real estate sector.

4. See Allen [1981]. There it is advocated that the real estate investor purchase one property each year for five years. At the end of the fifth year, the investor sells the first property, and buys another. A similar policy continues, with the second property sold, and another bought at the end of the sixth year.

5. Real estate trades, or like-kind exchanges, can qualify for the deferral of capital gains taxes.

6. Examples of retirement accounts that permit withdrawals are Individual Retirement Accounts (IRAs), employee deferred savings plans permitted under Sections 401(k) and 403(b) of the Income Tax Act in the United States, and Keogh plans for the self-employed.

7. Restrictions can arise on the dollar amount of losses that are deductible against earnings or other income, with a limit on the gross income of the taxpayer eligible to deduct the losses, and a restriction to active as opposed to passive real estate investments. "Passive real estate investments" refer largely to real estate partnerships. Tax regulations need not necessarily conform to this definition.

8. See Rosen [1981].

9. Other cases where rigid real estate markets have similar effects arise in rent control. Tenants in rent controlled units are less mobile; they tend to search for jobs only in the immediate area. The benefits of job switching must cover not only capital costs of moving, but the flow costs of the differential between real estate costs in the current and propsed location. Much of Europe, both Eastern and Western, suffers from real estate market immobility. The

effect of Proposition 13 is akin to rent control. Rent control renders tenants immobile. Property tax restrictions render property owners immobile.

A series of regulations is required to enforce the subsidy. Transfer of property to a spouse at any time, or to dependent children by testament through an estate, does not trigger a reassessment under Proposition 13, and the lower taxes remain.

# IV REAL ESTATE INVESTMENT:
## *Holding Financial Assets*

# 9 PASSIVE INVESTMENT: *Syndication, Limited Partnerships, and Real Estate Investment Trusts*

## Introduction

Active real estate involves the individual management of real estate properties. The owner is the manager. In active real estate management, the owner is responsible in varying degrees for administration, tenant selection, and maintenance. Some functions can be delegated to a property manager. Usually, active real estate investment involves the investor taking direct title to the property, whether or not the investor is a manager. Passive real estate investment does not involve the investor in a management role. The investment is through a security offering, and frequently the investor does not hold title to the property directly. Specific passive real estate investments are syndications, limited partnerships, and real estate investment trusts (REITs).

A syndication or limited partnership provides a passive real estate vehicle, which may be either income or tax oriented. The income oriented investment purchases a property with all or mostly cash, thus limiting leverage risk with a low loan-to-value ratio. Positive cash flow is generated immediately, but some income is protected by depreciation deductions in excess of economic rates. The tax oriented option is purchased with heavy leverage. The objective is to create losses in early years of a holding period, particularly through tax depreciation expense. The losses for tax purposes reduce income that is permitted to be sheltered by passive investments. In either limited partnership form, ownership is spread over many investors, reducing the risk of indivisibility or lumpiness of real estate investments. Passive investments solve the indivisibility in active real estate investments. A limited partnership can diversify risks by allocation of investment to several properties.

Prices paid by the passive real estate marketer, the ultimate investor, are liable to be "tax prices." The price of the property is increased; the expected future benefits are thus capitalized, assuming a particular marginal tax rate. The tax oriented partnership typically bases its rate of return calculations on the highest MTR available, and is limited to relatively few investors. Risk remains in both income and tax vehicles on future rents and prices. Passive real estate can be more illiquid than active real estate, because the investor is surrendering management and timing control.

Another passive real estate investment in physical property is the real estate investment trust (REIT). REIT units are traded as securities, some listed on major stock exchanges. REIT units sell at prices comparable with other listed securities, as opposed to prices of physical real estate, and this reduces the indivisibility of owning property directly. Shares are marketable and hence liquid. REIT investments compete with other equity issues and are not necessarily restricted by price to high tax rate individuals. The investor is surrendering management and paying fees to managers. In return, diversification, lower entry prices, and liquidity are obtained.

## Syndication and Limited Partnerships

### *Syndication*

A syndicate is any group combining to purchase real estate. It can take corporate, joint ownership, joint venture, or partnership forms. The corporate form does not provide tax benefits to the investors. Losses on real estate by a corporation cannot be counted as losses on tax returns of shareholders. The most common application of syndication under securities regulation covering real estate is the limited partnership. A prospectus must be sent to each potential purchaser. This prospectus describes the administration and management of the project, potential purchases, pro forma financial statements, and fees. The limited partnership form is focused on here because of its widespread application.

### *Limited Partnership*

The limited partnership combines the benefits of individual ownership with those of a corporation. A general partner manages the project. The general partner is usually a corporation with limited liability, and conveys this characteristic to the project. The individual investors, or limited partners, are at risk only for their initial investment. The limited liability avoids the risk of personal assets of the limited partners being claimed by creditors of the partnership. The limited partners are allowed to deduct the losses and share in the tax benefits, but the whole project has limited liability.

Despite the limited liability, because of the partnership structure, operating losses are deductible against certain other income. By comparison, the shareholder of a corporation reporting a loss cannot deduct this loss from any other income.

Although the investment is structured as a partnership, continuity is retained by having a corporation as general partner. The real estate investment has a lower risk of being dissolved because of the continuity of the corporation. Because full deductions of interest and depreciation expenses are claimable by individuals, limited partnerships are attractive to those with the highest marginal tax rate. Any reduction in marginal tax rates, by reducing the effect of the tax shield, affects tax oriented limited partnerships adversely.

For tax purposes, operating losses from business activity are deductible from some income of the limited partners. To permit the pass-through of losses, the legal form of organization must be a partnership and not an association, which is taxed as a corporation. The limited partnership has limited liability, transferability of interest, and continuity of life.

The corporate general partner can be the developer-builder. Although the limited partners have limited liability, the full amount of depreciation on the property can be claimed as a deduction, as opposed to only depreciation times $(1 - v)$, the equity ratio. The depreciation deduction is leveraged.

Suppose an investor purchases a real estate investment for $100,000, all of which is depreciable. Let the initial investment in the first year be $5,000. The remainder is payable as a promissory note to the syndicator of the limited partnership, usually as a nonrecourse loan with no claim against assets outside the investment. A nonrecourse loan establishes the limited liability. The project uses a straight-line depreciation schedule over 31.5 years, and a 10 percent interest rate is payable by the limited partner to the general partner or other lender on the note.

The investor is able to use leverage on the depreciation expense, and the straight-line rate of 3.175 percent produces a charge of $3,175. The interest expense on the 95,000 borrowed is $9,500, for a total interest and depreciation expense of $12,675. If, in the first year, the project generates operating income of $6,000, a loss of $6,675 is created on an investment of $5,000.

The typical real estate limited partnership requires a minimum investment of $5,000, except for certain pension accounts where the minimum is $2,000. Some have no mortgage debt, purchasing the properties with all cash, raised from the investors. The annual income is positive; and the limited partnership can distribute a dividend to the investors, partly sheltered by depreciation allowances. If there is mortgage debt, the write-off and deduction is greater, but the cash income is lower.

Some limited partnerships are organized as blind pools; these do not invest in specific properties, but, with a general fund, invest in several properties. Although this strategy spreads the risk by diversifying over a number of properties, there is a potential lack of accountability.

Limited partnerships have a thin market for secondary resale, because of their complex nature and because the market is restricted to relatively high-income and sophisticated investors. The general partner may sometimes be willing to find another buyer or repurchase the units, but typically at a deep discount. The lack of liquidity or marketability restricts investor diversification of a portfolio over various limited partnerships. The absence of a formal market for selling the limited partnership units creates a problem of valuation. There is no organized secondary market; although, potentially, a "stripped market," with tax shelter benefits already claimed, may develop. For tax oriented projects, the asset prices would be lower without the tax benefits. Tax oriented partnerships frequently assume that all losses are deductible at the highest marginal tax rate. This tax orientation implies that investors in tax-deferred accounts, such as pension funds, find it impractical to participate.

Losses are losses. While the partnership may have increased revenue in the future, the short-term promises losses to the investor, even if some of these are shared by the government through tax refunds. The guarantee is for short-term losses, and there is no guarantee of ultimate profits. Investment in limited partnerships entails some restriction in financial flexibility. The syndicator must provide tax identification numbers and information on all investors. Subsequent tax audits of the syndicator can involve direct claims against the limited partners. Legislative risk arises, in addition to the risk of changes in tax policy.

In a limited partnership organization, a financing proposal for a real estate project is presented to lenders. The financial proposal indicates how income and expenses are divided between the general partner and the limited partners. Also developed are projected annual income and expense statements over the holding period. The statements and other data are provided to potential limited partners in a prospectus.

## Limited Partnership Income: Cash-on-Cash and Holding Returns

### *Tax and Economic Income Statements*

The partnership itself is not taxable; all net income is transferred to the limited partners. Let $Y_{TAX}$ be net rental income, $a$ be net operating rental income per dollar of property after management and maintenance expenses, $r$ be the note interest rate, $\delta$ the tax depreciation rate, $u$ the structure-to-value ratio, and $\lambda$ the property tax rate. Then income for tax purposes of a limited partnership is

$$Y_{TAX} = aV - rB - (\delta u + \lambda)V$$

Dividing by $V$, the property value,

$$y_{TAX} = a - rv - (\delta u + \lambda)$$

The partnership pays no tax on this income, and passes it through to the limited partners. The income statement for tax purposes of the limited partners collectively (passed through from general partner, per dollar of property value) is:

**Tax Purposes Income Statement, Limited Partners, During Given Period**

| | | |
|---|---|---|
| Net operating rental income (gross rent less vacancy, allowances, maintenance, property management, general partner fees) | | $a$ |
| Less: | Interest expense (interest rate $r$ times loan-to-value ratio $v$) | $rv$ |
| Less: | Property taxes (property tax rate) | $\lambda$ |
| Equals: | Before-tax cash flow (BTCF) | $a - rv - \lambda$ |
| Less: | Depreciation expense permitted, tax purposes (allowed tax depreciation rate times depreciable portion $u$, $0 \leqslant u \leqslant 1$) | $\delta u$ |

Equals: Income for tax purposes $a - rv - \lambda - \delta u = y_{\mathrm{TAX}}$

Times: Marginal tax rate $\tau$
(assume same for all limited partners, and assume that income available to deduct losses)

Equals: Tax payable
(refund if negative) $\tau(a - rv - \lambda - \delta u) = \tau y_{\mathrm{TAX}}$

Income for tax purposes is the net rental income, less interest expense and property taxes, and less permitted depreciation. All variables are expressed as ratios of the property value. In the income for tax purposes, the rate of depreciation is that allowable by the tax laws. The tax payable is always the same, since income is treated similarly from any source, and is taxable. A loss may not necessarily be deductible against any income. The investor, if income for tax purposes is negative, is assumed to have another income source that can be sheltered by the losses on the real estate investment.

In a typical multiyear investment, in the early years, $Y_{\mathrm{TAX}}$ is negative, if tax depreciation expenses are large. Economic, or actual, depreciation is netted out in the change in market value of the property with time and age. All depreciation expenses can be claimed by the limited partners. Capital gains are excluded from the income in $a$, which is net of utilities and maintenance expenses.

The calculation of the effective rate of return is on a cash-on-cash basis. In the cash-on-cash method, the sources and uses of cash statement determines the rate of return. The return equates the present value of net cash receipts with the present value of net cash disbursements for a given holding period. Alternatively, the sources and uses of cash statement is calculated for different holding periods, until a target rate of return is achieved.

The economic income of the property is the sum of net income, tax benefits, and capital gains. Excluding accrued but unrealized capital gains or losses, the limited partner economic income (cash flow) statement (passed through from general partner, per dollar of property value) is

**Economic Income Statement, Limited Partnership, During Given Period (Year)**

Net operating rental income
(gross rent less vacancy, allowances

maintenance, property management,
general partner fees) $a$
Less: Interest expense (interest rate $r$ times loan-to-value ratio $v$) $rv$
Less: Property taxes (property tax rate) $\lambda$
Equals: Before-tax cash flow (BTCF) $a - rv - \lambda$

Less: Tax payable (MTR times $y_{TAX}$) $\tau y_{TAX}$
Equals: After-tax cash flow (ATCF) $= a - rv - \lambda - \tau y_{TAX}$

$$= a - rv - \lambda - \tau(a - rv - \lambda - \delta u)$$
$$= y_{EC} = (1 - \tau)(a - rv - \lambda) + \tau\delta u$$

Net economic income excluding capital gains is after-tax cash flow $y_{EC}$. Economic income is the sum of two components, with the capital gains suppressed. The net income after tax is $(1 - \tau)(a - rv - \lambda)$, or rental income, less interest and property tax, or cash flow without depreciation. The tax depreciation expense is a source of positive cash flow, of $\tau\delta u$, and this amount is added. All variables are expressed in percentage terms. Capital gains can be added at rate $h$. If they are deferrable indefinitely, such as with like-kind exchanges of property, they are not subject to taxation. Net economic income is the rental income, less interest expense, less property taxes, less tax payable. The tax and economic definitions of income differ, so the property investor must maintain two sets of books. The income $a$ is measured on a triple net (NNN) basis, net of maintenance and fees of the general partner.

### *Cash-on-Cash Returns*

The rate of return to investing in a limited partnership, cash-on-cash, requires the construction of sources and uses of cash statements. There are two statements, corresponding to the two decisions—hold or sell—faced by the investor in each time period. Under the hold cash flow statement, the investor retains the limited partnership unit. It is assumed that the investor has some choice in the hold or sell decision, though this choice is circumscribed in many limited partnerships.

In the if-hold cash flow statement, cash receipts and disbursements are reported for the limited partners collectively; they are assumed to face the same marginal tax rate. Cash receipts are the sources at date of purchase, and during the ownership period. At date of purchase, the promissory note funds are used in payment, contributed by the general partner or other lender to the limited partners. During ownership, positive net income of the property provides a source of cash. If negative, net income per dollar of value $y_{EC,t}$ at date $t$ is a cash disbursement. Cash disbursements at purchase are for the price of the property, for the payment of fees to the general partner, and for any points on the promissory note.

The if-hold cash flow statement is used to determine the effective rate of return, $r_e$, to real estate on a hold:

**Sources and Uses of Cash, Limited Partnership, If Hold Up to Time *t***
(cumulative over holding period)

**Cash Receipts**

Date of Purchase
Loan proceeds
Promissory note
Nonrecourse loan $B$

During Ownership Period
Cash flow after tax per dollar, year $t$ $y_{EC,t}$
Times: Property value $V$, year $t$
$y_{EC,t}V$
Times: Discounting factor
$1/(1 + r_e)^t$
Equals: Present value, after-tax cash flow (ATCF)
$\Sigma_{i=1}^{t} Y_{EC,i}/(1 + r_e)^i$

Present Value, Cash Receipts

$$B + \Sigma_{i=1}^{t} Y_{EC,i}/(1 + r_e)^i$$

**Cash Disbursements**

Date of Purchase
Purchase price $V$
Add: Sales fees and load
(LOAD times value $V$)
$\text{LOAD} \times V$
Add: Note fees and points
($p$ times promissory note $B$)
$pB$

Present Value, Cash Disbursements

$$= (1 + \text{LOAD})V + pB$$

(Divide by $V$, for per dollar of initial purchase price.)

$$v + \Sigma_{i=1}^{t} y_{EC,i}/(1 + r_e)^i \qquad = 1 + \text{LOAD} + pv$$

The effective rate of return $r_e$ is the only unknown and equates the present values of cash receipts and disbursements.

The rate of return for a hold can be determined at successive dates. It is for cash-on-cash, based on after-tax calculations, and is recalculated for various holding periods. For each successive date, the rate of return to selling is determined. Where the rate of return for a sell is the highest indicates the optimal holding period.

The partnership is assumed to receive all the lump sum proceeds from the limited partners in the initial period. The more common form of organization involves the limited partners making a continuing contribution of their equity portion over the life of the partnership.

The partnership is not taxable directly, so the income is distributed to the limited partners. The general partner collects a load from the limited partners. The load covers fees to the real estate or security brokers receiving commission on the project, the underwriting fees, the legal fees for the prospectus, and the costs of sales and marketing. On the promissory note, points and other closing fees are charged. Management fees are taken by the general partner, above other project expenses for interest, property taxes, maintenance, and utilities. Such pro forma statements are provided in the prospectus of the project.

The limited partners capital gains tax payable upon sale at date $t$ is

**Capital Gains Tax, Limited Partners, Date of Sale *t***

Purchase price, historical cost basis
(assuming no improvements or additions) $V$
Less: Cumulative depreciation claimed, tax purposes $D_t V$
Equals: Undepreciated basis, tax purposes $(1 - D_t)V$

Selling price, date $t$ $V_t$

Less: Undepreciated basis $(1 - D_t)V$
Equals: Capital gain, tax purposes $V_t - (1 - D_t)V$

Times: Tax rate $\alpha$ $\alpha[V_t - (1 - D_t)V]$
Equals: Capital gains tax $CGTAX_t$

All partners are assumed to have the same MTR, and capital gains taxed at rate $\alpha$ $(= \tau)$ if taxed as ordinary income.

It is assumed that no improvements or additions are made during ownership. If additions are made, they are added at historical cost to the basis. Under straight-line depreciation at rate $\delta$, the annual depreciation expense is $\delta V$, and the cumulative expense at year $t$ is $t\delta V$, so $D_t V = t\delta V$. If the rate of tax depreciation is $\delta_t$, varying by year $t$, then $D_t = \Sigma_{i=1}^{t} \delta_i$.

In the if-sell sources and uses of cash statement, if a sell occurs at time $t$, cash receipts are reported at the date of purchase, during ownership, and at the date of sale. The addition to the cash receipts from the hold statement is for date of sale. Cash received is the selling price. Physical cash need not change hands. If a note is provided by the limited partners to the buyer, to assist in financing the purchase price, the note is considered to be cash received. Cash disbursed at sale is for prepayment fees, capital gains tax, to pay-off of the initial promissory note, windup fees, and commissions.

The if-sell cash flow statement is used to determine the effective rate of return, $r_e$, to real estate on a sell:

**Sources and Uses of Cash, Limited Partnership, If-Sell at Time $t$**
(cumulative over holding period)

| Cash Receipts | | Cash Disbursements | |
|---|---|---|---|
| Date of Purchase | | Date of Purchase | |
| Loan proceeds | | Purchase price | $V$ |
| Promissory note | | Add: Sales fees and load | |
| Nonrecourse loan | $B$ | (LOAD times value $V$) | |
| | | LOAD × $V$ | |
| | | Add: Loan fees and points | |
| | | ($p$ × loan balance $B$) | $pB$ |
| During Ownership Period | | | |
| Cash flow after tax | | | |
| per dollar, year $t$ | $y_{EC,t}$ | | |
| Times: Property value $V$, year $t$ | | | |
| $y_{EC,t}V$ | | | |
| Times: Discounting factor | | | |
| $(1 + r_e)^{-t}$ | | | |
| Equals: Present value, after-tax cash flow (ATCF) | | | |
| $= \Sigma_{i=1}^{t} Y_{EC,i}/(1 + r_e)^i$ | | | |

| **Cash Receipts** | **Cash Disbursements** |
|---|---|
| Date of Sale | Date of Sale |
| Gross selling price $V_t$ | Real estate brokerage commission rate $n$ |
| | Times: Selling price $V_t$ |
| | Equals: Real estate commission $nV_t$ |
| | Add: Prepayment penalty rate $q_t$ |
| | Times: Promissory note $B$ |
| | Equals: Prepayment penalty $q_tB$ |
| | Add: Windup fees (paid to general partner at date of sale) $\mathrm{WINDUP}_t$ |
| | Add: Capital gains taxes (see below) $\mathrm{CGTAX}_t$ |
| | Add: Note balance, outstanding, nonrecourse loan $b_tB$ |
| **Present Value Cash Receipts** | **Present Value Cash Disbursements** |
| $B + \Sigma_{i=1}^{t} Y_{\mathrm{EC},i}/(1+r_e)^i$ | $= (1 + \mathrm{LOAD})V + pB$ |
| Add: $V_t/(1+r_e)^t$ | Add: $[nV_t + (b_t + q_t)B + \mathrm{CGTAX}_t + \mathrm{WINDUP}_t]/(1+r_e)^t$ |

The solution for $r_e$, cash-on-cash, is that rate of return equating the present value of cash receipts with the present value of cash disbursements.

At date of sale, the limited partnership is wound down, and the net sale proceeds are distributed. The limited partnership receives net sales proceeds, and deducts the prepayment penalty $q_tB$. Windup fees to the general partner $\mathrm{WINDUP}_t$ are paid. At sale, the total depreciation expense $D_t$ is subject to tax as a capital gain recapture. The net balance is subject to capital gains taxes at rate $\alpha$, in the hands of the limited partners. After taxes, the promissory note outstanding, $b_tB$, is either paid off or assumed by the buyer.

The response of the effective rate of return to changes in the variables is

| *Increase in Variable* | *Effect on Rate of Return $r_e$* |
|---|---|
| General partner fees: | |
| Load | Decrease |
| Windup fees | Decrease |
| Depreciation schedule: | |
| Writeoff period $T$ | Decrease |
| Annual rates $\delta$ | Increase |
| Taxes: | |
| Capital gains tax rate $\alpha$ | Decrease |
| Personal tax rate $\tau$ | Indeterminate |
| Property tax rate $\lambda$ | Decrease |
| Loan package: | |
| Contract interest rate $r$ | Decrease |
| Term $N$ | Increase |
| Frequency of compounding $k$ | Decrease |
| Points | Decrease |
| Prepayment penalty | Decrease |

Regarding the fees of the general partner, no imputation is made for the benefits provided by higher fees. If higher fees involve better service, and reduce the time and transactions costs of the limited partner, then the effect on the rate of return is indeterminate.

The fees paid to the general partner represent the price that the real estate investor pays to buy out the active management. From the total fees paid, the investor can calculate what the time spent on active management is worth. Time spent on active management is a random variable, in that variation arises over projects. Hence the time-cost estimate is an average. The fees paid to the general partner, if $\text{MANAGE}_i$, is the fee for year $i$, $i = 1 \ldots, t$ are

| | |
|---|---|
| Load | $\text{LOAD} \times V$ |
| Management fees | $\text{MANAGE}_i$ |
| Windup fees | $\text{WINDUP}_t$ |

The present value of the total fees is

$$\mathrm{LOAD} \times V + \sum_{i=1}^{t} \frac{\mathrm{MANAGE}_i}{(1+R)^i} + \frac{\mathrm{WINDUP}_t}{(1+R)^t}$$

at discount rate $R$.

This present value represents the cost to the passive investor. A complete comparison is not possible, since the limited partnership, in addition to freeing management time, may be more divisible, and more diversified than individual holdings, but less liquid. The limited partner has less control over the date of sale.

The rate of return for selling can be calculated for various holding dates, $i = 1, \ldots, t$. The rate of return to selling at date $t$ is $r_e(\text{sell},t)$. Then the optimal holding period, for timing, is that where $r_e(\text{sell},t)$ is the highest, on the cash-on-cash basis. If this best time to sell is $t^*$, then

$$t^* = \max_t r_e(\text{sell},t)$$

Recalculate $r_e$ from the if-sell cash flow statement each year, and choose the selling rate of return, cash-on-cash, that is highest. The calculation can be repeated every year until the depreciation benefits are exhausted, or beyond.

It is possible that the rate of return to holding continues to increase indefinitely, so that the owner should never sell. In this case, the criterion should be strengthened by adding "if $r_e(\text{sell},t^*) > r_e(\text{hold},t^*)$."

The investor could require returns to exceed a particular threshold. The returns are averages over a holding period, not marginal returns to holding for one more year. Where the effective $r_e$, as an average return, is decreasing, the marginal return is negative, so seeking the highest rate of return remains appropriate.

## Tax- and Income-Oriented Partnerships

### *Tax Laws*

Tax-oriented limited partnerships, through the interest payments on nonrecourse loans and the leveraging of tax depreciation expense, operate by creating a loss for tax purposes. After-tax cash flow (ATCF) exceeds before-tax cash flow (BTCF). The investment defers income into the future.

Certain features of the tax code are exploited by tax-oriented limited partnerships. If capital gains are taxed at rates below those of ordinary income, there is an incentive to shift income to capital gains. Such a shift can be accomplished with depreciation expenses. The prices of the properties offering tax benefits are higher than were the benefits to be removed. The potential investor may continue to receive no more than the prevailing rate of return facing one with the highest marginal tax rate.

A reform that treates capital gains as ordinary income and reduces the depreciation expense chargeable, reduces the benefit of the tax-oriented limited partnership. The reduction in tax depreciation expense is achievable by increasing the length of time over which a property can be depreciated, and by restricting the use of accelerated depreciation schedules.

The reduction of benefit for tax-oriented limited partnerships creates a market for income-oriented limited partnerships. Both are considered passive investments. Some investors in tax-oriented limited partnerships continue with tax losses, and nowhere to park them if deductibility is restricted.[1] A market develops for income-oriented limited partnerships, to provide the positive net income to shield losses on tax oriented deals. As long as depreciation expenses remain above economic rates, some of the cash flow from an income-oriented limited partnership is shielded. If capital gains are taxed on a realized but not accrued basis, the taxation can be deferred. Income-oriented partnerships offer no tax benefits. The payment is made mostly with cash and there is low leverage. The syndication spreads the risk by buying many properties.

Tax-oriented partnerships are highly leveraged, to provide larger deductions for the investor. Unlike income-oriented partnerships, tax-oriented partnerships are usually private, and not registered with the Securities and Exchange Commission. Fees are higher, and range up to 25 percent of the initial investment. Tax-oriented limited partnerships are geared toward maximizing initial year losses.

The calculation of cash flow is the same for both income and tax-oriented limited partnerships. The difference is in the degree of leverage offered. An income-oriented limited partnership reduces the debt load by making $v$ low. In the corner solution case, $v = 0$, and the properties of the limited partnership are paid for with all-cash transactions. The income-oriented limited partnership typically faces a low marginal tax rate, as cash flow is immediately positive. Individual and group pension funds, insurance companies, and trusts are potential investors.

### *Risk and Leverage*

The return to any real estate investment has three components. From the economic income statement, total income is

**Net Income, Including Capital Gains, During Period *t***
(per dollar of property value)

Net income—rental
Net operating income $a$
Less: Loan or note interest $rv$
Less: Property tax $\lambda$
Equals: Net income BTCF
(before-tax cash flow) $a - rv - \lambda$
Times: (1 less marginal tax rate) $(1 - \tau)$
Equals: Net income from operations ATCF
(after-tax cash flow) $(1 - \tau)(a - rv - \lambda)$

Add: Tax shield—depreciation recovery
Tax depreciation rate $\delta$
Times: Marginal tax rate $\tau$
Times: Fraction depreciable $u$
Equals: Tax shield, depreciation recovery $\delta\tau u$

Add: Accrued, unrealized capital gains
(net of economic depreciation) $h$

Net income, after-tax cash flow, and capital gains

$$y_{EC} = (1 - \tau)(a - rv - \lambda) + \delta\tau u + h$$

The net income is $y_{EC}$ under both tax- and income-oriented deals. Suppose $u = 1$, and the property is all depreciable, such as a condominium. Then the income net is

$$y_{EC} = (1 - \tau)(a - rv - \lambda) + \delta\tau + h$$

The one-period income per dollar of property value is $r_e(1 - v)$, where $(1 - v)$ is the equity ratio, so

$$r_e(1 - v) = (1 - \tau)(a - rv - \lambda) + \delta\tau + h$$

This one-period return is appropriate under constant straight-line depreciation. Then

$$r_e = [(1 - \tau)(a - rv - \lambda) + \delta\tau + h]/(1 - v)$$

$$= L[(1 - \tau)(a - rv - \lambda) + \delta\tau + h]$$

where $L$ is the leverage. If $v = 0$, for an all-cash, or income-oriented deal, $L = 1$. The standard deviation of the return, if the only variation is in the rate of return $a$, is

$$\sigma(r_e) = L(1 - \tau)\sigma(a)$$

If $L = 1$, then $\sigma(r_e) = (1 - \tau)\sigma(a)$, and the risk is smaller than $\sigma(a)$, because some is borne by the tax authorities.

### *Portion of Return Shielded*

On any investment, some return is shielded. Suppose capital gains are not present, so $h = 0$, or can be neglected. Then

$$r_e = L[(1 - \tau)(a - rv - \lambda) + \delta\tau]$$

where $r_e$ is the rate of return, and $\delta\tau$ is the portion shielded from taxation. The proportion shielded is

$$L\delta\tau/r_e = \delta\tau/[\delta\tau + (1 - \tau)(a - rv - \lambda)]$$

that is, the ratio of depreciation based income to after-tax cash flow.

All projects have a percentage of income shielded. Suppose the limited partnership has, per dollar of property value,

| | |
|---|---|
| Net operating income (10% net rent after operating expenses) | $a = 0.1$ |
| Interest rate | $r = 0.1$ |
| Loan-to-value ratio | $v = 0.9$ |
| Marginal tax rate (MTR) | $\tau = 0.3$ |
| Property tax rate | $\lambda = 0$ |
| Tax depreciation rate | $\delta = 0.03$ |

Then the ratio of depreciation income to ATCF is

$$\frac{\delta\tau}{\delta\tau + (1-\tau)(a - rv - \lambda)} = \frac{0.03 \times 0.3}{0.03 \times 0.3 + (1 - 0.3) \times (0.1 - 0.1 \times 0.9)}$$

$$= \frac{0.009}{0.009 + 0.7 \times 0.01} = \frac{0.009}{0.016} = 0.56$$

This example is relatively leveraged, and hence tax oriented. The rate of return is $r_e = 10 \times 0.016$, or 16 percent, with 56 percent of ATCF arising from shielded depreciation expense.

If $v = 0$ and there is no leverage, $\delta\tau/[\delta\tau + (1-\tau)a] = 0.009/(0.009 + 0.07) = 0.009/0.079$, or 11 percent shielded. The rate of return with all cash is income-oriented deal, is $0.7 \times 0.1 + 0.009 = 0.079$. The rate of return, excluding accrued capital gains, is 7.9 percent, 11 percent arising from shielded income. These rates of return are on an after-tax basis.

### *Tax Reform*

The effects of a tax reform on any of the variables can be determined. The rate of return for one period, cash-on-cash, after tax is

$$r_e = L((1-\tau)(a - rv - \lambda) + \delta\tau)$$

Suppose tax rates are changed, but $r_e$ is the return to investing in real estate and must remain the same to encourage investors to hold. Hold $r_e$ constant, or $dr_e = 0$, where $dr_e$ is a change in the rate of return; then change only $a$, the operating income, and $\tau$ the tax rate, as $da$ and $d\tau$. Then

$$\begin{aligned} 0 &= L(1-\tau)\,da - L(a - rv - \lambda)\,d\tau + \delta d\tau \\ &= L(1-\tau)\,da - L(a - rv - \lambda - \delta)\,d\tau \\ &= (1-\tau)\,da - (a - rv - \lambda - \delta)\,d\tau \end{aligned}$$

or

$$(a - rv - \lambda - \delta)\,d\tau = (1-\tau)\,da$$

and

$$da/d\tau = (a - rv - \lambda - \delta)/(1-\tau)$$

the ratio of net income for tax purposes to net income after tax per dollar earned. If net income for tax purposes is negative, then $da/d\tau < 0$, and when $\tau$ decreases, $a$ increases. A reduction in tax rates implies that operating income per dollar of property must rise. Rents rise, or property values fall. If net income for tax purposes is positive, the reverse is true; rents fall and property values rise. The effect of the tax law shift is indeterminate.

Intuitively, the "old line" landlord with large cash flow faces an increase in net income after tax, since marginal tax rates are reduced and the property is a source of current income. The tax shelter investor, a relatively recent buyer with negative cash flows, loses. Since one landlord cannot arbitrarily increase rents in a competitive market, the asset prices on the tax-shelter-oriented properties are likely to decline.

An income-oriented partnership faces a low tax rate, and a low leverage risk. For these calculations, capital gains are assumed to be taxed as ordinary income. If there is a preferential capital gains tax, the partnership has an additional return.

The tax-oriented limited partnership is heavily leveraged, with $\upsilon$ close to 1. A high marginal tax rate increases the value of the depreciation recovery. The prices of initial units may be adjusted to capitalize a high marginal tax rate. Income is taxed at the marginal tax rate. Depreciation recovery is subsidized at the marginal tax rate. Real estate projects have low operating income in early years, with projections of increases in the future. Higher marginal tax rates, coupled with a depreciation schedule in excess of economic depreciation rates, increase the recovery. If the investor has paid a higher initial price for the partnership unit, the internal rate of return requires a high marginal tax rate.

### *Bankruptcy and Foreclosure*

There are problems with projections of initial rental receipts. Since projects produce losses in early years, the failure of rental income to increase creates difficulties for the partnership.

One option for a partnership in distress is bankruptcy. A bankruptcy filing, such as under Chapter XI of the Federal Bankruptcy Act protects the investors and the syndication against creditors in the short run, and against lawsuits while a reorganization plan is constructed. Losses by investors can be curbed, but there are costs of having a trustee involved, and legal expenses.

The lender is permitted to foreclose on the property. Foreclosure implies a sale, and a realization for tax purposes, triggering capital gains taxes for the limited partners, even if the project is continuing with losses. The capital gains arise because the depreciated book value of the property is less than its market value in most cases. Bankruptcy is preferable to foreclosure, because the property remains unsold, and capital gains taxes are delayed. Bankruptcy reduces the credibility of the syndicator in future offerings.

The syndicator can lend funds to the partnership. Given the risk, lenders require high compensating interest rates. Fees payable to the general partner can be deferred, or financing renegotiated. Under renegotiation, mortgage payments are frequently allowed to accrue, or mortgage payments made as cash come in. Both the initial and accrued interest loans must be paid from future income, which includes cash received from sale of properties. Investors may receive nothing.

Another option for the investor is personal default on the payments to the partnership. Limited partners typically sign notes to the syndicators who set up the partnerships, agreeing to make payments to them. In some cases, the notes are backed by a surety bond or a bank letter of credit. In others, the only guarantee on the notes is the investors' promise to pay. If the notes are backed by a surety bond or bank, the bonding company or lender is likely to sue an investor who defaults for recovery. It is more difficult to default on a debt to a bank or bonding company than to a promoter. The notes are legally binding obligations of the investor, and default could restrict future investments by affecting the investor's credit rating.

A default triggers tax penalties. Consider an investor who has agreed to pay $10,000 per year for eight years on a building that produces $30,000 of losses from depreciation and interest charges each year. In the fifth year, the investor has paid $50,000 for $150,000 of losses undiscounted, that is, for $100,000 in net losses. On default, the entire losses are recaptured, a repayment of $30,000 at the 30 percent marginal tax rate. This tax trigger is equal to the $30,000 in payments owed to the partnership. The investor is not better off on an undiscounted basis for defaulting, on tax grounds alone.

## Securities Backed by Physical Real Estate

### *Master Limited Partnerships (MLPs)*

Developments in securities markets permit the issue of publicly traded issues backed by physical real estate. The master limited partnership (MLP) provides a solution to the problems of illiquidity and the absence of a secondary market for limited partnership units. The MLP issues publicly trade stock in exchange for greater flexibility in converting tax-oriented to income-producing investments. Several limited partnerships are combined, such as investments in commercial office buildings. MLPs retain the advantages of partnerships, by permitting interest and depreciation expenses to be passed through directly to investors. Syndicators combine a number of properties under one single MLP. One financing method for properties bought is the zero-coupon bond.

Debt holders, as opposed to equity holders for the MLP, lend a specific amount to the project, and receive no principal or interest payments until the term. The project in the short run has no interest expense, and is capitalizing its interest payment by adding it to the loan balance outstanding. It increases the short-run payout to the investor. With the payout sheltered by the depreciation deduction, the dividend from the MLP faces a low marginal tax rate, as seen from the proportion shielded calculations. As with other income-oriented projects, the tax shield is reduced if marginal tax rates are reduced, with the benefit of the depreciation deduction lessened. The net income from the unsheltered portion is increased.

In the MLP, limited partners in real estate investments contribute their units. The MLP holds the limited partnership units as assets. The MLP then issues security units, at a given par value, to the limited partner as payment. If the former limited partner desires liquidity, the MLP units can be sold on securities markets.

The company makes cash distributions to the holders, and lists the units on a stock exchange. The listing, and subsequent liquidity, reduces the transactions costs of leaving a limited partnership. The MLP has the advantage of providing liquidity on previously illiquid units. Income received from the partnerships is paid as a distribution to the holders. The units are advisable for a tax-free or tax-deferred account, such as a pension plan.

### *Real Estate Investment Trusts (REITs)*

REITs are investor owned real estate companies. REIT investors are able to hold a diversified portfolio of physical real estate. The REIT is liquid, since shares are bought and sold on exchanges. Shares are priced below 20 dollars, so investors can enter with low costs. The REIT pays a dividend based on net cash flow received. As the net cash flow is the sum of net income and a depreciation recovery, some of the income is sheltered.

REITs provide a method of holding real estate without restrictions in liquidity. The typical REIT owns income producing real properties paying dividends to shareholders. Shares are publicly offered, and bought and sold on stock exchanges. Under typical tax depreciation rules, economic income is less than cash flow. If dividends paid to shareholders are less than reported earnings, the excess is termed a return of capital and is not taxable. The return of capital reduces the cost basis, thus increasing the capital tax gains liability. The portion of the dividend representing the distributed capital gains, most of which arises from depreciation provisions, is termed the tax-sheltered portion.

When at least 95 percent of received income is distributed as dividends, the REIT is treated as an investment company, and is exempt from taxation. If the tax depreciation schedule exceeds the economic depreciation rate, a portion of the dividend paid is sheltered. As an example, CAL REIT, traded on the American Stock Exchange, could pay a 10 percent dividend, but 40 percent of this is sheltered.

One problem with REITs concerns the timing of the selling of the properties owned. For the investor holding the stock, a sale can trigger a capital gain at a personally inconvenient time. A solution is provided by the finite life REIT (FREIT). The finite life REIT follows a predetermined schedule of sales. A FREIT can pay a 7 to 10 percent dividend for the first 5 years, 35 to 50 percent sheltered. After a period of no more than 12 years, the FREIT sells its real estate portfolio completely and distributes the capital gains. The investor can dovetail a personal investment strategy to that of the REIT.

## Concluding Remarks

The limited partnership provides a method for passive real estate investing. In a passive real estate investment, the investor has no day-to-day management, and the financial arrangements are packaged by the syndicator. Another method of passive real estate investment is to purchase REIT shares that are publicly traded.

The rate of return on investment depends on tax and other considerations. A change in the tax environment affects the rate of return. Some partnership units are sold with heavy sales and marketing expenses, reducing the available funds for investment in real estate.

## Notes

1. The Tax Reform Act of 1986 divides individual income into three categories, earned, unearned, and passive. An alternative classification is into three ps, portfolio, passive and

paycheck. Earned income includes wages and salaries and active business income where the owner engages in management. Unearned income includes interest, dividends, and capital gains. Passive income is received from owned but not managed business, notably from limited partnerships. All three types of income are taxed at the same rate. Passive losses are deductible only against passive income, where previously they had been deductible against any income.

# 10 MORTGAGE SECURITIES

## Introduction

The investor in real estate is not restricted to either active or passive holding of physical property. As an alternative, financial assets backed by real estate can be held. The investor holds claims against the physical property by purchasing or selling securities secured by real estate. Mortgage securities are for real estate paper, or financial assets, as opposed to bricks, mortar, and land.

The development of resale mortgage markets attacks the illiquidity and inefficiency surrounding real estate finance.[1] Where real estate financial assets were previously in the form of mortgages held by the lender to term, and illiquid and undiversifiable, a market for mortgage resale (secondary market) has developed. Inefficiency arises from the valuation problem when a market is absent. Where mortgages do not have a secondary market, the lender cannot lay off risks. There are several types of financial risk on mortgages, including interest rates, inflation, refinancing, default, indivisibility, and lack of diversification.

Interest rate risk on mortgages, as on other long-term securities, arises because of the inverse relationship between interest rates and asset prices.[2]

As interest rates rise, the mortgage lender or mortgagee, as creditor, is at risk of capital loss. Inflation risk arises on long-term instruments such as FRPM mortgages. Since the interest rate and payment are constant, the real interest rate decreases with an increase in the rate of inflation.

Refinancing risk arises because borrowers can respond to declining interest rates. It is analogous to the exercise of a call option on municipal or corporate bonds.[3] As interest rates decline, borrowers on FRPMs refinance their mortgages to reduce their monthly or other periodic payments. A refinancing reduces the yield and return to the lender or holder, who is at risk from both rising and falling interest rates.

Mortgage borrowers or mortgagors have their financial resources and the value of the property as security or collateral. If either the financial resources or the property value declines, the probability of default increases. Some mortgages are guaranteed against default by the federal government. Mortgages not so guaranteed are subject to default risk. Mortgages are typically for relatively large unit sums, and not in the ten-dollar issue price of mutual funds. Individual investors in single or whole mortgages have difficulty diversifying their portfolio, implying a risk from these large-unit, or lumpy, investments.

The presence of these risks, in addition to the transactions costs of points and other loan fees, creates an inefficiency in mortgage financial markets. The development of resale mortgage markets reduces these risks to the individual lender, spreading them through the economy more efficiently. With a secondary market, the lender can sell a mortgage to another institution for portfolio purposes, as a whole mortgage. Alternatively, the lender sells the loan to be packaged as part of a pool, where tradeable and marketable securities are sold with the mortgages as collateral.

## Secondary-Market Securities

The market for secondary real estate securities has emerged following the development of intermediaries. These intermediaries buy whole mortgages from lenders, group them into pools, divide these pools into smaller units, and sell the units to individual investors as mortgage backed securities. Mortgage borrowers, usually on FRPMs, have their payments passed through to the investors in the mortgage backed security. Since the securities have effective terms the same as the FRPMs in the pool, they have similar characteristics of other long-term securities. The development of secondary mortgage markets in the United States has been associated with three intermediary agencies, the Federal Home Loan Mortgage Corporation (FHLMC—Freddie Mac), the Federal National Mortgage Association (FNMA—Fannie Mae), and the Government National Mortgage Agency (GNMA—Ginnie Mae). Ginnie Mae securities pay a blend of principal and interest; their income is subject to federal income tax, and to state income tax in some states, such as California. Ginnie Mae certificates are highly liquid. They generally come in a minimum denomination of $25,000.

### *Federal Home Loan Mortgage Corporation (FHLMC—Freddie Mac)*

The Federal Home Loan Mortgage Corporation (FHLMC—Freddie Mac) was created in 1970 to promote a secondary market for mortgages. The corporation is directed by the Federal Home Loan Bank Board (FHLBB), and buys mortgages from depository institutions and mortgage bankers meeting FHLBB criteria. Freddie Mac provides funds for mortgage lending by buying loans from lenders. Purchasers include conventional loans, with no government default guarantees; participation loans; and loans from the Federal Home Administration (FHA), Veterans' Administration (VA), and Farmers' Home Administration.

The FHA, created in 1934, is an agency within the Department of Housing and Urban Development. The FHA operates loan insurance and subsidy programs, focusing on residential mortgages. The FHA provides an insurance program, based on initial premium income collected by purchasers, to guarnatee the mortgage on properties with given price limits against loan default. Relatively low interest rates with low down payments arise. The premium charged for FHA insurance is ½ of 1 percent of the average principal outstanding during the year. The Veterans' Administration (VA) guarantees loans made by private lenders for eligible veterans of the United States Armed Forces. With these guarantees, veterans can purchase houses with no down payments. The maximum interest rate is set by the VA.

Freddie Mac buys loans from the existing mortgage portfolios of lenders. It extends forward commitments to buy as yet unextended loans. The funds for purchase are obtained by issuing securities, sold in bond or pass-through forms. Most loans purchased are FRPMs, but Freddie Mac is prepared to buy ARMs under certain circumstances. Requirements for ARMs purchased include limits on the periodic interest rate adjustment, on the lifetime maximum interest rate, and on negative amortization.

Freddie Mac provides a secondary market for conventional residential mortgages. Lenders sell mortgages to Freddie Mac to increase liqudity. Freddie Mac buys mortgages over the counter based on the amount; the loan-to-value ratio $v = B/V$; whether or not mortgage insurance has been included; and the term, age, and documentation. Mortgage insurance requirements depend on the $v$ ratio. Where $v > 0.8$, such insurance, to protect the lender in an amount equal to or greater than the loan balance, is required.

There are various types of Freddie Mac programs, under which the agency undertakes to purchase mortgages from lenders. In the whole-loan, single-family program, the lender must deliver the single-family mortgage to Freddie Mac within 60 days of the contract. Freddie Mac pays a 0.375 percent fee for servicing the mortgage. The institution servicing the mortgage need not be the original lender. Servicing includes the collection of payments, processing, remittance, and inspection of property when necessary. For a whole loan, on a multifamily structure, the criteria are the same as for single-family mortgages. The fee paid for servicing is 0.25 percent for the first $250,000 and 0.125 percent on the excess.

Under the Participation A program, Freddie Mac purchases 50 to 85 percent of eligible conventional multifamily mortgages. There is a required yield to Freddie Mac. The differential between the actual mortgage yield and this required yield is retained by Freddie Mac as a fee. Participation B applies to packages of single- and multifamily mortgages. For the latter, the purcahse obligation is limited to 50 percent. The same rules as for A apply.

Loans issued by the FHA, VA, and Farmers' Home Administration are guaranteed as to repayment of the principal loan balance by the "full faith and credit" of the United States Treasury. They are essentially free of default risk. Mortgage backed securities issued against these loans are free of default risk. Freddie Mac buys qualifying single-family residential mortgages, or makes commitments to buy such loans. Then securities are issued by the agency. Payments from these mortgages are passed through to the security buyer.

### *Federal National Mortgage Association (FNMA—Fannie Mae)*

The Federal National Mortgage Association (FNMA—Fannie Mae), acts to create a secondary market in residential loans. It buys mortgages, pools them, and sells securities issued in its own name backed by these pools.

The standard security is based on a 30-year loan term, but assumes prepayment after 12 years. Both conventional (nonguaranteed), and government guaranteed mortgages are purchased. Fannie Mae operates as a private corporation, though it is administered and regulated by the federal government. On loans in the Fannie Mae portfolio, the government permits a servicing fee, typically 0.35 percent annually of the loan balance. Fannie Mae provides lock-in guarantees for developers, on residential construction. It makes a precommitment to buy the loan upon issue, thus facilitating the completion of construction financing arrangements.

Fannie Mae has a mortgage purchasing procedure. It offers 4-month and 12-month forward commitments to guarantee the available funds to purchase mortgages at a predetermined yield. Auctions occur every other Monday. The sellers are banks, thrifts, insurance companies, mortgage bankers, and mortgage companies. Bids are submitted on a yield basis, and are reviewed for committal. A noncompetitive bid can be submitted at the average accepted bid. Yields are net to Fannie Mae after servicing fees. Yields are calculated on the *FNMA Yield Book,* based on a 30-year amortization schedule, and the assumptions that (1) the borrower prepays the loan after 12 years, and (2) a 0.375 percent annual servicing fee is paid to original lender. Any yield premium to the initial lender above the 0.375 percent is charged up front to the borrower as points. Approximately, to obtain a 0.25 percent higher yield over the 12 years, 1.75 points must be charged.

The sources and uses of cash statement is for the borrower,

$$(1 - p)B = MA(r_e/k,t) + \frac{B_t}{(1 + r_e/k)^t}$$

where

$$M = m(r/k,N)B$$

$$B_t = b_t B$$

$$b_t = 1 - \frac{A_t(r/k,N)}{A_N(r/k,N)}$$

The trade-off is between points to be charged by the primary lender $p$, and the desired yield $r_e$.

### *Government National Mortgage Association (GNMA—Ginnie Mae)*

The Government National Mortgage Association (GNMA—Ginnie Mae), created in 1968, is a wholly owned corporation of the United States Government, administered by the Department of Housing and Urban Development (HUD). Ginnie Mae guarantees securities backed by mortgages insured by the federal government or supported by the "full faith and credit" of the U.S. Treasury. Typical mortgages pooled are those issued under FHA, VA, or Farmers' Home Administration programs. The Farmers' Home Administration provides guarantees on mortgages made for farm home purchases. Ginnie Mae issues certificates against mortgage pools of at least two million dollars. The most popular trading vehicles in secondary markets for mortgage backed securities are those issued by Ginnie Mae, given the absence of default risk.

Ginnie Mae manages previously acquired mortgages in its own portfolio. It administers government lending on federal mortgage programs. It guarantees to support markets for mortgage pools. These government guaranteed pools are behind the issue of Ginnie Mae securities. On the securities issued by Ginnie Mae, all underlying mortgages are insured and guaranteed as to timely payment of principal and interest by the federal government, with the "full faith and credit" provision. The holder of a Ginnie Mae certificate is able to invest in a portfolio of mortgages without involvement in management or debt collection. Ginnie Mae certificates are marketable, providing liquidity.

A pass-through Ginnie Mae security is one where both principal and interest are paid to the holder. In the standard pass-through security, interest and debt repayment are passed through to the holder monthly. There is a reserve for delinquencies. The modified pass-through (MPT) security, more commonly issued, provides for less frequent payment to holders, such as quarterly.

Ginnie Mae issues mortgage backed bonds. Sinking-fund mortgage backed bonds are similar to the MPT securities, but principal is repaid in fixed amounts. Interest payments must be made regardless of mortgage collections. In staggered-maturity mortgage backed bonds, interest and principal are paid regardless of payments on the mortgage. Risk of default or slow payment on the mortgages is borne by the issuer. Ginnie Mae creates a public market for mortgages. It buys and sells mortgages guaranteed or issued through the VA, FHA, and Farmers' Home Administration. Ginnie Mae sells some mortgages, and pays a servicing fee of 0.44 percent, as opposed to the more common 0.375 percent. These mortgages are more attractive to servicing providers.

## Yields, Returns, and Prices: Mortgage Backed Securities

Mortgage securities have prices and yields based on a long-term FRPM. Suppose a security promises to pay the holder one dollar per year for $N$ periods, at interest rate $r$. The market price is based on supply and demand for the security, and expectations on the course of future interest rates. The price depends on the real rate of return on long-term bonds, the price of the call option, and a threshold marginal tax rate.

The mortgage backed security promises to pay the holder, on a modified pass-through basis, the principal and interest received from the ultimate borrower. There are fees to the servicing lender. Suppose the mortgage backed security is composed of a pool of mortgages with identical interest rate, term, conditions, and purchase date. The security slices the packaged mortgages into smaller dollar units palatable to the smaller investor.

The cash flow statement for a buyer of a mortgage security is

**Sources and Uses of Cash, Mortgage Security, to Term $N$**
**Cash Flow, Security Holder, No Prepayment**
(present value at purchase date, per dollar of loan)

**Cash Disbursements**

Date of purchase
Paid for security 1
Present value of cash disbursements 1

**Cash Receipts**

Received on mortgage payments
Payment per period $(k/k_1)m(r/k,N)$
Times: Annuity (present value of 1 per period) $A(r_e/k_1,K)$
Equals: Present value of cash receipts $(k/k_1)m(r/k,N)$

At purchase, the buyer pays one dollar for the security. In practice, the units are sold in \$25,000 blocks, except in unit trusts or mutual funds. In exchange, the buyer receives mortgage payments from the pool. Since the mortgages are identical, the payment is $m(r/k,N)$ per dollar invested per payment. The security issuer holds this payment, for $(k/k_1)$ periods, prior to passing it through to the investor. The frequency of payment on the mortgage is $k$, but the frequency on the modified pass-through security is $k_1$. At each payment date on the security, per dollar invested, the holder receives $(k/k_1)m(r/k,N)$. If the frequency of compounding is monthly, $k = 3$, and pass through is quarterly, $k/k_1 = 3$. This payment is capitalized over the expected term of the mortgage pool.

Suppose the security holder buys when the loans have been originated, and all loans are expected to be held until the balances are paid off. Then the security holder can expect to hold for $K = Tk_1$, where $T$ is the number of years on the mortgage contract, and $k_1$ is the number of payments made to the holder each year. The present value of a payment of one dollar for $K$ periods, at $r_e$ percent per year, the yield on the security, is $A(r_e/k_1,K)$. The product of the present value of the annuity, and the payment per dollar of investment, is the present value of the cash received over the term, at date of purchase. Equating the present value of cash receipts and disbursements produces the yield on the security as $r_e$.

The yield on the security if held to term $K$, $r_e(K)$ is solved from

$$1 = (k/k_1)m(r/k,N)A(r_e/k_1,K). \tag{10.1}$$

The price of this Ginnie Mae security at issue is one dollar, and the yield is $r_e(K)$, to term $K$.

There are differences between this yield and the effective borrowing cost to the mortgagor (borrower). For the borrower, points are subtracted from the loan. For every one dollar of loan borrowed, $(1 - p)$ cents are received at origination. Hence $(1 - p)$ is cash receipts for the borrower. The contract interest rate $r$ for the mortgage security holder is net of servicing costs, but gross of such costs for the borrower.

Mortgages are typically not held to term. They are prepaid at some date prior to $K$. Ginnie Mae securities are priced on the assumption of a 12-year prepayment. For prepayment at some date $t$ prior to $N$, the sources and uses of cash statement for the security holder is

**Sources and Uses of Cash, Security Holder, Prepayment at Specific Date $t$**
(present value at purchase date, per dollar of loan)

**Cash Disbursements**

Paid for security 1
Equals: Present value of cash disbursements 1

**Cash Receipts**

Received on mortgage payments
  Payment per period $(k/k_1)m(r/k,N)$
  Times: Annuity (present value of 1 per period) $A(r_e/k_1,t)$
  Equals: Present value of mortgage payments (MPT)

$$(k/k_1)m(r/k,N)A(r_e/k_1,t)$$

Plus: Balloon payment present value

Loan balance $b_t = 1 - A_t(r/k,t)/A_K(r/k,N)$

Plus: Prepayment penalty $q_t = \Sigma_{i=1}^{C} b_{t+i}$

Equals: Future value of balloon payment $b_t + q_t$

Times: Present value of 1 at date $t$ $1/(1 + r_e/k_1)^t$

Equals: Balloon payment present value

$(b_t + q_t)/(1 + r_e/k_1)^t$

Equals: Present value of cash receipts

$$(k/k_1)m(r/k,N)A(r_e/k_1,t) + (b_t + q_t)/(1 + r_e/k_1)^t$$

Cash disbursed is for the one dollar at security purchase date. The return after date $t$, $1 < t \leqslant K$, contains two components. The first is the present value of the mortgage payments passed through up to date $t$. This present value is the periodic payment $(k/k_1)m(r/k,N)$ times the present value of an annuity of one dollar for $t$ periods, that is, $A(r_e/k_1,t)$.

The outstanding loan balance at date $t$ is $b_t$ per dollar, also cash received by the security holder if the property is refinanced. This balance is discounted from date $t$ to the present, by the present value of one dollar $t$ periods ahead at $r_e$ percent annually, or $1/(1 + r_e/k_1)^t$. If there is a prepayment penalty, $q_t$, this is passed through and discounted. A prepayment penalty has $C$ payments. If the penalty provides for three months of interest, and $k = 12$, and $k_1 = 4$, then $C = 3$.

The yield is solved by equating the present value of the cash disbursed for security purchase, with the present value of the cash received for the mortgage payments and the balloon payment. The cash-on-cash return, over $t$, $r_e(t)$ is

$$1 = (k/k_1)m(r/k,N)A(r_e/k_1,K) + \frac{b_t + q_t}{(1 + r_e/k_1)^t}$$

or

$$1 = (k/k_1)m(r/k,N)A(r_e/k_1,K) + \frac{b_t}{(1 + r_e/k_1)^t} \tag{10.2}$$

where there is no prepayment penalty. The yield depends on the frequency of compounding on the mortgage $k$, on the security $k_1$, the contract interest rate net of servicing fees $r$, and the number of mortgage payments $N$. The MPT security is priced assuming prepayment before term, given the low probability of a borrower remaining in a property for 30 years.

By selling mortgages, a lender removes loans from its balance sheet, receiving cash in exchange. At origination, any points $pB$ are retained by the lender as a servicing fee. The borrower receives $(1-p)B$ in net loan. The lender carries loan amount $B$ on its balance sheet as an asset prior to sale, the total repayment obligation of the borrower. The lender sells a loan to the secondary market for $B$ dollars, for which it paid $(1-p)B$ dollars. Since each time a sale occurs, a margin $p$ is retained, more rapid loan turnover increases revenue for the lender through the points.

The net interest rate on the mortgage is the contract rate, net of fees. This net interest rate $r$ is constant, as mortgage backed securities are based on FRPM loans. For a mortgage with a 12 percent contract, and a 0.375 percent servicing fee, the net interest rate $r$ is 11.625 percent.

Suppose on the MPT the following data are given:

| | |
|---|---|
| Contract interest rate | $r = 0.1$ |
| Net interest rate after service fee | $r = 0.1 - 0.0375 = 0.09625$ |
| Term in years | $T = 30$ |
| Frequency of compounding mortgage per year | $k = 12$ |
| Frequency of compounding security per year | $k_1 = 4$ |
| Number of mortgage payments in computing yield (12 years) | $12 \times k = 144$ |
| Number of payments to term | $N = Tk = 360$ |
| Prepayment penalty | $q_t = 0$ |
| Number of payments, to term, made to holder of MPT security | $K = Tk_1 = 120$ |
| Number of payments, at yield date, made to holder of MPT security | $t = 12 \times k_1 = 48$ |

These parameters characterize the Ginnie Mae MPT security. The yield on the security is solved from

$$1 = \left(\frac{12}{4}\right) m \left(\frac{0.09625}{12,\ 360}\right) A(r_e/4, 48) + \left(\frac{b_{144}}{(1 + r_e/4)^{48}}\right)$$

where

$$m = \frac{0.09625/12}{1 - (1 + 0.09625/12)^{-360}}$$

is the fixed mortgage payment and

$$b_{144} = 1 - A_{144}/A_{360}$$

The future values of annuities have the form $A_t = [(1 + r/k)^{3t} - 1]/(r/k)$, so

$$A_{144} = \frac{(1 + 0.09625/12)^{144} - 1}{0.09625/12}$$

$$A_{360} = \frac{(1 + 0.09625/12)^{360} - 1}{0.09625/12}$$

are both fixed, implying $b_{144}$ is fixed. The loan balance is determined monthly. The payment to the mortgage security buyer is determined quarterly. The only unknown is the rate of return $r_e(48)$, the yield on the security at payment date 48, after the 12th year. The yield is obtained by solving the equation iteratively. This yield is the base used to determine an issue price for Ginnie Mae and other mortgage backed securities.

The sequence of payments on a mortgage backed security differs from the sequence on other long-term issues such as bonds. The pool does not have mortgages all of the same initial date or maturity. The prospect of repayment is partly random, and partly dependent on factors such as the differential between market and contract interest rates. Not all mortgages are prepaid after 12 years, and some can be prepaid in advance.

## Risk: Mortgage Backed Securities

The appearance is that mortgage backed securities, whether in bond funds on unit investment trusts, or pools, are riskless securities. Some are guaranteed as to principal repayment. Yet mortgage backed securities contain more risk than United States Treasury bonds or securities. While free of default risk, risks arise with Ginnie Maes and other mortgage backed securities. Some risks follow:

**Refinancing Risk.** Corporate and municipal securities have due and call provisions that permit the borrower to repurchase the securities at a specified price. The call option to refinance is exercised if yields have fallen below those at issue. If interest rates increase, the borrower does not refinance, and the capital loss is borne by the bondholder. If refinancing occurs, the yield on the pool behind the mortgage backed securities declines, implying that the initial yield is not guaranteed to term. A high interest rate mortgage is replaced by one carrying a lower rate. The probability of refinancing depends on the costs to the borrower, but refinancing risk is borne by the mortgage security holder.

Mortgage security asset prices decline when interest rates fall, as the value of the refinancing option to the borrower increases. The option is an asset of the borrower, such as a FRPM homeowner, and a liability for the lender or mortgage security holder. A capital loss is recorded in the security price, to match the increase in the price of the call option to refinance.

**Interest Rate Risk.** There is an inverse relationship between interest rates and security prices. If interest rates rise, the price of the security falls. The decrease depends on the term of the security. Longer-term securities fall further in price for a given percentage point increase in interest rates than short-term securities. This risk applies both to government and mortgage backed securities. For government securities held to term, the face interest rate return is received, even if the yield fluctuates over the period. For mortgage backed securities, even the face interest rate is not guaranteed.

**Default Risk.** There is no default risk on either mortgage backed securities such as Ginnie Maes or Treasuries, if the full faith and credit provision is applied. Default risk applies to other debt issues, such as for corporate securities, or mortgage securities without the government guarantee.

**Undiversified Risk.** This risk affects investors who hold large proportions of their total holdings in specific pools of mortgage backed securities, and are not diversified over the market. Mutual funds and unit trusts containing Ginnie Mae securities are available. In unit investment trust Ginnie Maes, the monthly payment is held constant. If yields decline, the constant payment implies that a larger proportion of principal is being repaid, reducing the amount invested, and reducing the ultimate term of the investment.

### *Interest Rate Risk*

Interest rate risk arises because the payment on the FRPM is fixed, while long-term interest rates can fluctuate. At date of issue, the mortgage payment is $M = m(r/k,N)B$, for loan balance $B$. The face value of the mortgage security issued is $B$, so

$$B = \frac{M}{m(r/k,N)}$$

$$= MA(r/k,N)$$

The payment $M$, frequency of compounding per year $k$, contract interest rate $r$, and number of payments $N$ are constant. If market interest rates increase from $r$ to $r_1$, the annuity changes to $A(r_1/k,N)$, and decreases. Higher interest rates reduce the present value of the sum of the mortgage payments received by the security holder. With the mortgage payment constant, the product $MA(r_1/k,N)$ is below $B$, no longer the value of the mortgage.

The capital value of the mortgage declines from $B$ to $B_1$, where

$$B_1 = MA(r_1/k,N) = m(r/k,N)BA(r_1/k,N)$$

and

$$B_1/B = m(r/k,N)A(r_1/k,N) = \frac{A(r_1/k,N)}{A(r/k,N)}. \qquad (10.3)$$

Then $B_1/B$ is the ratio of the value of the mortgage, per dollar of face value, respectively at interest rates $r_1$ and $r$. If $\sigma(B_1/B)$ is the standard deviation of the price of the mortgage:

$$\sigma(B_1/B) = \sigma\left(\frac{A(r_1/k,N)}{A(r/k,N)}\right)$$

There is no variation in the annuity $A(r/k,N)$, which is fixed. The value of the mortgage security declines from $B$ to $B_1$, or, in percentage terms, $(B_1 - B)/B$. The price of mortgage backed securities is negatively correlated with interest rates.

When interest rates rise, prices of mortgage backed and other long-term securities fall. When interest rates fall, normally the prices of mortgage backed securities rise. These securities are vulnerable to refinancing risk; and capital gains on falling interest rates do not necessarily accrue.

### *Refinancing Risk*

Mortgage security mutual funds hold various mortgage securities to provide diversification. Such mutual funds seek higher returns by buying securities selling at a premium. Securities selling at a premium are those with contract interest rates exceeding current market interest rates. Premium issues are likely to have the highest refinancing risk. Refinancing risk affects mortgage security mutual funds and holders in two ways. First, if the funds bought high-coupon pools, they paid above par, such as a price of $107 for $100 of principal. The borrower on refinancing exercises the call option and buys the mortgage for $100, so the fund bears the loss of the $7. Second, the fund must reinvest at market interest rates, lower than the contract rates replaced.

The greatest refinancing risk is on premium mortgage securities, those selling at above par value. The higher yields are obtained by taking on higher refinancing risk. Correspondingly, a lower-yielding fund, all else equal, has lower refinancing risk.

Prepayment or refinancing risk affects mortgage backed securities, but not federal government securities, though corporate and municipal issues face similar risk. Long-term bonds issued by corporations or municipalities typically have call provisions, where the borrower has the right to prepay prior to term. For mortgages, while there may be prepayment penalties, there are no restrictions against refinancing.

The yield on a mortgage backed security is higher than the yield on a federal government bond of similar face maturity, even with the same interest rate. The reason is the built-in expected prepayment. In the typical case, the prepayment is expected at 12 years, so a guaranteed mortgage backed security is comparable to a Treasury security of maturity of 12 years. If the borrowers on the mortgages prepay on average more rapidly than expected, the holders of the securities bear the refinancing risk.

Market yields on mortgage backed securities depend on the real return to investment in mortgages, the price of the call option, and the adjustment for taxation on returns. When interest rates fall, the holder of the security takes a capital loss, as the option is worth a positive price. When interest rates rise above the issue price, the call option is worthless to the borrower. To the extent that the initial yield included a premium for the security holder to act as an insurer, mortgage backed securities provide more protection against rising interest rates than do noncallable securities.

The yield on a mortgage backed security, after tax is

$$r_e(\text{GNMA}) = (1 - \tau)(r_e + r(\text{CALL})) \qquad (10.4)$$

where $r_e$ is the risk-adjusted rate of return to holding long-term securities. The interest rate premium the holder of the security receives to hold the call option as a liability is $r$(CALL), and $\tau$ is the marginal tax rate of the security investor. All income is taxed at the same rate, and GNMA is an acronym for Ginnie Mae. If the borrower wants the option to refinance, the call is bought at origination by the payment of a higher interest rate. The seller is the lender or ultimate holder, through the mortgage backed security.

With each mortgage payment, the borrower pays the holder, through CALL, a premium for the right to refinance. Part of the interest payment is a premium received for having sold a compound option to the borrower. In this compound option, if the borrower elects not to refinance, another option to refinance is issued. The borrower buys the call from the security holder, who acts as an insurer, collecting the premium monthly, but bearing the risk that the loan can be refinanced. The premium is paid by the interest rate differential between a callable and a noncallable security.

The market establishes an initial interest rate differential between mortgages, albeit government guaranteed, and Treasury securities, to compensate for refinancing risk. A risk premium is built into interest rates. If the investor guesses correctly as to a lower refinancing rate, there is an additional return.

If interest rates fall, more borrowers refinance, and the yield on the securities falls. As interest rates rise, fewer refinance, and the prices on mortgage securities do not decline as much as those on federal bonds. Mortgage securities have some hedge against rising interest rates, although there can be capital losses because of interest rate risk. The yield on mortgage securities depends on the inverse relation between bond yields and interest rates, the prepayment rate as a function of interest rates, and the receipt of premium interest income through CALL.

A mortgage security certificate at 12 percent, backed by 12.5 percent loans, could have 25 percent of its balance repaid each year if interest rates are 10 percent. At a price of 107.5, the 12 percent security would yield 9.18 percent over a weighted maturity of 3.5 years, assuming a 25 percent prepayment rate, or 2 percentage points over the yield on a five-year Treasury note.

There is undiversified refinancing risk, if an investor buys only one or two pools. There is variation in prepayment rates around a mean. Slower repaying pools are likely to be known to the market, and have a correspondingly high price. There is insider information on the prepayment quality of pools. The investor can obtain from brokers the one-month, three-month, and one-year prepayment histories of particular pools. Past performance on refinancing is no guarantee of future refinancing behavior.

Mortgage securities have a random date of maturity. The investor plans to hold securities based on a given repayment rate. If interest rates rise, the repayment rate falls, creating a longer term security. This repayment affects the term structure distribution of portfolios. An example of the effect of refinancing on yields on Ginnie Maes, as compared with Treasuries having approximately the same maturity as the average life of the mortgage backed security, is indicated in table 10–1.

The table applies to a 12 percent Ginnie Mae, priced at a 7 percent premium over par. The Treasury security is a 10 year note.

The holder of the security backed by a refinanced mortgage must invest the received proceeds at the current market rate. Suppose the refinancing takes place at date $i$, before the date $t$, the expected maturity. The market interest rate $r_1$ is less than the contract rate $r$. Both interest rates are measured net of service fees as the return facing the security holder. When refinancing occurs, the holder loses the investment with interest rate $r$, which is replaced with interest rate $r_1$.

The holder loses the investment and a cash flow over the life of the contract. The reduction in mortgage payment per dollar is

$$\Delta m = m(r/k,N) - m(r_1/k,N) \tag{10.5}$$

The payments are forwarded to the security holder at $k_1$ times per year, usually less frequently than the mortgage payments. The payment to the security holder is $(k/k_1)[m(r/k,N) - m(r_1/k,N)]$. There are $K - i$ periods for which the investment is lost. The present value of losing one dollar of payment per period, at a target interest rate $r_e$ is $A(r_e/k_1, K - i)$. One candidate for the target interest rate is $r$, the replaced interest rate. The present value of the capital loss of the investor is

**Table 10–1. Effect of Refinancing on Yields**

| *Prepayment Rate %* | *Average Life (years)* | *Ginnie Mae (% yield)* | *Differential with Treasuries* |
|---|---|---|---|
| 10 | 8.1 | 10.51 | +2.83 |
| 20 | 4.4 | 9.65 | +2.29 |
| 30 | 2.8 | 8.68 | +1.50 |
| 40 | 2.0 | 7.59 | +0.49 |
| 50 | 1.5 | 6.34 | −0.76 |
| 60 | 1.2 | 4.85 | −2.15 |

$$\text{CAPLOSS} = (k/k_1)[m(r/k,N) - m(r_1/k,N)]A(r_e/k_1,K-i) \tag{10.6}$$

A corresponding gain is made by the mortgage borrower, from having exercised the call option to refinance.

This calculation of capital loss on refinancing assumes that the holder was the original investor. If the investor purchased the security when interest rates were above $r$, the issue price, the capital loss when interest rates fall to $r_1$ is greater. The loss depends on the market interest rate $r_1$ on new mortgages, and the date of refinancing $i$.

A mortgage borrower has the right at any time to redeem the loan at the nominal face value, prior to maturity. A FRPM carries an American call option, with the borrower able to buy back the loan from the security holder. The exercise price is the amount of loan balance outstanding, but the market price of the mortgage, based on current interest rates, could be higher.

At date $t$, the nominal face-value loan balance is

$$B_t = b_t B$$

$$= \left[1 - \frac{A_t(r/k,t)}{A_N(r/k,N)}\right] B$$

Per one dollar of initial loan, $b_t$ is the price payable for refinancing at date $t$, with the call option. The option is only valuable if the current market interest rate $r$ is lower than the contract rate $r$.

The security holder has the right to collect $M = m(r/k,N)B$, for $N - t$, periods, given current date $t$. The present value of this right is

$$B_{1t} = MA(r_1/k,N-t)$$

$$= m(r/k,N)BA(r_1/k,N-t)$$

Per one dollar of loan

$$b_{1t} = B_{1t}/B = m(r/k,N)A(r_1/k,N-t)$$

$$= \frac{A(r_1/k,N-t)}{A(r/k,N)} \tag{10.7}$$

If interest rates decline, to $r_1$, $A(r_1/k,N-t)$ increases, since the future is discounted less. Then the price of one dollar of holding mortgage debt, $b_{1t}$, increases.

The borrower, such as a FRPM homeowner, retains the option of buying out the mortgage at balance $b_t$ per dollar. The price is not constant, but declines with time. The borrower buys an asset with a market price of $b_{1t}$ for $b_t$. The mortgage option price is

$$\begin{array}{ll} b_{1t} - b_t & \text{if } r_1 < r \\ 0 & \text{if } r_1 \geqslant r \end{array}$$

If the mortgage call option has price $\text{CALL}_t$, the expected value is

$$E(\text{CALL}_t) = \int_0^r (b_{1t} - b_t) f(r_1)\, dr_1 - p \qquad (10.8)$$

where $f(r_1)$ is the probability density function of market interest rates. The transactions costs of refinancing are summarized by the points payable per dollar $p$.

The value of the option, upon exercise, represents a loss to the holder of the mortgage security. The option price $E(\text{CALL}_t)$ at exercise date $t$ is the expected loss to be faced by a holder of a mortgage backed security, as compared with a noncallable security. The yield on a Ginnie Mae or comparable callable security must widen, as compared with a noncallable security, if interest rates are expected to decline.

Municipal bonds are more comparable with mortgage backed securities than are Treasury issues. The yield on a taxable security, such as a Treasury issue, is $r_e(1 - \tau)$, after tax, where $r_e$ is the long-term rate of return, and $\tau$ is the marginal tax rate. The yield on a Ginnie Mae, or other mortgage backed security, is

$$\begin{aligned} r_e(\text{GNMA}) &= (1 - \tau)[r_e + r_e E(\text{CALL}_t)] \\ &= r_e(1 - \tau)[1 + E(\text{CALL}_t)] \end{aligned} \qquad (10.9)$$

The call option has asset price $E(\text{CALL}_t)$, to appear on the balance sheet of the security holder as a liability. The premium received, in interest, is the holding cost per period on the option, the product of a return to real estate securities and the asset price, that is, $r_e E(\text{CALL}_t)$.

The yield equation can be applied to table 10-1. The Ginnie Mae yield for a 8.1-year term is 10.51 percent, and the Treasury security is 7.68 percent. Use 7.68 percent as $r_e$, and assume the same risk on both securities except for the call option. Then

$$r_e E(\text{CALL}_t) = 0.0283$$

so

$$E(\text{CALL}_t) = 0.0283/0.0768$$

$$= 0.3685$$

From table 10–1, the expected call option prices (per one dollar of mortgage loan) are:

| *Average Term* | *Expected Price, Call Option* |
|---|---|
| 8.1 | 0.3685 |
| 4.4 | 0.3111 |
| 2.8 | 0.2089 |
| 2.0 | 0.0690 |
| 1.5 | 0 |
| 1.2 | 0 |

The zero prices occur when the option is worthless. As the term increases, the refinancing risk increases. On the 8.1-year average term, the call option is worth over one-third of the face value of the mortgage itself.

## Collateralized Mortgage Obligations (CMOs)

### *Payment Sequencing*

A collateralized mortgage obligation (CMO) diffuses the refinancing risk in mortgage backed securities. The CMO is sold as a form of serial bond, with staggered maturity dates, and backed by a pool of FRPM loans. Investors seeking a short-term security buy the shortest-term class of the CMO. Refinancing risk is not eliminated, since prepayment is accelerated as interest rates fall.[4]

The CMO is issued at interest rates competitive with other long-term securities, but in classes. The lower-ordered classes, labeled alphanumerically toward A and 1, receive first claim on the principal repayments and other equity until their obligations are completely discharged. When the obligations of one class are completely discharged, the next class moves to the top in terms of priority.

Consider an offer of a CMO from Salomon Capital Access Corporation from a "tombstone" listing, an advertisement indicating the basic terms of issue of a security and the principal issuers and managers. A prospectus contains the details of the solicitation. Some of the information supplied in the listing is indicated in table 10-2. The bonds are collateralized by finding agreements between the issuer and finance subsidiaries of savings institution participants and by related notes issued by them; the notes are secured by Ginnie Mae and Freddie Mac certificates. The bonds are not insured, and the issuer has no significant assets other than those pledged as collateral.

For many investors, CMOs are preferable to Ginnie Mae pass throughs because they remove uncertainty about timing the repayment of principal. With Ginnie Maes, depending on the direction of interest rates, borrowers have random refinancing rates, which produces an uneven flow of principal payments.

CMO paybacks are more predictable, and act as an ordinary bond because investors can choose in advance either a short, medium, or long payback schedule. Investors with a short-term CMO receive all principal payments from the pool until the bonds in their class are paid off. Then holders of the next class, who initially receive only interest, start receiving all remaining principal until the group has been paid off.

The investor chooses a term by buying securities of a particular class. Each class has a given maturity. Then principal or interest payments are allocated by the maturity selected by the investor. This characteristic makes these securities more like bonds than Ginnie Maes, by systematically allocating the refinancing risk.

CMOs are bonds collateralized by mortgages, or certificates issued by Ginnie Mae, Fannie Mae, or guaranteed through agencies such as the Veterans' Administration.[5] The bonds are secured by a collection account

**Table 10-2. Tombstone Listing**

| *Dollar Quantity* | *Yield %* | *Class* | *Term (approximate)* | *Issue Price* |
|---|---|---|---|---|
| 96,420,000 | 7.90 | A | 17 years, 9 months | 99.937 |
| 4,790,000 | 7.35 | B | 18 years, 3 months | 90.812 |
| 37,420,000 | 7.30 | C | 21 years, 6 months | 86.625 |
| 5,820,000 | 7.25 | Z | 26 years, 10 months | 64.660 |

on principal and interest from the mortgage pool. Scheduled payments on the certificates or mortgages pledged to secure the bonds, together with reinvestment earnings at an assumed reinvestment rate, are sufficient—regardless of the rate of payment on the certificates—to make timely payments of interest on the bonds, to begin payment of principal of each class of bonds not later than its first mandatory payment date, and to retire each class not later than its stated maturity. The bonds are not necessarily insured.

A CMO involves selling the equity that accumulates as payments are made on a mortgage backed security.[6] A CMO is a bond like security backed by a pool of mortgages, whose cash flows are repackaged to create securities of different maturities, divided into classes. Proceeds of a CMO are slightly less than the cost of the mortgage pool behind it, the difference being the implicit investment of the issuer. The mortgage pool accumulates additional funds, termed residuals, as additional equity.

### *Residual Equity*

Residual equity arises from several sources. Since interest and principal payments on the CMO are made quarterly and mortgage payments are usually made monthly, there is investment income while the mortgage income is held. Interest rates on the mortgages backing the CMO exceed those on bonds, producing additional equity. Equity arises because rating aggencies insist on conservative projections on cash flows from mortgages. Cash flows realized tend to be greater than projected, producing more income for the issuer.

Prior to the development of the CMO, residuals were taken as a return on the implicit investment. Capital is tied up, for the income arises slowly over the term of the security, as payments on the underlying mortgages are made. If a financial firm purchases a package or pool of mortgages, it can sell the equity accruing from those mortgages as a CMO security.

By selling equity, issuers receive the full effect of the income stream at the date of sale. Selling residuals permits the financial firm to remove the CMOs from the balance sheet. The CMO frees capital; and this is important since mortgage bankers operate on thin margins. If the mortgages backing the CMO are not insured, there can be default risk. This default risk is off the balance sheet, implying additional capital requirement, in owners' equity, to insure against default.

Consider the sequence of payments. The balance on a mortgage at date $t$ is $b_t$ per dollar of loan. A contract interest rate $r$, net of service fee, is received by the investor in the mortgage backed security. The interest received per dollar is $rb_t$ at date $t$, and the mortgage multiplier is $m(r/k,N)$. The principal repaid at time $t$ is

$$m(r/k,N) - rb_t$$

per dollar of loan borrowed. This principal payment, the difference between the constant mortgage multiplier and a declining interest payment—since $b_t$ decreases with $t$—is increasing in $t$. By comparison, the holder of a bond receives only interest during the term, and all principal is repaid at the end. The principal payments are:

| | *Bond (Treasury, Corporate)* | *Mortgage* |
|---|---|---|
| Date $= t = 1,\ldots,N-1$ | 0 | $m(r/k,N) - rb_t$, each $t$ |
| Date $= t = N$ | 1 | $m(r/k,N) - rb_N$ |

The principal payments on the government bond are akin to those of the "one hoss shay" of Oliver Wendell Holmes. The one hoss shay vehicle operates until it falls apart. The payments are zero throughout, and 1 in the last. The holder of the government bond has no equity buildup, receiving the initial price, the one dollar paid, at the end of the term. By comparison, the investor in the mortgage backed security receives an equity buildup of $m(r/k,N) - rb_t$, separate from an investment paying interest rate $r$. Even if both securities paid the same interest rate, this equity buildup, or residual, remains. The prospect arises, unlike with other long-term securities, of packaging residuals for sale as a security. The interest portion can be sold as another security.

Suppose the contract interest rate on a Treasury security of similar maturity is $r_1$ percent annually. The differential in interest rates is $r - r_1$. The differential in mortgage multipliers is $m(r/k,N) - m(r_1/k,N)$. This capitalized interest rate differential is another part of equity that can be sold to another investor.

The borrower pays interest and principal payments more frequently than the pass-through to the investor holding the security behind the mortgage. The mortgage multiplier is $m(r/k,N)$ per dollar of loan, and the buildup of payments prior to their modified pass through is $(k/k_1)m(r/k,N)$ per dollar of loan. With $k = 12$ and $k_1 = 4$, the intermediary is holding three months of payment prior to pass through, and receives a return on this amount. The contribution to residual, at the opportunity cost of funds $r_e$, is

$$r_e(k/k_1)m(r/k,N)A(r_e/k_1,N)$$

The contribution is the product of the opportunity cost of funds in an alternative investment $r_e$, the number of periods when the payments are held or warehoused prior to payment $(k/k_1)$, the mortgage multiplier on the original loan $m(r/k,N)$ and an annuity capitalizing the payments over the term of the mortgage. The servicer can reflect the various sources of residuals, of additional equity on its economic, as opposed to accounting, balance sheet, the assumptions for which are

1. Compounding occurs at the frequency of mortgage payments.
2. Loan balance, date $i$, is $b_i = [1 - A_i(r/k,i)/A_N(r/k,N)]$, $i = 1,\ldots,N$.
3. Calculation is an approximation of CMO residual equity sources.
4. $N = Tk$, $K = Tk_1$; $T$ is term in years; $k$ is number of mortgage payments per year; $k_1$ is number of MPT payments per year; $t_1 = t/(k/k_1)$, the number of MPT payments made when the borrower has made $t$ payments.

## Sources and Uses of Cash, Investment in CMO, Over Holding Period to Date *t* (Residual Equity)

### Cash Disbursements

Date of Purchase
Purchase price of CMO security 1

### Cash Receipts

During period of ownership
Principal receipts capitalized
Mortgage payment $m(r/k,N)$
Times: Present value, one dollar, capitalized over $t$ $A(r_e/k,t)$
Equals: Present value, mortgage payments
$m(r/k,N)A(r_e/k,t)$
Less: Present value, interest payments
Mortgage interest rate $r$
Times: Discounted loan balance, each payment
$\Sigma_{i=1}^{t} b_i/(1 + r_e/k)^i$
Equals: Interest portion $r\,\Sigma_{i=1}^{t} b_i/(1 + r_e/k)$

Equals: Present value, principal receipts
$m(r/k,N)A(r_e/k,t) - r\,\Sigma_{i=1}^{t} b_i/(1 + r_e/k)^i$

Plus: Interest rate differential

Mortgage payment, at contract rate $m(r/k,N)$

Less: Mortgage payment at bond rate $m(r_1/k,N)$

Equals: Payment differential $[m(r/k,N) - m(r_1/k,N)]$

Times: Present value, one dollar, capitalized over term $A(r_e/k,t)$

Equals: Present value, interest rate differential (stripping the call option from the mortgage) $[m(r/k,N) - m(r_1/k,N)]A(r_e/k,t)$

Plus: Warehousing factor (held before pass through)

Opportunity cost of funds $r_e$

Times: Mortgage payment $m(r/k,N)$

Equals: Foregone interest cost, one mortgage payment $(r_e/k)m(r/k,N)$

Times: Number of payments held $\text{FAC}[(k/k_1) - 1] = [(k/k_1) - 1] \times [(k/k_1) - 2] \times \cdots$ (since mortgage payments made at end of period)

Equals: Foregone interest, per MPT $(r_e/k)m(r/k,N)\text{FAC}[(k/k_1) - 1]$

Times: Present value, one dollar annuity, capitalized over number of payments to holder $A(r_e/k_1,t_1)$

Equals: Present value, warehousing $(r_e/k)m(r/k,N)\text{FAC}[(k/k_1) - 1]A(r_e/k_1,t_1)$

Plus: Balloon payment

Loan balance outstanding, time $t$ $b_t$

Times: Present value discounted $1/(1 + r_e/k)$

Equals: Present value, balloon payment $b_t/(1 + r_e/k)^t$

The investor in a CMO receives payments on residual equity. The payment of the principal is the difference between the mortgage payment and the interest-only portion, capitalized at the security yield, over the holding period. This component is termed the principal receipts capitalized. The interest rate differential between mortgages and bonds is capitalized, and added. The warehousing factor is the interest received by the servicer, while waiting to forward the mortgage payment to the security holder. Suppose three months of mortgage payment are warehoused. The first payment receives two months of interest, since mortgage payments are made at the end of the month. The second payment receives one month of interest, and the third payment receives no interest.

The investor is entitled to recover a balloon payment if the mortgage is prepaid. The yield on the CMO residual equity security, for term $t$—$r_e(t)$—is solved by equating the cash disbursed, or one dollar, with the present value of the receipts from the principal payments, the interest rate differential, the warehousing factor, and the balloon payment. If the residual equity portion is packaged into one security, then

$$1 = m(r/k,N)A(r_e/k,t) - \frac{r\sum_{i=1}^{t} b_i}{(1+r_e/k)^i} + [m(r/k,N) - m(r_1/k,N)]A(r_e/k,t)$$
$$+ (r_e/k)m(r/k,N)\text{FAC}\{[(k/k_1) - 1]A(r_e/k_1,t_1)\} + \frac{b_t}{(1+r_e/k)^t} \quad (10.10)$$

The yield on this security is $r_e(t)$, the return for a security of maturity date $t$. The CMO can be offered in different maturities. For accounting purposes, since the security is sold in classes, all residuals are collected, and paid to the class holding the shortest maturity. If the buyer pays a premium or discount of $p$, the cash disbursed is $1 - p$ instead of 1, with $p < 0$ for a premium.

The remaining portion of the payment is packaged into a bond-like security. The payments are interest only, there is no call option, and interest is paid on the MPT basis, such as quarterly. The bond portion can be marketed separately. The assumptions of the bond portion of the balance sheet are: time $t$ augments in units of the MPT, such as quarterly; $t = 1, \ldots, K, K = Tk_1$; $T$ is term in years; $k_1$ is number of payments per year to MPT holder. For the residual equity portion, time augments with the mortgage payment, such as monthly.

### Sources and Uses of Cash, Investment in CMO, Bond Portion, to Date $t$

**Cash Disbursements**

1

**Cash Receipts**

Interest payments
- Interest rate, bond, annual $r_1$
- Divide: Number of payments held $(k/k_1)$

Equals: Interest received, per dollar, at MPT payment $r_1(k_1/k)$
Times: Present value, annuity of one dollar per payment $A(r_e/k_1,K)$
Equals: Present value, cash received $r_1(k_1/k)A(r_e/k_1,K)$

Plus: Balloon payment
Prepayment of principal invested 1
Times: Present value, of one dollar $K$ periods ahead $1/(1 + r_e/k_1)^K$
Equals: Present value, balloon repayment $1/(1 + r_e/k_1)^K$

The cash-on-cash return on the bond is $r_e = r_1$ at issue, if the bond is not sold at a premium or discount. If the bond is sold at a discount $p$, which is a premium if $p < 0$, then, equating the sources and uses of cash

$$1 - p = r_1(k_1/k)A(r_e/k_1,K) + (1 + r_e/k_1)^{-K} \qquad (10.11)$$

The market interest rate is used for $r_e$. If the market interest rate increases, the present value of the annuity decreases, and the present value of the bond repayment decreases. The price of the bond decreases from the issue price $1 - p$.

The above analysis applies to any stripped security where the interest portion has been removed. The interest payment contains no call option, though more rapid repayment than projected can remove the investment. The interest payments are not guaranteed indefinitely, and the ultimate term of the interest-only or bond portion CMO is not $K$, but is likely to be shorter. The principal receipts are capitalized at the frequency of compounding on the mortgage. The discrepancy in frequency of compounding is taken in the warehousing term.

With the CMO, mortgage equity is sold as a security. The lender or intermediary reflects the inflow from the sale of the security as cash on the accounting balance sheet, increasing liquidity. Lenders are subject to regulation or supervision on capital adequacy, or on the ratio of (assets – liabilities) divided by owners' equity. By reducing both assets and liabilities in the same dollar amount, the capital-adequacy ratio improves for a given amount of owners' equity. Incomplete markets for these packages produce effective rates of return above the contract interest rate $r_1$.

Yields on the CMO are similar to those on long-term government securities, but below those on long-term mortgages, such as those in the pool. The investor has the advantage of being able to choose a term. Short- or medium-term securities are backed by FRPM mortgages, by adjusting the stagger on the payments. The yield equation is stripped in packaging the CMO. The contract interest rate $r$ is replaced by the long-term Treasury equivalent $r_1$, and sold in the CMO. The warehousing factor is sold in the CMO. The payment of $m(r/k,N)$ per dollar is split between principal and interest; and the principal portion is credited to the priority CMO holders.

## Yields on Mortgage Pools

It has been assumed that all mortgages in a pool have the same contract provisions. In practice, a given pool has varying dates of maturity and contract provisions. The interest rate, points, and prepayment penalty vary, even if the term is the same on all mortgages. Within the pool, each mortgage must have its yield to maturity computed from the sources and uses of cash:

**Sources and Uses of Cash, Investor in Mortgage Backed Securities, Date *t***
(per dollar of loan)

**Cash Disbursements**

Purchase of security 1
Equals: Present value, cash disbursements

**Cash Receipts**

During period of mortgage
Receipts of payments on MPT basis
Accumulation prior to payment $(k/k_1)$
Times: Mortgage multiplier, contract $m(r/k,N)$
Times: Present value, annuity to date $t$ $A(r_e/k,t)$
Equals: Present value, payments passed through
$(k/k_1)m(r/k,N)A(r_e/k_1,t)$

Plus: Balloon prepayment $b_t/(1 + r_e/k_1)^t$
Equals: Present value, cash receipts

Equating cash disbursed and cash received,

$$1 = (k/k_1)m(r/k,N)A(r_e/k_1,t) + b_t/(1 + r_e/k_1)^t \qquad (10.12)$$

to solve for the cash-on-cash yield of the mortgage. If the mortgage is purchased at a discount from face value, such is reflected by $1 - p$. The yield $r_e$ is for one mortgage. The yield equation must be computed for each mortgage in the pool.

When all mortgages are identical, the loan balances $B$ are irrelevant. If mortgages are not identical, the loan balances for each are used as weights. The yield on the $i$th mortgage, is $r_{e,i}$, $i = 1,\ldots,I$, where $I$ mortgages are in the pool.

The effective yield is for the expected prepayment date $t$, $t = 1,\ldots,K$. The balance of each loan is $B_i$, for $i = 1,\ldots,I$, where there are $I$ loans in the pool. The average yield over the pool is

$$r_{\bar{e}} = \frac{\sum_{i=1}^{I} r_{e,i} B_i}{\sum_{i=1}^{I} B_i} \tag{10.13}$$

There are other methods of aggregation over loans. What is sought is an index of the effective interest rates, as $r_e = r_e(r_{e,1},\ldots,r_{e,I})$; the weighted mean is not necessasrily the appropriate measure of yield.

Some loans carry higher interest rates because the properties, borrowers, or lenders are, or are perceived to be, more risky. A higher interest rate compensates for higher risk. A higher yield does not necessarily signal a more attractive investment, but possibly more risk. No correction for the risk is applied in the average yield with the heterogeneous properties and borrowers.

## Mortgage Equity

The flip side of refinancing is mortgage equity. When the market interest rate exceeds the contract rate $r$, the borrower obtains equity on the loan, at the expense of the lender or holder of the mortgage security. The borrower who does not sell the property realizes a capital gain from mortgage equity. The borrower who sells the property cannot realize the capital gain on the mortgage, because FRPM loans are not transferable.

The owner not selling the property pays an interest rate $r$, when the market interest rate $r_1$ is higher. The owner selling the property loses the investment in the FRPM. Replacement financing must be conducted at $r_1$. A saving in interest per dollar of $r_1 - r$ arises from not moving.

The mortgage multiplier for the borrower, under existing financing, is

$m(r/k,N)$, for number of payments $N$, and frequency of compounding $k$. At market replacement interest rates, the mortgage multiplier is $m(r_1/k,N)$. The saving in payment, as compared with market rates, is $m(r_1/k,N) - m(r/k,N)$ per dollar of loan. Over $t$ periods, the annuity is $A(r_e/k,t)$. The capital value of the saving, or mortgage equity, is

$$\text{MOREQ} = [m(r_1/k,N) - m(r/k,N)]A(r_1/k,t) \quad (10.14)$$

using the market interest rate as the effective rate.

Provided the borrower retains title, it is possible to sell this equity to another investor. There are potentially billions of dollars of mortgage equity locked in, and illiquid. Financial markets could be made more efficient by the unlocking of mortgage equity.

Mortgage equity provides the borrower with another option contract in the package with a FRPM loan. When interest rates fall, the borrower has the option of refinancing. When interest rates rise, the borrower has the option of not selling.

The first option is

$$\text{if } r_1 > r \quad \text{then MOREQ} = [m(r_1/k,N) - m(r/k,N)]A(r_1/k,t)$$

$$\text{if } r_1 < r \quad \text{then MOREQ} = 0.$$

If $f(r_1)$ is the probability distribution of market interest rates, $r_1$, $0 < r_1 < \infty$, expected mortgage equity per dollar of loan is

$$E(\text{MOREQ}) = \int_r^{\infty} [m(r_1/k,N) - m(r/k,N)]A(r_1/k,t)f(r_1)\,dr_1 \quad (10.15)$$

This estimate overstates illiquid mortgage equity. Mortgage equity cannot be sold if FRPMs have a due-on-sale clause. Otherwise, the property value would be increased by the mortgage equity at sale time. The property is more valuable to the existing owner than to a subsequent owner.

If $V$ is the market value of the property, then

$$V = \text{VAPP} \qquad \text{if property sold}$$

$$= \text{VAPP} + E(\text{MOREQ}) \qquad \text{if property not sold}$$

where VAPP is the value of the physical real estate. If the owner sells, and attempts to replace the property with an identical one, financing at rate $r_1$

must be paid. The owner is less willing to sell. As interest rates rise, although VAPP declines, mortgage equity increases. A market inefficiency arises, since the property is more valuable to the current owner than any other.

Mortgage equity is an increase in owners' equity arising from purely financing considerations. If the financing cannot be sold, or mortgages are not assumable, this mortgage equity is not transferable, providing an incentive for the owner to hold the property longer, thereby reducing the level of real estate transactions. The supply of available property is reduced, which increases the price of real estate.

Defeasance provides a method of capitalizing the benefits of having a low interest rate mortgage without selling the property, losing the investment, and triggering capital gains taxation. Defeasance operates best when a property has a low interest rate mortgage as a liability, and the owner seeks to unlock mortgage equity. The owner buys a portfolio of securities whose maturity matches exactly that of the mortgage. The securities are placed in an irrevocable trust, and the interest is used to pay the mortgage obligation.

Since market interest rates exceed those on the mortgage, the owner is able to buy more face value in securities than the amount of the loan. The mortgage has been exchanged for securities whose price reflects movements in interest rates.

Suppose an investor has an apartment worth $150,000, with a $100,000 loan carrying straight interest at 8 percent. Market interest rates are 10 percent. The multiplier, or times gross, is 10, so the gross income is $15,000. The $8,000 of interest can be serviced by $80,000 of bonds. There is $20,000 of mortgage equity, in addition to the $50,000 of balance-sheet equity. The balance-sheet equity is the market value less the loan balance. There is no depreciation or depreciated balance, and no other expenses other than for interest.

If financial accounting regulations, specified by the Financial Accounting Standards Board (FASB), permitted a writedown of the mortgage balance, mortgage equity is included on the balance sheet.

**Balance Sheet, Investor, Recognizing Mortgage Equity, Given Date**

| Assets ($) | | Liabilities and Owners' Equity ($) | |
|---|---|---|---|
| Real estate | 150,000 | Mortgage (book value) | 100,000 |
| | | Less: Writedown for mortgage equity | 20,000 |
| | | Mortgage (market value) | 80,000 |
| | | Owners' equity | 70,000 |

The owners' equity is $50,000 of equity in the property, or $150,000 less $100,000 in the book value of the mortgage, plus $20,000 of mortgage equity. The mortgage is a FRPM paying straight interest with no assumption. The mortgage equity arises from having the right to pay a lower interest rate than that prevailing in the market. If the owner takes no action, and does not recognize the mortgage equity, total owners' equity is $50,000.

If FASB or other financial accounting procedures prevent the use of mortgage equity, a defeasance is an alternative. Suppose the funds to purchase the securities are borrowed at 10 percent, with proceeds from the gross income. Securities with a redeemable value at term of $100,000 can be bought for $80,000, yielding the 10 percent. The income statement is, neglecting operating expenses and with no defeasance,

**Income Statement, During Period *t*, No Defeasance**

| | $ |
|---|---|
| Revenue | |
| Gross income | 15,000 |
| Less: Expenses | |
| Interest | 8,000 |
| Income after debt service | 7,000 |

Defeasance dominates either not purchasing the securities, or selling the property. If preferential tax rates apply to capital gains, defeasance dominates. Even where capital gains not taxed preferentially, the $80,000 borrowed is matched against a $100,000 mortgage, effectively unlocking the $20,000 of mortgage equity.

**Income Statement, During Period *t*, Defeasance**

| | | $ |
|---|---|---|
| Revenue | | |
| Gross income from rental | | 15,000 |
| Plus: Financial revenue | | |
| Yield on securities: interest | | 8,000 |
| Plus: Capital gain on security | | 2,000 |
| Total revenue | | 25,000 |
| Less: Expenses | | |
| Interest, mortgage | 8,000 | |
| Interest, securities | 10,000 | |
| Total expenses | 18,000 | |
| Net Income | | 7,000 |

It is assumed that 10 percent ($2,000) of the capital gain is assigned each period to income.

The income statements indicate the same net income with or without defeasance. The owner, however, may be able to include the book value of the securities purchased as an asset on the balance sheet. The difference between the book value and market value of the securities is equal to the mortgage equity. The capital gain on the security need not be recognized as current income.

## Self-Insured Mortgage Security (SIMS)

Mortgage insurance is offered to protect the security holder against default risk. Particularly on large whole loans, mortgage insurance is either expensive or unavailable, depending on default risk. For example, a premium of 0.3 percent of the loan balance annually by the borrower is required to upgrade a mortgage security to a premium rating.[7] If the intermediary, the packager of the mortgage securities, bears the risk internally by self-insuring the loans, this premium is eliminated and the mortgages are more marketable. With self-insured mortgage security (SIMS), the intermediary retains a portion of the offering, as the last class to be paid, in a subordinated position.

Tax regulations permit an issuing intermediary to divide a mortgage backed offering into more than one class, as with CMOs, and pass principal and interest through itself without paying tax. Senior holders, in higher denominated classes, closer to A in the alphabet and 1 in numbering, obtain principal and interest first. Junior holders, including the issuer in a subordinated position, absorb losses up to the size of their holding before senior holders lose their investment. With the subordinated position, other holders must be paid in full before any payments are made in this class. The percentage held by the issuer in subordinated form is effectively the pool insurance rate.

Investors have no claim on the issuer beyond the subordinated position. Given this feature, the issue counts as a sale of assets for regulatory and accounting purposes. The trade-off for the issuer is between an insurance premium and the risk of losing a subordinated investment. Investors do not receive mortgage insurance, a risk, since the self-insured firm may not be able to survive a large series of claims.

SIMS is issued directly by a thrift, bank, or other lender. SIMS permit a lender to pool and sell securities backed by its mortgage portfolio, acting as its marketer, without requiring outside insurance purchase.

## Real Estate Securities

Real estate securities include common stock secured by commercial real estate and real estate municipal investment grade and junk bonds. The securities are backed either by physical properties or mortgages. Real estate securities permit large placements to be made at one time. A mortgage or piece of real estate is sold to investors in the form of stock, bonds, or partnership interests. By selling bonds to the public instead of borrowing from an insurance company, savings in financing costs are effected.

Income for the future is uncertain and also the stability of the tenants, as for all commercial development. Some projects are so highly leveraged that interest payments alone cannot be covered by the rental income, or the interest-coverage ratio is less than one. Secondary markets for bonds secured by commercial real estate are thin, which leads to illiquidity problems. There is greater risk if equity financing is applied when debt financing is unobtainable. Sometimes the properties are not yet built, or interest payments cannot be covered until into the future.

Junk bonds describe seucrities with low or no rating. Junk bonds carry high coupon interest rates, with high degrees of risk. Real estate junk bonds are analogues of the corporate issues used in arbitrage and in leveraged buyouts and takeovers. The bonds are backed by second or higher-order mortgages. Unlike corporate takeover junk bonds, some real estate junk bonds have low interest rates, but carry an equity kicker. The lower interest rates reduce the carrying charges, at the cost of surrendering some equity. Other variants include thrifts issuing certificates of deposit, particularly for pension accounts, for investment in second mortgages.

Other securities secured by real estate include STRIPS (Separate Trading of Registered Interest and Principal of Securities) and CATS (Certificates of Accrual of Treasury Securities). These securities represent ownership of interest or principal payments. They can be issued against various types of securities. The yields on stripped securities are derived analogously for the CMOs. They are not callable if issued on Treasury securities.

## Municipal Bonds

### *Marginal Investor*

A bond is a debt obligation or promise to pay by a corporation, government, or government agency. The bond issuer is obligated to repay the investment plus interest at a set date, but there is risk of default. Higher-quality bonds pay lower yields, though in real estate some bonds carry an option to receive equity in exchange for a lower interest rate.

Municipal bonds, together with property taxes on real estate, form the chief revenue sources of local and municipal governments providing the services for owners of real estate. Municipal bonds are free of federal income taxes, and free of state and local income taxes if the holder is a resident of the state of issue. The effective marginal tax rate for an individual facing state tax is, on a taxable investment, $\tau_f + \tau_s(1 - \tau_f)$, where $\tau_f$ is the federal marginal tax rate, and $\tau_s$ is the state marginal tax rate, if state income taxes are deductible in calculating federal tax liability.

An investor in the 28 percent federal marginal tax bracket has $\tau_f = 0.28$, and suppose $\tau_s = 0.1$. Then $\tau_s(1 - \tau_f) = 0.1 \times (1 - 0.28) = 0.1 \times 0.72 = 0.072$, and $\tau_f + \tau_s(1 - \tau_f) = 0.28 + 0.072 = 0.352$, or 35.2 percent. The total marginal tax rate is

$$\tau = \tau_f + \tau_s(1 - \tau_f)$$

This calculation applies to individual taxation. Let $r_e$ be the yield on a taxable security. A municipal bond of identical risk and maturity characteristics need pay only $r_e(1 - \tau)$ as a yield to buyers. The actual yield on the municipal security is determined by the market. If the market yield is $r_e(\text{MUNI})$, then

$$r_e(\text{MUNI}) = r_e(1 - \tau^*)$$

where, as with the active real estate investor, $\tau^*$ is the threshold marginal tax rate above which the investment is attractive. Then

$$r_e(\text{MUNI}) = r_e - r_e\tau^*$$

$$r_e\tau^* = r_e - r_e(\text{MUNI})$$

$$\tau^* = \frac{r_e - r_e(\text{MUNI})}{r_e} = 1 - \frac{r_e(\text{MUNI})}{r_e} \qquad (10.16)$$

For an individual or corporation with marginal tax rate greater than $\tau^*$, the tax-free security is held, otherwise the taxable security is held. The

1986 Tax Reform Act severely restricted the demand and supply of municipal bonds. On the demand side, financial institutions are no longer permitted to exclude interest income or municipal bonds. On the supply side, industrial development bond issues have been restricted. The same individual faces different marginal tax rates on other investments, such as pension funds. Tax-free securities are not appropriate for pension funds, since the current marginal tax rate is zero, whether inside or outside the funds. Treasury securities and other direct federal government issues are not subject to state and local income taxes. Corporate long-term bonds and Ginnie Maes are not exempt from state and local income taxes unless stated.

The marginal tax rates on securities relevant to real estate, in currently taxable accounts, are

| | |
|---|---|
| Ginnie Maes (and corporate issues) | $\tau = \tau_f + \tau_s(1 - \tau_f)$ |
| Treasuries (direct federal issues) | $\tau = \tau_f$ |
| Municipal bonds (in state) | $\tau = 0$ |
| Municipal bonds (out of state) | $\tau = \tau_s$ |

All securities face a marginal tax rate of zero in tax-deferred accounts. If the following data on market yields, for corresponding securities, are $r_e = 0.1$ and $r_e(\text{MUNI}) = 0.08$, then

$$\tau^* = 1 - [r_e(\text{MUNI})]/r_e$$

$$= 1 - (0.08/0.1) = 0.2$$

The threshold marginal tax rate is 20 percent. The investor with the 35 percent marginal tax rate holds municipal bonds. The comparable yield for $r_e$ should be for a Ginnie Mae or corporate bond, and not a Treasury security.[8] The Ginnie Mae includes a call option, as does a municipal bond, while the Treasury security has no call option.

Bonds are rated by various agencies. Three rating agencies are Standard and Poor, Moody and Fitch. The ratings are:

| *Credit rating* | *Standard and Poor* | *Moody* | *Fitch* |
|---|---|---|---|
| Prime | AAA | Aaa | AAA |
| Excellent | AA | Aa | AA |
| Good | A | A | A |
| Average | BBB | Baa | BBB |
| Speculative | BB | Ba | BB |
| Highly speculative | B | B | B |
| Poor | CCC | Caa | CCC |
| Default probable | CC | Ca | CC |
| Default imminent | C | C | C |

While Standard and Poor's and Fitch have the same categories, the actual rating received varies between the firms. The first four categories are investment grade. The remaining categories are speculative. Junk bonds are those with below-investment grade, or no rating. Standard and Poor adds a + or − sign after the letter rating, to distinguish credit ratings within a group. Moody adds a number to the rating, with a lower number indicating a better rating.

In the municipal sector, Moody rates short term notes

| *Credit rating* | *Moody* |
|---|---|
| Best quality | MIG1 |
| High quality | MIG2 |
| Favorable | MIG3 |
| Some risk | MIG4 |

### *Types of Municipal Bonds*

Municipal bonds are issued for various real estate financing purposes. Direct loan program housing bonds (DLHBs) finance new construction. Developers receive a mortgage loan from the issuing agency, frequently a state agency, for a specific purpose. The usual purpose is the construction of low-income housing. The bonds are secured by the mortgage payments of the owner-occupiers, and sometimes carry a state guarantee against default. Some DLHBs carry insurance, either from the federal government or a private insurer. The insurance need not cover all risks, such as developer default or failure to complete construction on time, on budget, or satisfactorily, as opposed to owner-occupier default.

With a DLHB, the owner-occupiers are households who, through insufficient income and wealth, are unable to purchase a house in the price range constructed. A subsidy or buydown from an outside agency can be involved. Without insurance, the buyer of the bond bears risks of payment or repayment of the subsidy, price movement or deterioration of the property, and management of the project.

Mortgage purchase bonds (MPBs) are used to buy existing mortgage pools. The issuing agency, typically from the state, sells housing revenue bonds, and buys mortgages directly from thrifts. The thrifts use the proceeds for extension of other mortgages. The bonds are secured by mortgage payments.

Municipal bonds are issued for construction of rental housing, notably under Section 8 of the National Housing Act. Section 8 provides for rent subsidies to be paid to low-income tenants. These subsidies are adjusted for expected inflation. Risks to the buyer are withdrawal of subsidies and deterioration of property or management. With federal guarantees on repayment, and the rents being placed into an escrow account to support the payment to the bond buyer, Section 8 type municipal bonds reduce the risk to the investor. Under Section 8-11b, for multifamily construction, proceeds from municipal bond issues cover developer costs, debt services for one year, capitalized interest, and expenses. The security is the rent from the project.

Where there is no security other than the project itself, the investor in the municipal bond has to examine various operating ratios. Such ratios are useful checks for other real estate investments. Various ratios are:

Operating ratio = operating and maintenance expenses ÷ operating revenues
Interest coverage ratio = net revenues ÷ interest payment
Debt service ratio = net revenue ÷ debt service
Debt service safety margin ratio = debt service ÷ gross revenue
Debt ratio = net debt ÷ (working capital + plant)
Net takedown ratio = net revenue ÷ gross revenue

Criteria can be established that the ratios exceed or fall below certain levels.

Types of municipal bonds are:

| *Category* | *Collateral Support* |
|---|---|
| General obligation (GO) bonds and notes | Local tax revenue, mainly taxes on residential property |
| General obligation (GO) securities | Leases on buildings |

| *Category* | *Collateral Support* |
|---|---|
| Limited or special tax bonds | Particular property assessments |
| Revenue bonds | Specific local projects, such as toll roads or bridges |
| Letter of credit bonds | Guaranteed by lender |
| Double-barrelled bonds | Special issue, and general tax revenue |
| Housing bonds | Mortgage payments (owners) or rental payments (tenants) |

Municipal bonds are not free of default risk, because a municipality or issuing authority has the prospect of collapse or loss of revenue. Pools of insurance companies, such as the Municipal Bond Insurance Association (MBIA), and the American Municipal Bond Assurance Corporation (AMBAC), insure the principal and interest payment on municipal bonds, permitting their upgrading to AAA by Standard and Poor. Other insuring agencies are the Federal Guaranty Insurance Corporation (FGIC) for municipal bonds with federal involvement, and some specialized agencies such as the Health Industry Bond Insurance Corporation (HIBI).

Municipal securities are available for short terms. Tax-free commercial paper is typically sold for 15–45 days. Tax anticipation notes (TANs), secured by the prospect of taxes, are for less than three years.

Packages of municipal bonds are sold to investors as tax-free bonds funds or unit trusts. Funds trade by buying and selling municipal bonds. The investor in the fund pays a management fee for administrative expenses. The costs of trading, in brokerage and other commissions, are not part of the expenses, but are subtracted in calculating the net income of the fund. Municipal bond unit trusts do not trade. An initial portfolio is retained until maturity and is typically sold with a front-end load. Buyers of bond funds obtain diversification and liquidity, at the cost of expenses, management fees, and, potentially, a load. The higher the fees, the lower the rate of return to the holder, if the managers are unable to produce additional returns.[9]

Some characteristics of municipal bonds include the credit rating or quality, the yield to maturity, current yield, the security, the presence of call or put provisions, and liquidity. In terms of liquidity and divisibility, municipal bonds are sold in units of $5,000, but one bond is viewed as $1,000. A round lot is $25,000 of a unit, with smaller amounts being odd lots, potentially less liquid and subject to sale at a large discount. Since July 1, 1983, municipal bonds are sold in registered form, where the name of the owner of the bond is recorded for security. Most older bonds are in bearer form, where interest is paid to the holder. Holding a larger amount of fewer bonds loses diversification, but the transactions costs of selling are reduced.

Municipal bonds have call and put provisions. The call provision is the equivalent of refinancing, except that the buyer has some limit on the date of call. With a call provision, the issuer has the option of repurchasing the security at specific dates, with maximum prices, not necessarily par. This provision protects the issuer against declining interest rates by permitting refinancing at lower rates, with this risk borne by the buyer. Some municipal bonds have no call provisions; others have call protection by placing a lower limit on the date of refinancing. Call protection prevents exercise on a 25-year bond prior to 5 years. With a put provision, the buyer is protected against interest rate risk on the upside. The issuer undertakes to buy the bond back at minimum prices, at specific dates. The typical provision undertakes to buy back at the issued par price, up to a certain date. Call provisions shift downside interest rate risk to the buyer from the issuer, and put provisions shift upside interest rate risk to the issuer from the buyer.

One measure of the yield on a municipal bond is

$$r_e = rB/P$$

where $B$ is the face value issued, $r$ the contract interest rate, and $P$ the market price of the municipal bond. The assumption is for an infinite holding period. This yield excludes the possibility that some municipal bonds are sold at issue at either a discount or premium. Using $p$ as the equivalent of points, and being either positive or negative, an approximation of the yield is

$$\bar{r} = r + p/T$$

where $T$ is the term in years. This approximation differs from the calculations used elsewhere, in that the discount of premium is capitalized at a constant average rate. Mortgage points, by comparison, are capitalized at a declining balance rate.

The average price used for yield calculation is the mean of the current market price and the price at term. If the price of the bond on redemption is $P_T$, then

$$\bar{P} = (P + P_T)/2$$

and the yield is approximately

$$r_e = \bar{r} P_T / \bar{P}$$

Suppose a bond with a price of $1,000 at maturity is bought on the market at issue at $980, with a contract interest rate, or coupon rate of 8 percent. The term of the bond is 20 years. Then $r = 0.08, T = 20, P = 980, P_T = 1000$, and $p = 0.02$. For a buy at discount, $p > 0$; and for a buy at a premium, $p < 0$. Total income is based on the redemption price of $1,000, so annual income, is $\bar{r} P_T = (0.08 + 0.02/20) \times 1000 = 84$. The average price is $990, so $r_e = 84/990$, or 8.484 percent. The current or running yield is $r/P$.

Interest payment on bonds is made twice annually. For a purchase not on one of the two days that interest is paid, accrued interest is added, and the purchaser buys at a price that include accrued interest. The buyer pays the seller interest on a 360-day year basis. The added accrued interest at purchase is $BrD/360$, where $D$ is the number of days of interest. The number of days of interest is obtained by subtracting the last date interest was paid from the date of purchase.

Municipal bonds are issued in serial, term, and zero-coupon forms. Serial bonds involve the issue being divided into various maturities, and corresponding coupon interest rates. Purchase along various terms is determined by comparison of yields on a specific issue with the prevailing term structure. Term bonds have one date of redemption. Zero-coupon bonds pay all interest at maturity. At issue, they are sold at a deep discount, and the price increases toward maturity, as interest is earned.

The plot of the sequence of yields from a serial bond against maturity is the yield curve, the compensation of the investor for holding a longer term. The yield curve for a particular issue can be compared to some average, to determine whether a maturity is above the market in yield. A flatter yield curve provides less reward for the additional risk of investing for the long term.[10] The relative return for short-term municipal bonds is higher, and there is additional risk of the yield curve steepening. The relative yield of longer-term bonds is expected to increase, with capital losses for current holders.

Zero-coupon bonds pay no direct interest to the holder. The interest payments are factored into the price of the bond, sold at a deep discount. Zero-coupon bonds are less expensive to purchase, and all reinvestment occurs at the stated yield. In the early years, as with a mortgage, most of the price increase represents the implicit interest payment, and there is risk of call. By having the interest payments capitalized, there is more risk of price fluctuation than with other municipal bonds. The holder of the zero-coupon bond receives no income, with the interest being part of the return.

Zero-coupon municipal bonds, or compound interest bonds (CIBs) are issued by municipalities in connection with real estate and industrial development lending. Interest is compounded semiannually and paid with the principal at maturity. This feature assures a high total return on investment, and is tax free. CIBs have an active secondary market.

Municipal bonds have typically thin secondary markets. The option tender bond (OTB) increases liquidity. Issued as long-term bonds with maturities ranging from 25 to 30 years, these securities are more similar to short-term bonds. The interest rate is adjusted periodically to reflect changes in short-term interest rates. The bond owner has the option of tendering the bond to the trustee for payment at part value, or of accepting the new rate.

On the short-term front, tax anticipation notes (TANs) are backed by local taxes and have low risk. Tax allocation notes are backed by real estate taxes. General obligation notes are not backed by specific taxes. Commercial paper, usually sold in units of $100,000, is offered as a short-term, tax-free investment.

## Municipal Bond Risk

### *Types of Risk*

The risks on municipal bonds include default, liquidity, capital loss, credit rating, and tax and legislative policy. The municipality (issuing agency) can default. Some municipal bonds are insured, but the insurance benefit depends on the resources of the insurer. For housing bonds, deterioration of a neighborhood reduces the value of the security for the bond. In small amounts, illiquidity arises, involving higher transactions costs of sale. Capital losses arise with movement in interest rates, and the exercise of call or put options. The credit rating of the issuer can be increased or decreased, affecting the yield. Some bonds can lose their tax exempt status, or the legislation exempting the income from taxation can change. A change in marginal tax rates affects the threshold rate and relative yields.

The presence of a call option implies that a premium for refinancing is built into the price of municipal bonds. The call premium operates analogously to that for mortgage backed securities in pricing refinancing risk. The holder is exposed to upside interest rate risk, with capital losses.

On interest rate risk, some issuers undertake to protect bondholders by buying back the bonds at face value after a certain date, regardless of market price.

### *Risk Layoff—Swapping*

The holders of municipal bonds are individuals or corporations subject to federal and state taxes. Interest rate risk can be hedged through bond swapping. Bond swapping involves having some of the capital losses shared with the government through tax-loss selling. Capital gains are not taxed on an accrued, but on a realized basis. Suppose a municipal bond has coupon interest rate of $r$, price $P$, and term $T$ at issue. Market interest rates on municipal securities increase to $r_1 > r$. To achieve a market yield, the price on the initial issue declines to $P_1$, and the holder has an accrued but unrealized capital loss. A change in marginal tax rates affects the threshold rate and relative yields.

The capital loss $P_1 - P$ is realized by selling the security, producing a tax loss, and recovering $\tau(P_1 - P)$ as a tax refund. The buyer, assuming no change in portfolio preferences, buys another bond with similar characteristics. Buying back the same bond within 31 days counts as a wash sale, and the tax deduction of capital losses is not applicable.

There may be additional costs of premature realization, particularly if the bond is illiquid. Even if the date of tax saving is delayed, swapping is a method of partially laying off the risk of a capital loss from an increase in interest rates. If interest rates decline, the buyer holds the bond and does not sell.

The swapping strategy is not confined to municipal bonds, but is applicable to Ginnie Maes and all securities. For municipal bonds, while the interest is not taxable, capital gains are taxable, and losses are deductible. The strategy requires that capital gains are taxed on an accrued but unrealized basis. The holder of the security has an American put option, the right to sell upon a price drop, on any day, triggering a tax recovery. The put option is not exercised, and is worthless, if the price of the municipal bond increases.

The municipal bond is purchased for $P$, a fixed basis for capital gains calculations. Market prices for municipal bonds, dependent on interest rates, call options for the issuer, and tax policy, are $P_1$, but random, with probability distribution $f(P_1)$, over $0 \leqslant P_1 < \infty$. The investor holds a put option to sell capital losses to the tax authority. The option price, PUT, is

$$\text{PUT} = \tau(P - P_1) \qquad \text{if } P_1 < P$$

$$= 0 \qquad \text{if } P_1 \geqslant P$$

Suppose the option is exercisable immediately. The expected value of the saving is, where $c$ is the roundtrip transaction cost of selling the bond and buying another with the same characteristics,

$$E(\text{PUT}) = \tau \int_0^P (P - P_1) f(P_1)\, dP_1 - c. \qquad (10.17)$$

The tax recovery is the marginal tax rate, combined state and federal, $\tau$, times the expected capital loss, less the roundtrip commission. Securities with gains in the portfolio are retained. If there is a limit on deductibility of capital losses, some capital losses face a marginal tax rate of zero, though unused losses are carried forward.

If transactions costs are high, as with odd lots, the value of the put is reduced. The put option is an asset for the bondholder, but a contingent liability for the tax authorities. High tax rates spur purchase of municipal bonds, and increase the value of the put. If transactions costs are the same for all marginal tax rates, or $c$ is independent of $\tau$, then

$$\partial E(\text{PUT})/\partial\tau = \int_0^P (P - P_1) f(P_1)\, dP_1 > 0.$$

and the put option is worth more to those in higher tax brackets. In equilibrium, the market prices all contingent claims, including this put option. Since this option depends on tax rates, only a threshold marginal tax rate is priced. The price of the put option depends on the distribution of bond prices $f(P_1)$ and the basis price $P$.

## Secondary Real Estate Securities Markets

### *Mortgage Exchange*

Liquidity and efficiency are increased by a mortgage exchange, where whole individual mortgages or packaged products can be bought and sold.[11] Almost two-thirds of the volume of mortgage securities traded are MPTs and CMOs. The rest is mortgage backed agency debt, whole loans, builder bonds, mortgage revenue bonds, and brokered CDs for real estate.

With trading in real estate debt instruments exceeding that in stock markets, an argument can be made for a mortgage exchange. The six principal market makers in real estate securities are Morgan Stanley, Merrill Lynch Capital Markets, Alex. Brown and Sons, Salomon Brothers, and First Boston, with the last two controlling about 60 percent of the market. Potential inefficiency lies in the sale of whole and pools of mortgages and loans, as opposed to the securities themselves. An electronic mortgage exchange increases information, reduces price dispersion, transactions costs, and possibly interest rates.

A national mortgage exchange can trade debt of mortgage related agencies, mortgage securities, mortgage revenue bonds, CMOs, pools of mortgages, and individual mortgages. Members of an exchange can be institutional investors, large issuers of mortgage securities, and broker dealers. Such an exchange could increase competition and liquidity, given that the current market is concentrated and contains price dispersions and arbitrage opportunities. Securities initially would be dominated by FRPMs, because of the heterogeneity of conditions behind ARMs. It can be argued that the additional gap in bid-asked spreads on mortgage securities arises because of refinancing risk.

In the United States, the six largest firms are among those permitted by the Federal Reserve to trade government securities. These designated broker dealers are the only ones with bookie screens, and thereby with access to pricing information on federally backed mortgage securities.

### *Mortgage Backed Securities for ARMs*

Mortgage backed securities have been principally issued against FRPMs. There are limited secondary markets for ARMs. This absence has led to thrifts and other lenders having perverse incentives. FRPMs are sold with higher overall secondary market risk, at the expense of ARMs that have more incomplete secondary markets.

The thrifts and other lenders do not necessarily intend to hold the FRPMs in their portfolios, so other than the need to determine qualifying standards for resale, limited risk management arises. Lenders are permitted to recognize the points and fees as current income, and act solely as loan brokers. There are more limited secondary markets for ARMs, and greater risk of having to hold them in the portfolio. The lender is prevented from increasing the velocity or frequency of transactions and thus reducing points and fee income, by holding portfolio loans.

ARMs have characteristics that could be useful to potential securities buyers. ARMs carry less interest rate risk to the lender or security holder, since interest rates are flexible and move in the same directly as the market. Borrowers with ARMs have lower default rates.

The problem with ARMs lies with the heterogeneity of variables in the issuance of the mortgage. The packaging of the security could commence with certain characteristics such as no negative amortization, no going-in rate subsidy, and limits on the periodic and ultimate caps. The interest rate index could be restricted, such as one on Treasury notes, with a specific margin contained. Thrifts and other lenders have incentives to steer borrowers toward ARMs that have an immediate secondary market, providing working capital for new originations.

An ARM backed security has yields moving in the same direction as interest rates. Long-term securities, such as bonds and stocks, have asset prices negatively correlated with interest rates. An ARM security provides diversified protection against interest rate risk. By comparison, FRPM securities prices move in the opposite direction to interest rates. The ARM backed security has some characteristics of an inflation-indexed bond. When interest rates increase because of an increase in inflation, the yield increases. The security is appealing to those who require current income and inflation protection, such as retirees.

## Concluding Remarks

Real estate markets have become more liquid, as financial claims have been developed and issued against physical properties and mortgages. Mortgages trade in secondary markets, either pooled or sold as collateral for certificates. The mortgage backed securities most free of default risk are those with loans guaranteed by the full faith and credit of the United States Treasury. Other mortgages are subject to default risk, but markets are capable of pricing this risk. The development of mortgage markets permits potential buyers of long-term securities access to alternative markets.

Risks in holding mortgage backed securities arise from interest rates and refinancing. Mortgages are bonds promising to pay an annuity over a long term. The blend of interest and principal payments provides an opportunity to separate the two. A stripped security can pay interest or principal only.

Mortgage backed securities are issued for FRPMs, notably on single-family residential property, but on other properties such as apartment buildings. Shorter-term securities can be offered, backed by ARM mortgages. ARM loans require the borrower to accept a part of the interest rate and inflation risk, and reduce the refinancing risk by permitting contract interest rates to remain close to market rates. This reduction in risks can be packaged into securities that have low risk of capital gain or loss, but fluctuation in the interest rate and payment received. ARM backed securities are attractive to those seeking income at lower capital risk, including insurance companies, pension funds, pensioners, and corporations seeking short-term parking places for funds.

## Notes

1. The term "revolution" has been applied by Downs [1986].

2. As interest rates rise, asset prices fall so that the rate of return—the product of the interest rates and asset price in the limit—is competitive with alternative investments.

3. Municipal or corporate bonds can be called at a particular price and date, prior to maturity. The issuer exercises this provision if interest rates fall below those at issue.

4. There can be some refinancing at interest rates in excess of contract rates. Borrowers change locations for reasons other than interest rates, and their FRPM loans are not assumable by subsequent buyers. The ultimate holders receive nonnegative inflows at all interest rates.

5. The VA effectively covers a large part of down payment equity. Lenders can then extend loans to qualifying veterans involving no down payment.

6. Principal firms in the mortgage security sector are Salomon Brothers and Drexel Burnham Lambert. Principal firms in the development of CMOs are Salomon Brothers, Morgan Stanley, Lomas and Nettleton and PaineWebber.

7. Complete bond rating will be discussed in the section on municipal bonds.

8. A rule of thumb used for purchase of municipal securities is based on $r_e(\text{MUNI})/r_e$, using comparable municipal and federal government securities. When the ratio exceeds some target, effectively $1 - \tau^*$, then buy municipal bonds. One example is to buy when the ratio exceeds 0.7, and not to buy below. There are problems with any rule of thumb. Tax rates and policy can change, affecting the criterion. The call option premium varies with interest rate expectations. Effectively, $r_e(\text{MUNI}) = r_e + E(\text{CALL})$, where $E(\text{CALL})$ is the expected interest rate premium the borrower must apy to retain the call option to refinance. The ratio should be framed with the return on callable securities, such as Ginnie Maes, as $r_e$. The implications can be substantially different for purchasing decisions.

9. In an efficient market, such returns are elusive. A high management fee can be in excess of 0.6 percent annually. Managed funds are compared with each other, so it is important not to be ranked at the bottom of a table. A strategy for such avoidance entails following the leader, buying and selling when other funds are so doing. This strategy need not produce returns for the fund holders, and generates churning, or high portfolio turnover rates. Some funds indicate higher yields obtained by investing in risky securities. Buyers of unit trusts obtain diversification, with less or no liquidity, at the cost of a load.

10. A source of information on municipal bonds is the periodical *The Bond Buyer.* Its Blue List contains the par values of secondary offerings, and the 30-day supply of new municipal bonds, indicating the supply. The placement ratio indicates how new issues are selling, rela-

tive to existing issues. If there is a large overhang, there is a relatively large supply of new issues.

11. The market for mortgage securities has exploded. In 1981 trading volume was $0.5 trillion, about half of which was MPT modified pass-through securities, including CMOs. In 1985, the volume was $2 trillion, substantially larger than the volume of trading on all stock exchanges.

# 11 MORTGAGES AND MORTGAGE SECURITY HEDGING

## Introduction

Mortgages and mortgage backed securities are vulnerable to interest rate, refinancing and other risks. Hedging these risks, or shifting them elsewhere, is accomplished either by taking an opposite position to that held. This hedging is achievable by taking opposite positions either in the mortgages or securities themselves, or in options (claims on the securities). There can be arbitrage opportunities in such trading. Markets for such strategies may be incomplete, with no full matching of terms. There are administrative and transactions costs of setting up markets, and charges for trading, brokerage services, taxes, and fees. While securities can be bought or sold short, options are limited in term, and are not available over all maturities. Mortgage risk arises on the quality of borrower and property that may not be replicated identically in a secondary security.

To eliminate certain types of risk, hedgers take an opposite position in the futures market to that owned in the cash market. Speculators take the same position in both cash and futures markets, if they feel they have a better expectation than the market as to the future course of interest rates. Speculators are willing to take increased risk; hedgers lay off risk.

There are risks on future interest rates, suggesting the opportunities for a market. Advance commitments are made on mortgages, but interest rates are unstable prior to commitment. The lender seeks protection for potential losses on warehoused mortgages during a holding period.

### Hedging: Opposite Positions

Hedging can be achieved by selling short securities highly positively correlated with those held long. For a portfolio containing mortgages or mortgage securities, such securities are sold short, to eliminate the risks of rising interest rates and capital loss, or falling interest rates and refinancing. A thrift holding mortgages in its portfolio sells short similar mortgages not owned. Such mortgages have similar term, interest rates, and maturity. A speculative strategy entails increasing or amplifying the risk by taking a long, or hold, position in mortgage securities similar to the mortgages held.

The development of secondary markets for mortgage securities facilitates such laying off of risk and short selling strategies. The thrift or other lender need not carry out the hedge with mortgages, but with mortgage securities. A specific trading vehicle is Ginnie Mae modified pass-through (MPT) securities. The lender sells short these securities, while being long on mortgages. As opposed to hedging, lenders willing to accept additional risk engage in speculation taking the same position in both mortgage and securities markets. A complete hedging strategy eliminates interest rate risk. A speculative strategy for a lender long on mortgages involves purchasing Ginnie Mae securities.

Consider three parties to a real estate financial transaction, a developer, a bank, and a pension fund. The developer constructs the project, the bank is an intermediary, and the pension fund is the ultimate holder of the mortgage. The developer seeks a guaranteed interest rate. The bank is to lend the funds for the development, but does not intend to hold the loan in the mortgage portfolio. Rather, the bank intends to sell the loan to the pension fund.

Suppose there is no hedging. There are two dates of relevance, date of the agreement and the future date for delivery. The lender signs on the agreement date to distribute funds on the delivery date. Since the financing is long term, the asset price of the mortgage is vulnerable to fluctuations in interest rates between the dates of agreement and delivery. The lender is providing a FRPM with a guaranteed interest rate, delivered in the future.[1] On the agreement date, the developer and the bank undertake that the funds will be dispersed according to some fixed interest rate. Also on the agreement date, the bank sells the mortgage to be delivered on the delivery date to the pension fund. Since the bank is not holding the mortgage in its portfolio, or warehousing, the lender has no risk. It acts as a broker between buyer and seller only. Were the bank to warehouse the mortgage, hedging could be required.

The buyer (the pension fund), is subject to interest rate risk. If interest rates decline between the agreement and delivery dates, the bank receives service loan fees, and the pension fund receives a capital gain on the mortgage. The pension fund is holding an asset promising to pay a stream of funds at rates above those in the market. There is refinancing risk to the mortgage buyer. The developer, depending on transactions costs, may seek to refinance the loan at the lower market rates. Any gain to one party in this transaction comes at the expense of the other. If refinancing does not occur, the capital gain to the ultimate lender (the pension fund) is an opportunity loss to the borrower. This zero-sum game in returns involves risk to both parties, for the changes in interest rates or prospects of refinancing are unknown. Hedging reduces or eliminates the risk, and leaves the zero-sum returns unchanged, at a cost of writing the appropriate contracts.

If interest rates rise during the period until delivery, the fund takes a capital loss. The pension fund can hedge its position. It is obliged to take delivery of the mortgage at delivery date. The mortgage is a contingent liability, and the buyer is effectively in a short position on the mortgage. As a complete hedge, the pension fund can buy and hold equivalent mortgage securities as assets. By being long on the mortgage securities, and short on the mortgage, the fund has a complete hedge.

Ginnie Mae contracts of the same value as the mortgage are purchased on the agreement date. On the delivery date, the pension fund sells the Ginnie Mae securities and takes delivery of the mortgage. If the bank warehouses the mortgage during the period between agreement and delivery, it has a long position. The mortgage is an asset on the bank's balance sheet. To hedge its position, the bank sells short Ginnie Mae securities not owned. The asset of the mortgage is balanced by the liability of the mortgage securities. At the agreement date, the bank becomes the seller of the Ginnie Mae securities to the pension fund, and the buyer of these securities on the delivery date. If the Ginnie Mae securities are perfectly positively correlated with the mortgage, the interest rate and refinancing risks are hedged.

On the agreement date, the developer and bank undertake an agreement that loan proceeds will be disbursed effective on the future delivery date. The bank sells the mortgage into the secondary market, with the deal made on the current December 1 price, but with the sale effective February 1. Suppose the loan is for $100 million, with a FRPM contract at 8 percent. The agreement date is December 1, and the delivery date is February 1.

If there is no hedging, the sequence of events is as follows:

**No hedging**

| *Agreement Date* | *Bank* | *Secondary Market* | *Futures Market* |
|---|---|---|---|
| December 1 | Loan made to developer at 8 percent | Sell mortgage to secondary market at December 1 price, to be delivered on February 1. Price is 99 22/32 | No activity |

The price is quoted per $100 of par, in units of 1/32. Suppose rates fall between December 1 and February 1, from 8 percent to 7 percent. Assume that the developer makes no attempt to refinance.

| *Delivery Date* | | | |
|---|---|---|---|
| February 1 | Pay funds to developer | Receive funds from mortgage sale at 99 22/32 per 100, but now market price is 107 12/22 | |

The bank has lost an opportunity to make 107 12/22 instead of the 99 22/32 contracted for. If interest rates rise, to 10 percent, the market price is 86 12/32, but the bank receives 99 22/32, in excess of the market price. The bank bears the interest rate risk.

If there is hedging through long and short positions on the mortgage securities, the transactions are:

**Hedging**

| *Agreement Date* | *Bank* | *Secondary Market* | *Futures Market* |
|---|---|---|---|
| December 1 | Loan made to developer. Funds payable February 1. | *Sell* mortgage to secondary market, for delivery February 1. Price is 99 22/32 at 8 percent | *Buy* future contract. GNMA contract at 99 22/32 |
| *Delivery Date* | | | |
| February 1 | Pay funds to developer | Receive funds from mortgage sale at 99 22/32 per 100, but now market price is 107 12/32. | *Sell* future contract at market of 107 12/32 |
| | | Opportunity loss is 7 22/32 | Profit is 7 22/32 |

The transactions cancel, and the risk of loss from interest rate fluctuations is eliminated. If interest rates increase, a profit is made on the mortgage and a loss is made on the contract. There are costs of setting up the hedge. These costs include brokerage fees for the round-trip buying and selling of the mortgage securities used for the hedge, and recording and administrative costs. The benefit is the reduced risk to all parties.

On the reverse side, the buyer of the mortgage, the pension fund, sells the future contract on December 1, and buys it back on February 1. Otherwise, any interest rate profit by one firm, such as the bank, comes at the expense of the other, such as the pension fund.

There are problems in construction financing that create the opportunities to set up markets for interest rate risk. The parties must make commitments in advance, with future interest rates unknown. The mortgages are warehoused for a period, and the lender holds the financing in its portfolio prior to making a secondary market sale.

The warehousing institution, here the bank, takes the risk of holding the mortgage in its portfolio. In the residential market, mortgage brokers take the risk of holding mortgages prior to sale to the secondary market. By taking an opposite position in the securities market, interest rate risk is hedged. The hedging vehicle is typically not perfectly identical to the asset at risk. The hedge is not perfect, and losses can arise.

The use of a Ginnie Mae contract for hedging eliminates the default risk on the security, though not necessarily on the mortgage itself. Interest rate risk is not hedged, and refinancing risk is not eliminated. If interest rates decline sufficiently during the warehousing period of December 1 to February 1, the developer finds it profitable to refinance. If there is less refinancing activity on the mortgage pools behind the specific Ginnie Mae securities owned, the bank takes losses. The bank loses the mortgage, and the capital gains it would have made, and takes capital losses on its short Ginnie Mae position.

A particular trading unit for interest rate futures, used since October 20, 1975, on the Chicago Board of Trade, is a GNMA MPT certificate for $100,000 at 8 percent per annum. Prices are quoted as percentage of par. The daily trading range has a minimum 0.03125 percent of par or $31.25 per contract, and a maximum of $750 per contract. Delivery occurs in March, June, September and December.

The conversion from yield to price is based on the *GNMA Yield and Price Equivalent Tables.* The typical trading security assumes simple, uncompounded monthly payments of interest and principal at interest rate $r$ on a 30-year mortgage, with prepayment in 12 years.[2] The mortgage multiplier is $m(r/12, 360)$, at the contract interest rate. The present value of the payments over the period up to 12 years, with monthly payments, is $m(r/12, 360)A(r_e/12, 144)$, where $r_e$ is the effective yield. The interest rate $r$ is net of service charges, and is the passed through rate. Per one dollar of loan, the sources and uses of cash are:

**Sources and Uses of Cash, Mortgage Security Investment**
(per one dollar invested)

**Cash Receipts**

During holding period

Mortgage multiplier $m(r/12, 360)$

Times: Present value of annuity of one dollar per year, compounded monthly $A(r_e/12, 144)$

Equals: Present value, passed through mortgage payments $m(r/12, 360)A(r_e/12, 144)$

Projected balloon payment, at expected duration of loan

Loan balance outstanding $b_{144} = 1 - A_{144}/A_{360}$

Times: Present value of one dollar, compounded monthly 144 periods hence

Equals: Present value, balloon payment $b_{144}/(1 + r_e/12)^{144}$

Present value, cash receipts

$m(r/12, 360)A(r_e/12, 144) + b_{144}/(1 + r_e/12)^{144}$

Cash Disbursements

Date of purchase

Purchase price of security 1

Equating the sources and uses of cash, to determine the cash-on-cash return, the rate of return is

$$1 = m(r/12, 360)A(r_e/12, 144) + \frac{b_{144}}{(1 + r_e/12)^{144}} \tag{11.1}$$

where $r_e$ is the yield, for having paid one dollar for the security. The GNMA contract is traded in units of $100,000. Points and fees on the mortgage pool are taken out by the lender in advance.

The hedger exposed to risk from having sold a mortgage or mortgage security, buys a mortgage security contract. This strategy is long or buy hedging. If interest rates fall, and the contracts gain in price, there is a balance of the capital loss on the mortgage. There are effects of both capital loss and refinancing, but both risks are hedged by taking the opposite position with the mortgage security. If interest rates fall, and the contracts fall in price, the mortgages are sold for above the initial issuing price. The risk of the mortgage is laid off to the market. The hedger surrenders potential profit from interest rates or refinancing, but the risk is eliminated. For an institution relying on servicing fees, and points for revenue, such as a thrift, a hedging strategy eliminates the risk arising from warehousing the mortgages and securities. There are transactions costs for buying and selling the contracts.

The hedger exposed to risk from having a mortgage or mortgage security as an asset sells short a mortgage security. This strategy is short or sell hedging. Speculative, as opposed to hedging strategies, imply taking the same position in both markets. The investor who holds mortgages as assets buys mortgage securities. The investor who has sold a mortgage, but retains the risk of interest rates or refinancing, for having sold ahead, sells short a mortgage security.

## Hedging: Option Trading

### *Option Pricing*

An alternative method of hedging mortgage or mortgage security risk is to use options. Instead of selling mortgage securities short to balance a long mortgage position, the hedger or speculator takes a position in the options market.

An option gives the holder the right to purchase or sell a security at a specific price on a specific date. The specific price is the strike, exercise, or contract price. The specific date is the maturity or exercise date. Options to purchase securities written by individuals are calls. Options to sell securities are puts. An American option can be exercised prior to the maturity date. A European option can only be exercised on the maturity date. Since an American option provides more flexibility than a European option, it sells for a higher price. Options issued by corporations are warrants or rights. Rights are usually issued for a short and warrants for a long time period. A contract to purchase commodities is a commodity option. An option contract to purchase or sell mortgage securities can be used as a hedging vehicle.

Any contingent claim on the liability side of the balance sheet can be viewed as an option. The characteristics are a predetermined price and maturity date. Insurance policies where a particular price is paid on a certain date can be priced as options throughout the period they are in force. Convertible preferred shares have an option characteristic.

Options can be used to hedge a mortgage portfolio. An investor who owns a security, such as a mortgage backed security, or has a long position, sells short call options in that security, should a market for such options exist. Where the security pays a cash return, such as a mortgage payment, the option model can be extended. While such payouts are unlikely for stocks, they are the rule for FRPM loans and securities. Hence option pricing is particularly appropriate for mortgages and mortgage securities.

The price of an option is derived from an equilibrium hedging condition.[3] The price is based on a European call, and the security pays no dividends. The assumptions are:

1. The short-term interest rate is known and constant.
2. The price of the underlying security follows a random walk in continuous time with a variance proportional to the square of the price. The distribution of the logarithm of the security price is normal, or the price is distributed lognormal. The variance is constant over time at $\sigma^2$.

3. The security pays no interest, and there are no buying or selling transactions costs. If interest is payable, it arises at a constant rate.
4. The security is divisible and short selling is permitted.

The relationship between the price of a security and its option is indicated in figure 11-1. On the horizontal axis is the price of the security. Suppose there is a mortgage backed security with price $y$, on which an option is written. The price of the option is $P$ per unit, on the vertical axis. The option provides the right to sell one unit of the security at $\gamma$ dollars at the maturity date $t$.

The maximum price of the option, max $y$, occurs along a 45-degree line for $y = P$, since the option cannot sell for more than the security. The minimum price, or min $P$, is given by

$$\min P = \max(0, y - \gamma)$$

Suppose the option provides the holder the right to sell one unit of the security at $\gamma = \$20$ on a given maturity date. If the price of the security is $y = \$25$ at that date, the investor makes a \$5 profit, but if the price of the

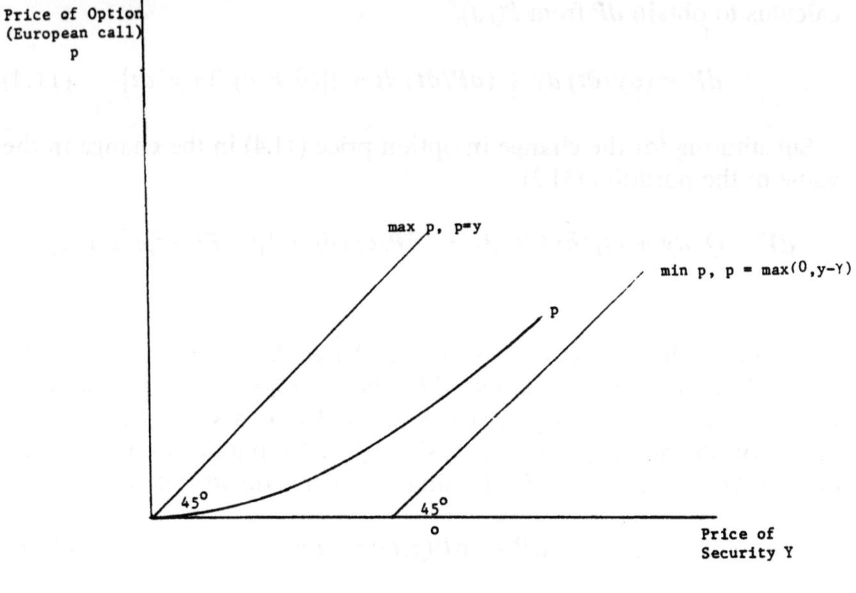


Figure 11-1. Option Pricing

security is \$15, the option is worth zero. As the maturity decreases, the option price path tends towards min $P$, but can vary within the boundaries, for a given security price sequence. The price of the option is more volatile than the price of the underlying security.

With a complete option market in equilibrium, the risk of holding the security can be hedged by selling short an appropriate number of call options. Suppose the security being held is a Ginnie Mae or other residential or commercial mortgage backed security. Let the quantities held of the security and its option be $Q_y$ and $Q_P$ respectively. Then the value of the portfolio is

$$V = yQ_y + PQ_P \tag{11.2}$$

the sum of the value of the security holding $yQ_y$ and the value of the option holding is $PQ_P$. Suppose prices change, but the quantities held do not. The change in value of the portfolio is

$$dV = Q_y\,dy + Q_P\,dP \tag{11.3}$$

Now the price of the option $P(y,t)$ is dependent on the price of the security and time. The security price is stochastic, and so stochastic calculus is required to obtain the change in the option price $dP$. Using stochastic calculus to obtain $dP$ from $P(y,t)$,[4]

$$dP = (\partial y/\partial t)\,dy + (\partial P/\partial t)\,dt + \tfrac{1}{2}[(\partial^2 P/\partial y^2)\sigma^2 y^2\,dt] \tag{11.4}$$

Substituting for the change in option price (11.4) in the change in the value of the portfolio (11.3)

$$dV = Q_y\,dy + Q_P(\partial y/\partial t)\,dy + (\partial P/\partial t)\,dt + \tfrac{1}{2}[(\partial^2 P/\partial y^2)\sigma^2 y^2)\,dt] \tag{11.5}$$

The value of this portfolio is stochastic. Perfect hedging implies that the value of the portfolio is unaffected by the appropriate short position on the call option, if the mortgage security is held as an asset. The price of the option on the mortgage security is $P = P(y,t)$. Taking the total derivative, $dP = (\partial P/\partial y)\,dy + (\partial P/\partial t)\,dt$. Holding time constant, $dt = 0$, so

$$dP = [\partial P(y,t)/\partial y]\,dy \tag{11.6}$$

The overall portfolio will change by

$$dV = Q_y\,dy + Q_P\,(\partial P/\partial y)\,dy \tag{11.7}$$

To be fully and completely hedged, the value of the portfolio after the strategy should be unchanged, or $dV = 0$. Then substituting

$$0 = Q_y + Q_P\,\partial P/\partial y \tag{11.8}$$

or $-Q_y = Q_P\,\partial P/\partial y$, and $Q_y/Q_P = -\partial P/\partial y$, and $Q_P/Q_y = -1/(\partial P/\partial y)$. If the ratio of the quantity held of the security to that of the call option, $Q_y/Q_P$, is equated with the response of the option price to the security price, $-\partial P/\partial y$, then the portfolio is fully hedged. The portfolio is fully hedged in that the value of the total portfolio is unaffected, or $dV = 0$, by any change in strategy. To be hedged against any risk from fluctuation in the price of the security, for each one unit of the security or $Q_y = 1$, $Q_P$ must be $-1/(\partial P/\partial y)$. The number of call options sold short is $\partial y/\partial P$, the change in the security price with respect to the option price. Substituting these quantities in the change of the value of the portfolio

$$dV = -\left(\frac{1}{\partial P/\partial y}\right)\left[\left(\frac{\partial P}{\partial t}\right) + 0.5\left(\frac{\partial^2 P}{\partial y^2 \sigma^2 y^2}\right)\right] dt$$

With the security priced at \$15, and $\gamma = 20$, the price of the option is \$5. If the slope of the option price, the security price line, is ⅓, the hedged portfolio is constructed by buying one unit of the security and selling three call options short.

The equilibrium condition is that two securities that are perfect substitutes earn the same return. Then the rate of return on the portfolio is the riskless rate, since the risk has been hedged away. Let this riskless return be $\rho$. Then the percentage rate of return is

$$dV/V = \rho\,dt$$

Since $V = y - P/(\partial y/\partial y)$, then

$$dV = dt\left[\rho y - \left(\frac{\rho P}{\partial P/\partial y}\right)\right]$$

$$= -\left(\frac{1}{\partial P/\partial y}\right)\left[\left(\frac{\partial P}{\partial t}\right) + 0.5\left(\frac{\partial^2 P}{\partial y^2 \sigma^2 y^2}\right)\right] dt$$

implying

$$\rho y - \left(\frac{\rho P}{\partial P/\partial y}\right) = -\left(\frac{1}{\partial P/\partial y}\right)\left[\left(\frac{\partial P}{\partial t}\right) + 0.5\left(\frac{\partial^2 P}{\partial y^2 \sigma^2 y^2}\right)\right]$$

whereupon

$$\frac{\partial P}{\partial t} = \rho P - \frac{\rho y\, \partial P}{\partial y} - 0.5\left(\frac{\partial^2 P}{\partial y^2 \sigma^2 y^2}\right) \tag{11.9}$$

is the relation of the price movement of the option in time, a differential equation subject to the boundary condition that at the maturity date $t$

$$P_t = \max\,(0, y_t - \gamma) \tag{11.10}$$

where $y_t$ is the price of the security at the exercise date, and $P_t$ is the price of the option at the exercise date. Solution of this differential equation requires a specification as to the behavior of the security price movement.

### *Security Price Movements*

Some results on the behavior of security prices are required to complete the option pricing specification. If $y$, the mortgage security price, has a lognormal distribution, then the probability density function of $y$ is

$$f(y) = 2\pi^{-0.5} y^{-1} \sigma^{-1} \exp\left[-0.5\left(\frac{\ln y - \mu}{\sigma}\right)^2\right] \qquad 0 < y < \infty \tag{11.11}$$

where $y$ is variable and strictly positive. The logarithm of the security price, $\ln y$ is distributed normally with mean $\mu$ and variance $\sigma^2$. The expected value of $y$ is $\mu + \sigma^2/2$. The price of the mortgage security currently is $y$, and $y_1$ at time 1. The relative price is $w_1 = y_1/y$, and the ratio of the mortgage security price at exercise date to the current price is $y_t/y$. Then

$$\begin{aligned} k_t = y_t/y &= (y_1/y) \times (y_2/y_1) \times \cdots \times (y_t/y_{t-1}) \\ &= \prod_{s=1}^{t} w_s \end{aligned} \tag{11.12}$$

where $w_s = (y_s/y_{s-1})$ and $\ln w_s = \ln y_s - \ln y_{s-1} = \Delta \ln y_s$, the percentage change in the security price. This percentage change $\ln w_s$ is assumed to be independently and identically normally distributed as $n(\mu,\sigma^2)$ where $\mu$ is the mean percentage increase, and $\sigma^2$ the variance. Now

$$\ln y_t - \ln y = \sum_{s=1}^{t} \ln w_s \tag{11.13}$$

is the percentage increase in the security price between the current date and $t$, the exercise date. Under the independent and identical specification, since a sum of normal distributions is normally distributed, $\ln y_t - \ln y$ is distributed $n(\mu t,\sigma^2 t)$. The probability that the security increases in price by between 0 and 5 percent annually is equal to the probability that it decreases in price between 0 and 5 percent annually.

Without imposing the restriction that the security prices are independently and identically distributed, and with $k_s = y_s/y$, the relative price of the mortgage security at exercise date $s \leqslant t$ to the current date is

$$f(k_s) = 2\pi^{-0.5} k_s^{-1} \sigma_s^{-1} \exp\left[-0.5\left(\frac{\ln k_s - \mu_s}{\sigma_s}\right)^2\right] \qquad 0 \leqslant k_s \leqslant \infty$$

where $\ln k_s$ is distributed $n(\mu_s,\sigma_s^2)$.

### Call Option

A call option provides the right to buy the mortgage security at exercise date $t$, at exercise price $\beta$. The price of the mortgage security at the exercise date is $y_t = k_t y$, or $k_t = y_t/y$. If $y_t > \beta$, the option with European feature has a positive terminal, or exercise date price $c_t = y_t - \beta$. The price of the option is

$$\begin{aligned} &\text{if } k_t > \beta/y \qquad \text{then } c_t = y_t - \beta > 0 \\ &\text{if } k_t < \beta/y \qquad \text{then } c_t = 0 \end{aligned} \tag{11.14}$$

The exercise price of the option is $\beta$, and the current price of the security is $y$. So $\beta/y$ is the target ratio. Any increase in the actual relative price of the security $k_t = y_t/y$ in excess of $\beta/y$ implies that the option has a positive price. Otherwise the option is worthless. The distribution of the exercise date call option price is truncated over the random variable $k_t$, with $\beta$, the exercise price, $t$ the exercise date, and $y$, the current price all fixed. If $k_s > \beta$, for $s < t$, then the option is in the money. An in the money option is one whose prire, prior to the exercise date, exceeds the exercise price. The expected price of the call option at exercise date is

$$E(c_t) = y\int_{\beta/y}^{\infty} (k_t - \beta/y) f(k_t)\, dk_t$$

$$= y \exp(\rho_t) N\left[\frac{\rho_t + \sigma_t^2/2 - \ln(\beta/y)}{\sigma_t}\right] \tag{11.15}$$

$$- \beta N\left[\frac{\rho_t - \sigma_t^2/2 - \ln(\beta/y)}{\sigma_t}\right]$$

This result, and others an option pricing, is derived in the appendix. Here $\rho_t = \mu_t + \sigma_t^2/2$ is the geometric mean and $N(w)$ is the distribution function of $n$ the normal distribution evaluated at $w$. The expected current price $c$ of the option is

$$E(c) = yN\left[\frac{\rho_t + \sigma_t^2/2 - \ln(\beta/y)}{\sigma_t}\right]$$

$$- \beta \exp(-\rho_t) N\left[\frac{\rho_t - \sigma_t^2/2 - \ln(\beta/y)}{\sigma_t}\right] \tag{11.16}$$

If the relative incomes $w_s$ in $k_t = \Pi_{s=0}^{t} w_s$ are independently and identically distributed (iid) as lognormal, $\rho_t = \rho t$ and $\sigma_t^2 = \sigma^2 t$.[5] The expected current price of the option $E(c)$ is

$$E(c) = \lambda yN\left[\frac{\rho t + \sigma^2 t - \ln(\beta/y)}{\sigma t^{0.5}}\right]$$

$$- \lambda\beta \exp(-\rho t) N\left[\frac{\rho t - \sigma_t^2/2 - \ln(\beta/y)}{\sigma t^{0.5}}\right] \tag{11.17}$$

### *Put Option*

A put option on the mortgage security provides the right to sell. Let the exercise price be $\gamma$. Then the target ratio is $\beta/y$. If the ratio of the security price at the exercise to the current date $k_t = y_t/y$ exceeds $\gamma/y$, the option is worthless. If $k_t$ is below $\gamma/y$, the option has a positive price.

The European put option, with exercise price $P_t$ at date $t$ is

$$\begin{aligned} &\text{if } k_t > \gamma/y \qquad \text{then } P_t = 0 \\ &\text{if } k_t < \gamma/y \qquad \text{then } P_t = y_t - \gamma > 0 \end{aligned} \tag{11.18}$$

The expected exercise date price of the put option is

$$\begin{aligned} E(P_t) &= \lambda y \int_0^{\gamma/y} (k_t - \gamma/y) f(k_t)\, dk_t \\ &= \beta N\left[\frac{\ln(\gamma/y) - \mu_t}{\sigma_t}\right] - y \exp(\rho_t) N\left[\frac{\ln(\gamma/y) - \mu_t - \sigma_t^2}{\sigma_t}\right] \end{aligned} \tag{11.19}$$

The current price of the option is

$$\begin{aligned} E(P) = \beta \exp(-\rho_t) N&\left[\frac{\ln(\gamma/y) - \rho_t - \sigma_t^2/2}{\sigma_t}\right] \\ - yN&\left[\frac{\ln(\gamma/y) - \rho_t + \sigma_t^2/2}{\sigma_t}\right] \end{aligned} \tag{11.20}$$

Under the independent and identical specification $\rho_t = \rho t$ and $\sigma_t^2 = \sigma^2 t$, so

$$\begin{aligned} E(P) = \beta \exp(-\rho t) N&\left[\frac{\ln(\gamma/y) - \rho t - \sigma^2 t/2}{\sigma t^{0.5}}\right] \\ - yN&\left[\frac{\ln(\gamma/y) - \rho t + \sigma^2 t/2}{\sigma t^{0.5}}\right] \end{aligned} \tag{11.21}$$

The option pricing model can be applied to any contingent claim on a firm or individual. In real estate markets, contingent claims include insurance policies providing a certain pay-off at a particular date. Mortgage insurance can be priced as an option, if there is a specific pay-off date. The model has been applied to the pricing of risk-adjusted deposit insurance for lenders. Thrifts are subject to deposit insurance protection, and the benefit of deposit insurnace is an additional asset to some lenders. Another application lies in the brokerage sector, where there are frequently production targets or quotas established for brokers. The firm has an option on the services of the real estate sales people.

### *Options Behavior*

Options are used by holders of mortgage portfolios to hedge their interest rate risk. Options are available against broadly based indexes of securities, and if these move in directions opposite to interest rates, an options trading strategy lays off interest rate risk. All interest rates do not move in tandem. Mortgage interest rates may not decline when interest rates on long-term securities decline, if holders of whole loans or mortgage backed securities require compensation for potential refinancing risk.

The investor purchasing a long-term United States Treasury bond obtains a security with no refinancing option. The holder of a mortgage security has sold an American call option, exercisable at any time, in addition to investing in a long-term bond, even if the term is similar to that on the Treasury seucrity. As interest rates in the market decline, particularly on long-term securities, the holder of the Treasury security obtains a capital gain. The holder of the mortgage security and the call option seller finds that the call option is worth more to the buyer. To compensate for the increased liability on the call option, the interest rate on the bond component of the mortgage security, or interest rate on the underlying mortgages, must be increased.

As interest rates rise, capital losses are obtained on both securities. The refinancing rate on the pool of mortgages behind the mortgage security declines, and the price of the call option declines and can become worthless. Interest rates on mortgage securities need not move in tandem with interest rates in general.

The investor holding mortgage securities long, and desiring to hedge, buys a call option in similar securities. The effect of the hedge is to lock in current prices for the mortgage securities. This option conveys the right to buy at a predetermined price, the strike price, until the option expires, typically in three months or less.

With a perfect hedge, the holder of mortgage securities sells call options short to satisfy the equilibrium condition. The hedge is perfect if the call options are on the exact security held. The call option on the mortgage security provides the right to buy that security, itself a package of a bond and a refinancing or call option for the borrower—a liability for the lender.

The price of an option depends on how close the strike price is to the actual price, the time remaining before the option expires, and demand and supply. An option purchase is pure speculation in that for every buyer of a call, there must be a seller who has the opposite view. Naked sellers sell options that are not owned. If they are selling calls, they gain if the exercise date price of the mortgage security does not exceed the strike price. The seller of a put option gains if the exercise date price of the security remains above the strike price. These investors are selling term insurance for portfolios.

The buyer of an option has limited losses. The limit is the amount paid for the option. The seller of an option has unlimited risk. Regardless of the terminal price, the seller is required to honor the contract.

Suppose the underlying mortgage security price is 100 on a given date, January 21, and call options exist. In buying a call option, an option buyer, seeking to hedge or speculate, buys 10 calls at a a strike price of 101, expiring March 31, or 10 March 101 calls. The security has until March 31 to increase one point. The current price of the call option is 3/16 dollars, with options quoted in 1/16 units, and this price can be determined from the pricing model. If the contract entails buying 1000 options each for one unit of the mortgage security, the cost is $3000/16, or $187.50. The buyer has potential control over 1000 units of the mortgage security, each currently priced at 100, or $100,000 of assets. The investor has large potential leverage, with the attendant risk. A trading vehicle is the 8 percent Ginnie Mae certificate with units of $100,000. If the security fails to increase to $101 by the exercise date, the buyer of the call option loses the investment of $187.50. The seller of the call option must make good on any realized price above $101. The buyer of the call option is paying for insurance, and the seller acts as an insurer.

Out-of-the-money options are calls where the strike price exceeds the current security price, or put options where the strike price is below the current security price. If the mortgage security price has already exceeded the strike price, on a call option, it is "in the money." In the above case, as in-the-money option occurs where the security price exceeds 101 prior to March 31, and an investor holds March 101 calls.

The short term of options requires regular, almost continuous trading, and watching the market. Unless one is a professional trader, it is difficult to maintain contact with the market. The trader must keep buying and selling options to maintain a hedged position, which generates commissions and transactions costs. Not all securities have options written.

### *Risk with Hedging and Speculation*

There are several problems with hedging and speculation. A matching problem arises between the mortgages to be hedged and the securities to be used as the hedging vehicle. Mortgages are heterogeneous in characteristics of the borrower and the property. Ginnie Mae securities themselves are based on different pools. Unless the behavior of the security exactly matches the behavior of the borrowers on payment, prepayment, and default the risk is incompletely hedged. Since real estate and borrowers are heterogeneous, this matching is likely to be incomplete.

There are accounting restrictions. The Financial Accounting Standards Board (FASB) has regulations as to how a hedged position can be reflected on financial statements. The FASB requires a high correlation between the security used as the hedging vehicle and the mortgage portfolio being hedged against.

A hedging strategy implies that profits are surrendered to reduce risk. Profits otherwise to be made as capital gains on mortgages are lost on the hedge. There are transactions costs of commissions, fees, and supervisory time. Nevertheless, it is possible to reduce both interest rate and refinancing risks through hedging mortgage securities. Speculation entails increasing both forms of risk, if an investor has expectations about the future course of interest rates and refinancing that are believed superior to the market.

### Mortgage Securities and Straddle Options

A straddle option involves the simultaneous purchase or sale of a put and call. With a FRPM mortgage, if the market interest rate falls below the contract rate, the borrower can exercise the right to refinance, depending on transactions costs. The refinancing right is a continuous call option. If the interest rate rises, the lender has no right to call the loan, and the borrower has the right to mortgage equity, or below-market financing costs.

The holder of a mortgage, either in whole form, or as part of a mortgage security, is effectively the seller of a straddle option to the borrower. The payment for the straddle option package comes in the form of a higher interest rate than on a pure bond. The mortgage security holder is expecting that market interest rates, even if volatile, do not deviate substantially from the initial contract rate. If there is low deviation, the seller of the straddle, the mortgage security holder, benefits, by collecting the interest rate premium, the option payment. If there is a large deviation, the buyer of the straddle, the borrower, exercises whichever option is in the money. With a large decline in interest rates, the borrower refinances. With a large increase, the borrower does not refinance, and the lender or security holder assumes a capital loss. The seller of the straddle acts as an insurer against both upside and downside interest rate risk for the buyer of the straddle.

Even with no hedging, the buyer of a mortgage security is the seller of a straddle option package to the borrower on a FRPM. The mortgage security holder bears the risk of capital losses if interest rates rise, and refinancing if interest rates fall. For bearing these risks on open options to put and call the mortgage, premiums are paid by the borrower in the form of higher interest rates for a FRPM than on a ARM. The mortgage security holder, as for any straddle option seller, benefits, and retains the premium, if future interest rates remain within a narrow range, close to current rates. The greater the weight of the distribution of interest rates toward the tails, of high or low rates, the greater the risk of loss for the straddle holder.

The term "lender" is applied to describe an investor holding a mortgage or mortgage backed security as an asset, or in a long position. The "borrower" is the person making payments on the mortgage. These payments may be passed through to the lender via a mortgage backed security. The risk requiring hedging is the same, regardless of whether the lender is a thrift institution with a portfolio mortgage or an individual investor in a Ginnie Mae security.

The contract interest rate paid on a FRPM mortgage, subsequently packaged into a security, is based on an expected interest rate assumed to apply in the immediate period ahead. In this period 1, let the expected interest rate be $E(r_1)$. On a single-period basis, the fixed contract interest rate $r$ on the mortgage is

$$r = r(\text{ARM}) + P[E(r_1,p)] + c[E(r_1,p)] \qquad (11.22)$$

where $r(\text{ARM})$ is the interest rate applied for adjustable rate mortgages on similar properties and borrowers, but providing no restriction on short-run interest rate movements. The price of the call option to refinance $c$ depends on market interest rates expected on newly issued FRPMs, and the transactions costs of refinancing, summarized by points $p$. As the rate of points increases, refinancing is less likely. As interest rates fall, refinancing is more likely, so the option is more valuable to the borrower. The option $P[E(r_1,p)]$ refers to the capital gain or loss to the lender, as the borrower exercises the right to retain the mortgage.

The premium on the mortgage is

$$r - r(\text{ARM}) = P[E(r_1,p)] + c[E(r_1,p)]. \qquad (11.23)$$

The premium is the interest rate differential between the FRPM and an

ARM on a comparable property and borrower. The lender, either the holder of the mortgage or mortgage backed security, receives this differential as a premium from the borrower. In exchange for the premium, the lender bears the risk by holding as liabilities the two options, respectively priced at $P$ and $c$. Having sold the options, the lender must make good on them should they be exercised. The interest rate $r_1$ is random, so the lender carries the risk.

The ex post, or realized, yield to the lender depends on the behavior of the two options in the straddle package sold to the borrower. If the difference between the actual interest rate $r_1$ and the contract rate $r$ is zero, neither option is valuable. The borrower does not elect to refinance, so $c = 0$, and there are no capital gains or losses from interest rate movements, so $P = 0$. Then the realized yield premium $r_e$ on the FRPM mortgage is

$$\text{if} \quad P = 0 \quad \text{and} \quad c = 0 \qquad \text{then} \quad r_e = r - r(\text{ARM})$$

and the insurer (the lender) makes no payment.

More generally, the lender would carry the two options on the balance sheet as liabilities. If the actual interest rate $r_1$ is any number except that expected, or $E(r_1)$, one or both of the two options has a nonzero price. The yield premium on the FRPM mortgage investment is

$$r_e = r - r(\text{ARM}) - P(r_1,p) - c(r_1,p) \tag{11.24}$$

The interest rate $r(\text{ARM})$ covers the risk of the property and borrower. The remaining components of the yield premium cover the financial, as opposed to the physical, aspects of the real estate investment.

The put option, or interest rate risk option, can have a positive or negative price $P$. The put option is held as a liability by the lender. If $P$ is positive, interest rates for new FRPMs exceed $r$, the contract rate. A capital loss is obtained by the lender, since funds lent on existing loans receive a higher interest rate on new loans. If interest rates for new FRPMs are lower than the rate on the contract, the lender has a capital gain, treated as a negative liability, or an asset, with $P$ negative.

For the put option if $p = 0$ or capital gains or losses from interest rate movements,

$$P(r_1,p) > 0 \qquad \text{if}\, r_1 < r$$

$$P(r_1,p) = 0 \qquad \text{if}\, r_1 = r$$

$$P(r_1,p) < 0 \qquad \text{as}\, r_1 < r$$

For the call option to refinance, if $p = 0$

$$c(r_1,p) > 0 \qquad \text{if } r_1 < r$$
$$c(r_1,p) = 0 \qquad \text{if } r_1 \geqslant r \tag{11.26}$$

There are no transactions costs of refinancing. If there are points or other charges, the above conditions do not hold. As general interest rates fall, $r$(ARM), the market interest rate on continuously adjustable rate mortgages, declines also. The premium received on the FRPM, or $r - r$(ARM) increases, but so does the risk to the lender. The option to refinance, $c$, becomes more valuable as interest rates decline, so the lender is vulnerable to the loss of the high interest rate investment. Additional compensation for the risk is required, so the premium increases. A decline in interest rates, for given transactions costs $p$, implies that $P(r_1,p)$ becomes negative, that is, the lender obtains a capital gain. The lender is holding an asset returning a higher interest rate than that prevailing in the market.

The effective yield to the holder of a FRPM has three components. The first is the premium, the differential between the fixed contract interest rate $r$ and the interest rate prevailing on fully adjustable ARMs, $r$(ARM). This premium is paid by the borrower for interest rate and refinancing flexibility. The second is the liability for payment on the put option, representing interest rate risk. This option is carried as a liability by the lender, but is an asset if interest rates decline, generating a capital gain. The third component is the refinancing option with price $c$. This option is always a liability to the lender.

The condition for the lender to lose on the options regardless of the movement of interest rates is

$$c(r_1,p) > |P(r_1,p)| \qquad \text{if } r_1 < r$$
$$P(r_1,p) > 0 \qquad \text{if } r_1 > r \tag{11.27}$$

The borrower benefits both ways. If interest rates decline, the refinancing effect outweighs the capital gain on the mortgage. If interest rates rise, the refinancing option is worthless, and the lender absorbs all the capital loss. The premium yield to the lender $r_e$ is lower than the interest rate differential $r - r$(ARM).

The lender cannot benefit if interest rates rise.[6] The net return on the mortgage contains two risky components, for $c$, or refinancing risk, and $P$, interest rate risk. The holder seeks to hedge these risks, as the borrower has transferred the risks to the lender.

The pricing of $P$ is determined by recalculation of the capital loss at each changed interest rate, with refinancing constant. The refinancing loss requires estimation of the propensity to refinance when interest rates change.

### Mortgage Backed Security Purchase Warrants

Mortgage backed security purchase warrants provide a mechanism for reducing the refinancing risk on Ginnie Maes and on callable bonds. Purchase warrants permit the buyer to hedge, conveying the right to buy 8 percent Ginnie Mae securities one year in the future. The warrant buys the right on May 1 of a given year to buy $1,000 face value of Ginnie Maes at an exercise price dollars on May 1 one year ahead. Suppose the Ginnie Mae securities are trading at $912.50. If interest rates fall, the warrant permits the holder to continue having the right to buy the Ginnie Mae security, as opposed to losing this right if the securities alone are held and the underlying mortgages are refinanced. The price of the warrant is determined analogously to that for an option.

If the price of underlying securities falls, the warrant price falls. If the Ginnie Mae price rises, the warrants rise in price. Warrants are fully transferable, creating a secondary market. Warrants are more volatile in price, because of the leverage involved. Small changes in the price of Ginnie Maes can have large effects on warrant prices. Warrants are of interest to holders of Ginnie Mae securities and other holders of callable debt, such as corporate bonds. Both holders are at risk if interest rates fall and refinancing takes place. As interest rates fall, corporations call bonds and mortgage holders refinance, prepaying the mortgage, leaving the Ginnie Mae holder with no investment. Warrants permit holders to profit if interest rates fall, hedging the refinancing risk.

Fluctuations in prices of Ginnie Maes arise from various risks, including risks from interest rates and refinancing, implying a demand for hedging vehicles. Hedging by conventional methods, such as short selling, does not work effectively because of refinancing risk.

Normally, sellers delivering Ginnie Maes can deliver 5 percent more or less than promised. Under warrants, investors taking delivery of warrants are guaranteed a variation of 2.5 percent, giving a better chance of having all securities paid for.

Warrants reduce but do not elimiante refinancing risk. The risk hedged is that a specific Ginnie Mae position will not have a higher than average refinancing. if all of the mortgages behind a given Ginnie Mae are refinanced, there is no security. Yet Ginnie Maes as a whole remain in the market, so the warrant enables the purchase of another security at a guaranteed price. The price of the Ginnie Mae behind the warrant is affected by the average tendency to refinance when interest rates fall. Only the undiversified refinancing risk is hedged.

### Concluding Remarks

Mortgages are long-term investments. Risk arises from there being FRPM securities over 30 years, and the future is uncertain. With a mortgage, the borrower has the propensity to pay off the loan early, thereby exposing the ultimate holder to a removal of the investment. When interest rates rise, the borrower tends not to refinance or to move, another risk potentially requiring hedging. Those long on the mortgage market, or the ultimate holders of the mortgage, can seek to hedge their positions. Long holders include institutional investors, such as pension funds and insurance companies, lenders such as thrifts, and individual investors in mortgage backed securities. Short selling of the securities or call options are alternative hedging methods.

A completely hedged strategy removes all the risk from a given holding. The player, no longer receiving any more than the riskless rate of return from the investment, is presumably receiving income from other activities. In real estate, such income can include fees, commissions, and points. Hedging is not without risk. The securities being sold short, or where options have been written, may not be identical to those being hedged against. There are transactions costs of commissions and monitoring for firms engaged in risk management. Hedging is only profitable if the saving in risk outweighs the cost of buying the insurance, and the transactions costs.

# APPENDIX 11 EXPECTED OPTION PRICES

## Call Option

The terminal price of the security is $y_t = k_t y$, or $k_t = y_t/y$. The exercise price is $\beta$. Then if $y_t > \beta$, the option with European feature has a positive terminal, or exercise date, price $c_t = y_t - \beta$. The option test is

$$\text{if} \quad k_t > \beta \qquad \text{then} \quad c_t = y_t - \beta > 0$$

$$\text{if} \quad k_t < \beta \qquad \text{then} \quad c_t = 0$$

This is a truncated distribution over the random variable $k_t$, with $\beta$ the exercise price, $t$ the exercise date, and $y$ the current price all fixed. If $k_s > \beta$, for $s < t$, then the option is "in the money." Here $k_s$ is the relative price at some date prior to exercise. The expected price of the call option at exercise date is

$$E(c_t) = y\int_{\beta/y}^{\infty}(k_t - \beta/y)f(k_t)\,dk_t$$

$$= y(2\pi)^{-0.5}\sigma_t^{-1}\int_{\beta/y}^{\infty}\left(\frac{k_t - \beta/y}{k_t}\right)\exp\left[-0.5\left(\frac{\ln k_t - \mu_t}{\sigma_t}\right)^2\right]dk_t$$

If $k_t$ is lognormally distributed,

$$E(c_t) = y(2\pi)^{-0.5}\sigma_t^{-1}\int_{\ln(\beta/y)}^{\infty}\exp(x_t)\exp\left[-0.5\left(\frac{\ln x_t - \mu_t}{\sigma_t}\right)^2\right]dx_t$$

$$- \beta(2\pi)^{-0.5}\sigma_t^{-1}\int_{\ln(\beta/y)}^{\infty}\exp\left[-0.5\left(\frac{x_t - \mu_t}{\sigma_t}\right)^2\right]dx_t$$

Changing variables, defining $x_t = \ln k_t$,

$E(c_t) =$

$$y(2\pi)^{-0.5}\sigma_t^{-1}\exp(\mu_t + \sigma_t^2/2)\int_{\ln(\beta/y)}^{\infty}\exp\left[-0.5\left(\frac{\ln x_t - \mu_t - \sigma_t^2}{\sigma_t}\right)^2\right]dx_t$$

$$- \beta(2\pi)^{-0.5}\sigma_t^{-1}\int_{\ln(\beta/y)}^{\infty}\exp\left[-0.5\left(\frac{x_t - \mu_t}{\sigma_t}\right)^2\right]dx_t$$

This price is based on the difference between two normal distributions $n(\mu_t + \sigma_t^2, \sigma_t^2)$ and $n(\mu_t, \sigma_t^2)$, so

$$E(c_t) = y(2\pi)^{-0.5}\sigma_t^{-1}\exp(\mu_t + \sigma_t^2/2)\int_{\beta 1}^{\infty}\exp(-0.5v^2)\,dv$$

$$- \beta(2\pi)^{-0.5}\sigma_t^{-1}\int_{\beta 2}^{\infty}\exp(-0.5v^2)\,dv$$

where $v$ is has the standard normal density function $n(0,1)$ with mean 0 and variance 1 and $\beta 1 = [\ln(\beta/y) - \mu_t - \sigma_t^2]/\sigma_t$ and $\beta 2 = [\ln(\beta/y) - \mu_t]/\sigma_t$. Then

$$E(c_t) = y\exp(\rho_t)N\left[\frac{\rho_t + \sigma_t^2/2 - \ln(\beta/y)}{\sigma_t}\right] - \beta N\left[\frac{\rho_t + \sigma_t^2/2 - \ln(\beta/y)}{\sigma_t}\right]$$

where $\rho_t = \mu_t + \sigma_t^2/2$ is the geometric mean and $N(v)$ is the distribution function of $n$ evaluated at $v$. The current price of the option is

$$E(c) = yN\left[\frac{\rho_t + \sigma_t^2/2 - \ln(\beta/y)}{\sigma_t}\right]$$

$$- \beta \exp(-\rho_t)N\left[\frac{\rho_t - \sigma_t^2/2 - \ln(\beta/y)}{\sigma_t}\right]$$

If the relative prices $w_s$ in $k_t = \Pi_{s=0}^{t} w_s$ are independently and identically distributed (iid) as lognormal, $\rho_t = \rho t$ and $\sigma_t^2 = \sigma^2 t$. Hence

$$E(c) = yN\left[\frac{\rho t + \sigma^2 t - \ln(\beta/y)}{\sigma t^{0.5}}\right]$$

$$- \beta \exp(-\rho t)N\left[\frac{\rho t - \sigma_t^2/2 - \ln(\beta/y)}{\sigma t^{0.5}}\right]$$

The call option can be applied to the derivation of bonuses, such as those paid to securities or real estate brokers. Suppose the bonus specifies rate $\lambda$ if the price exceeds a given amount. Then

$$\text{if} \quad k_t > \beta \qquad c_t = \lambda y_t > 0$$

$$\text{if} \quad k_t < \beta \qquad c_t = 0$$

The expected price of the option to receive a bonus is

$$E(c_t)$$

$$= \lambda y \int_{\beta/y}^{\infty} k_t f(k_t)\, dk_t$$

$$= \lambda y (2\pi)^{-0.5} \sigma_t^{-1} \int_{\beta/y}^{\infty} \exp\left[-0.5\left(\frac{\ln k_t - \mu_t}{\sigma_t}\right)^2\right] dk_t$$

$$= \lambda y (2\pi)^{-0.5} \sigma_t^{-1} \exp(\mu_t + \sigma_t^2/2) \int_{\beta/y}^{\infty} \exp\left\{-0.5\left[\frac{(x_t - \mu_t - \sigma_t^2)^2}{\sigma_t^2}\right]\right\} dx_t$$

rearranging the exponent, with the area under the integral $n(\mu_t + \sigma_t^2, \sigma_t^2)$.[7] Hence

$$E(c_t) = \lambda y (2\pi)^{-0.5} \sigma_t^{-1} \exp(\mu_t + \sigma_t^2/2) \int_{\beta 3}^{\infty} \exp(-0.5 v^2)\, dv$$

where $\beta 3 = [\ln(\beta/y) - \mu_t - \sigma_t^2]/\sigma_t$ so

$$E(c_t) = \lambda y \exp(\rho_t)[1 - N(\beta 3)]$$

$$= \lambda y \exp(\rho_t)\left\{1 - N\left[\ln(\beta/y) - \left(\frac{\rho_t + \sigma_t^2/2}{\sigma_t}\right)\right]\right\}$$

The current expected price of the call option is

$$E(c) = \exp(-\rho t)E(c_t)$$

$$= \lambda y N\left[\frac{\rho_t - \sigma_t^2/2 - \ln(\beta/y)}{\sigma_t}\right]$$

$$= \lambda y N\left[\frac{\rho t - \sigma^2 t/2 - \ln(\beta/y)}{\sigma t^{0.5}}\right]$$

if the i.i.d. form holds. The mean return is used as the discount rate $\rho$.

### *Put Option*

The terminal price of the security is $y_t = k_t y$, or $k_t = y_t/y$. The exercise price is $\gamma$. Then if $y_t > \gamma$, the option with European feature has a positive terminal, or exercise date price $P_t = y_t - \gamma$. The price of the put option is

$$\text{if} \quad k_t > \gamma \qquad \text{then} \quad P_t = 0$$

$$\text{if} \quad k_t < \gamma \qquad \text{then} \quad P_t = y_t - \gamma$$

This is a truncated distribution over the random variable $k_t$, with $\gamma$, the exercise price; $t$, the exercise date; and $y$, the current price all predetermined and not random. If $k_s < \gamma$, for $s < t$, then the option is in the money. The expected price of the put option at exercise date is

$$E(P_t) = \lambda y \int_0^{\gamma/y} (k_t - \gamma/y) f(k_t)\, dk_t$$

$$= \lambda y (2\pi)^{-0.5} \sigma_t^{-1} \int_0^{\gamma/y} \left(\frac{k_t - \gamma/y}{k_t}\right) \exp\left[-0.5\left(\frac{\ln k_t - \mu_t}{\sigma_t}\right)^2\right] dk_t$$

If $k_t$ is lognormally distributed

$$E(P_t) = \lambda\beta(2\pi)^{-0.5}\sigma_t^{-1}\int_0^{\ln(\gamma/y)} \exp\left[-0.5\left(\frac{x_t-\mu_t}{\sigma_t}\right)^2\right] dx_t$$

$$- \lambda\gamma(2\pi)^{-0.5}\sigma_t^{-1}\int_0^{\ln(\gamma/y)} \exp(x_t)\exp\left[-0.5\left(\frac{\ln x_t-\mu_t}{\sigma_t}\right)^2\right] dx_t$$

Changing variables, defining $x_t - \ln k_t$,

$$E(P_t) = \lambda\beta(2\pi)^{-0.5}\sigma_t^{-1}\int_0^{\ln(\gamma/y)} \exp\left[-0.5\left(\frac{x_t-\mu_t}{\sigma_t}\right)^2\right] dx_t$$

$$- \lambda y(2\pi)^{-0.5}\sigma_t^{-1}\exp(\mu_t+\sigma_t^2/2)\int_0^{\ln(\gamma/y)}$$

$$\times \exp\left[-0.5\left(\frac{\ln x_t-\mu_t-\sigma_t^2}{\sigma_t}\right)^2\right] dx_t$$

the difference between functions of two normal distributions $n(\mu_t+\sigma_t^2,\sigma_t^2)$ and $n(\mu_t,\sigma_t^2)$. Hence

$$E(P_t) = \lambda\beta(2\pi)^{-0.5}\sigma_t^{-1}\int_0^{\gamma 1} \exp(-0.5v^2)\, dv$$

$$- \lambda y(2\pi)^{-0.5}\sigma_t^{-1}\exp(\mu_t+\sigma_t^2/2)\int_0^{\gamma 2} \exp(-0.5v^2)\, dv$$

where

$$\gamma 1 = [\ln(\gamma/y) - \mu_t]/\sigma_t \text{ and } \gamma 2 = [\ln(\gamma/y) - \mu_t - \sigma_t^2]/\sigma_t$$

$$E(P_t) = \lambda\beta N(\gamma 1) - \lambda y \exp(\rho_t) N(\gamma 2)$$

The current price of the option is

$$E(p) = \lambda\beta\exp(-\rho_t)N(\gamma 3) - \lambda y N(\gamma 4)$$

where

$$\gamma 3 = \frac{\ln(\gamma/y) - \rho_t - \sigma_t^2/2}{\sigma_t}$$

$$\gamma 4 = \frac{\ln(\gamma/y) - \rho_t + \sigma_t^2/2}{\sigma_t} = \gamma 3 + \sigma_t^2/2$$

Under the iid specification $\rho_t = \rho t$ and $\sigma_t^2 = \sigma^2 t$.

The put option can be applied to production and sales targets for brokers. The test is

$$\text{if } k_t > \gamma \quad P_t = 0$$

$$\text{if } k_t < \gamma \quad P_t = \lambda y_t$$

where $\lambda$ is some penalty. The expected price of the option imposing a penalty is

$E(P_t)$

$$= \lambda y \int_0^{\gamma/y} k_t f(k_t)\, dk_t$$

$$= \lambda y (2\pi)^{-0.5} \sigma_t^{-1} \int_0^{\gamma/y} \exp\left[-0.5\left(\frac{\ln k_t - \mu_t}{\sigma_t}\right)^2\right] dk_t$$

$$= \lambda y (2\pi)^{-0.5} \sigma_t^{-1} \exp(\mu_t + \sigma_t^2/2) \int_0^{\gamma/y} \exp\left\{-0.5\left[\frac{(x_t - \mu_t - \sigma_t^2)^2}{\sigma_t^2}\right] dx_t\right\}$$

rearranging the exponent, with the area under the integral $n(\mu_t + \sigma_t^2, \sigma_t^2)$,

$$E(P_t) = \lambda y (2\pi)^{-0.5} \sigma_t^{-1} \exp(\mu_t + \sigma_t^2/2) \int_0^{\gamma 5} \exp(-0.5 v^2)\, dv$$

where $\gamma 5 = [\ln(\gamma/y) - \mu_t - \sigma_t^2]/\sigma_t$

$$E(P_t) = \lambda y \exp(\rho_t) N(\gamma 2)$$

The current price of the put option is

$$E(P) = \exp(-\rho_t) E(p_t)$$

$$= \lambda y \exp(\rho_t) N\left[\frac{\ln(\gamma/y) - (\rho_t + \sigma_t^2/2)}{\sigma_t}\right]$$

$$= \lambda y N\left[\frac{\ln(\beta/y) - (\rho t + \sigma^2 t/2)}{\sigma t^{0.5}}\right]$$

if the relative prices are independently and identically and lognormally distributed.

### Moment Generating Function for a Lognormal Distribution

$$E(y)^g = E[\exp(gx)] = M_x(g) = \exp\{g\mu + g^2\sigma^2/2\}$$

where $g$ is an arbitrary constant. Where $g = 1$,

$$E(y) = \exp\{\mu + \sigma^2/2\}.$$

When $g = 2$

$$E(y)^2 = \exp\{2\mu + 4\sigma^2/2\} = \exp\{2(\mu + \sigma^2/2) + 2\sigma^2/2\}$$

$$= \exp 2\{\mu + \sigma^2/2\} \exp(\sigma^2) = E(y)^2 \exp\{\sigma^2\}$$

$$\text{var}(y) = E(y^2) - [E(y)]^2 = [E(y)]^2 \exp(\sigma^2) - [E(y)]^2$$

$$= [E(y)]^2[\exp(\sigma^2) - 1]$$

### Geometric Mean

$$E(y) = \exp(\mu + \sigma^2/2)$$

$$\ln E(y) = \mu + \sigma^2/2$$

$$\mu = \ln E(y) - \sigma^2/2$$

$$\mu + \sigma^2 = \ln E(y) + \sigma^2/2$$

If $\ln E(y) = \rho$, then $\mu = \rho - \sigma^2/2$ and $\mu + \sigma^2 = \rho + \sigma^2/2$.

### Notes

1. An alternative in this case is for the lender not to guarantee the interest rate in advance, but to provide the market rate at the time of delivery. This procedure, applied when mortgage closing lengths are long, shifts the interest rate risk from lender to borrower. The borrower may then require a hedging strategy.

2. If the contract interest rate on the mortgages is $r$, the yields and prices, on an 8 percent coupond Ginnie Mae with prepayment at 12 years, the standard trading contract, as from the *GNMA Yield and Price Equivalent Tables,* are:

| *Yield* | *Price* |
|---|---|
| 7.00 | 107 12/32 |
| 8.00 | 99 22/32 |
| 9.00 | 92 22/32 |
| 10.00 | 86 12/32 |
| 11.00 | 80 20/32 |
| 12.00 | 75 13/32 |
| 13.00 | 70 21/32 |

3. The option pricing model is developed in Black and Scholes (1973), and Merton (1973).

4. The security price is assumed to move with geometric Brownian motion, or the rate of change in price is $dS/S = \pi\, dt + \sigma\, dz$, where $\pi$ is the instantaneous rate of return expected on the security $S$, $\sigma$ is the instantaneous variance, and $dz$ is a Wiener process. See McKean [1965, 1969], or Merton [1973]. Under the Brownian motion assumption, the derivative above is obtained by Ito's lemma. The derivative would be $dC = (\partial C/\partial S)dS + (\partial C/\partial t)dt$ if $S$ were not stochastic, and the assumption of Brownian motion effectively adds only one second order term.

5. Now

$$k_t = y_t/y = \prod_{s=1}^{t} w_s, \text{ and } \ln k_t = \ln y_t - \ln y = \sum_{s=1}^{t} \ln w_s$$

Under the independent and identical (iid) specification of the distribution, $\ln w_s$ is distributed $n(\mu,\sigma^2)$, $s \in [0,t]$.

6. A modified specification is for the call option to refinance to be, if points are zero

$$c(r_1,p) > 0 \qquad \text{if } r_1 < r$$

$$c(r_1,p) < 0 \qquad \text{if } r_1 > r$$

As interest rates rise, the rate of refinancing falls below that expected in the premium. If the market interest rate exceeds the contract rate, the lender saves only the transactions cost of finding a new borrower.

7. A general result on completing the square in the exponent is

$$\exp(x)\exp\{-0.5[(x-\mu)/\sigma]^2\}$$

$$= \exp[x - 0.5(x^2 - 2x\mu + \mu^2)/\sigma^2]$$

$$= \exp[-0.5(x^2 - 2x\mu + \mu^2 - 2x\sigma^2)/\sigma^2]$$

$$= \exp\{-0.5[((x-\mu-\sigma^2)^2 - \sigma^4 - 2\sigma^2\mu)/\sigma^2]\}$$

$$= \exp(\mu + \sigma^2/2)\exp[-0.5(x-\mu-\sigma^2)^2/\sigma^2]$$

The last expression is the production of the geometric mean of $x$, the random variable, and the exponential term for a standardized normal variable with mean $\mu + \sigma^2$ and variance $\sigma^2$.

# 12 MORTGAGE BANKING: DIRECT LENDERS

## Introduction

The demand for funds in real estate comes from the investment in physical property and from the securing of financing for investment in such property. Thus far, emphasis has been on the demand side, from investors in real property, and financial assets secured by real property. While investors in mortgage securities are effectively lenders, the supply of funds comes from institutions engaged in mortgage banking. Mortgage banking entails intermediation—provision of real estate financial services—in addition to lending. The term *direct lender* is used to describe the party engaged in lending to the borrower. Direct lenders include depository institutions such as thrifts and commercial banks, or a mortgage banker or broker, lending borrower funds not on deposit. The purchaser of a mortgage security is an indirect lender.

Mortgage bankers and mortgage brokers make decisions between holding loans in the portfolio or selling the loans in the secondary market. With guidelines established on underwriting standards for sale of mortgages by public and quasi-public agencies, the direct lender is able to obtain liquidity for mortgages. The standards for qualifying borrowers and underwriting permit mortgages to be tradable, either in whole or unit form or in packages.

The largest direct lenders for residential mortgages have been depository thrift institutions—savings and loan associations and mutual savings banks. Among nondepository lenders, pension funds and life insurance companies participate in commercial and industrial real estate development. Other nondepository direct lenders include the financing subsidiaries of automobile producers.

The development of secondary markets for mortgages implies that a lender does not have to bear interest rate and inflation risk, nor necessarily to continue carrying the loan on financial statements.[1] By carrying a given loan on the financial statements, the lender restricts its ability to make other loans and receive servicing fees. The primary mortgage market has emerged as one where the direct lender, interfacing with the borrower, has the objective only of collecting servicing and up-front fees, and not necessarily of holding the mortgage. The separation of primary and secondary mortgage markets increases the efficiency of real estate financing, because liquidity is increased and risk is diversified. Among direct lenders, first discussed are depository mortgage bankers, including thrifts. Given that thrifts have had a central role in mortgage lending, the focus is on these as opposed to other depository institutions. Nondepository mortgage lenders are then considered.

## Mortgage Banking

Mortgage bankers are in the business of direct lending on the security of improved real estate, or as purchasers of mortgage securities. Mortgage brokers are agents whose function is to intermediate between borrowers and lenders; they provide banks with business in real estate loans. For mortgage bankers and brokers, two main sources of income are sales commissions, paid out of points and origination fees, and servicing fees on mortgages outstanding. Efficiency in converting deposits to loans, and the spread between borrowing and lending interest costs, are additional sources of income for depository direct lenders holding mortgages as assets.

Mortgage bankers advance funds directly, while brokers do not usually advance funds. Mortgage banking and brokerage have grown because of national standards for purchase in the secondary market. These standards arise from the Federal National Mortgage Association which stands ready to buy mortgages under credit stringency. The agency provides a secondary market for federally underwritten mortgages. The Government

National Mortgage Association is a guarantor of eligible mortgages, especially for mortgage pools. A large proportion of mortgage banker loan originations are purchased by Fannie Mae and Ginnie Mae.

Mortgage bankers sell loans to investors, based on standards imposed on the borrowers and property. Servicing a mortgage involves the receipt of payments of principal and interest from the borrower, and the setting up and maintenance of escrow accounts for property tax and insurance payments if applicable. The servicer forwards mortgage payments to the ultimate lender. The servicer can be one depository or nondepository institution, and the lender, or recipient of the funds, another. If the lender is indirect, the payments are passed through a series of intermediaries. On a portfolio loan, the mortgage borrower makes payments to the servicer, who forwards them to the direct lender. On a loan sold to the secondary market, the borrower makes the payment to the servicer, who forwards it to the agency managing the pool of mortgages of which the loan is part. The pool then makes the payment to the investor.[2]

The servicer acts as the agent for the ultimate investor, being willing to inspect the property should payments not be maintained. If the property is sold or otherwise changes hands or title, the record keeping is maintained. On foreclosure or delinquency, the servicer commences legal proceedings.

Fees for a mortgage include origination fees, paid up-front, for the points, appraisal, and application. Kickbacks and referral fees are forbidden under the Real Estate Settlement and Procedures Act (RESPA), but mortgage brokers can receive a fee for their services, if licensed to deal in real estate or exempted by statute.[3] Other fees are for the subsequent servicing of payments. A typical fee is 0.375 percent of the principal balance, and reduce the pass-through to the ultimate investor.

## Thrifts

The supply of funds comes from all depository institutions, but thrifts have historically concentrated on providing real estate financing. The discussion thus focuses on the thrifts, as opposed to commercial banks.

The thrift industry—savings and loans associations and mutual savings banks—contains depository institutions analogous to commercial banks, totalling over 3000 institutions. Deposits in thrifts are held as liabilities. Depositors in thrifts are insured against failure by federal deposit insurance. Thrifts can be covered by both the Federal Deposit Insurance Corporation (FDIC), founded in 1933, and the Federal Savings and Loan Insurance Corporation (FSLIC). There is federal regulatory authority through the Federal Home Loan Bank Board (FHLBB), with twelve regional Federal Home Loan Banks, the analogoues of the Federal Reserve System. The Federal Home Loan bank was established in 1932. The system provides liquidity to thrifts, and membership is required for thrifts in FSLIC.

Regulatory restrictions typically limited thrifts to holding in their portfolios either whole loans or mortgage backed securities. Tax policy permitted a deferral of current income earned from real estate financial assets. Deregulation of thrifts occurred with the passage of the Depository Institutions Deregulation and Monetary Control Act (DIDMCA) of 1980, and the Garn–St. Germain Act of 1982, applicable to federally chartered thrifts. Federally chartered thrifts are permitted to invest up to 30 percent of their total assets in nonmortgage loans, including consumer loans, commercial paper, and corporate securities. Up to 10 percent of assets can be invested in commercial loans other than for real estate. In exchange, they are required to hold reserves at the central bank.

On the liability side, the bulk of deposits in thrifts prior to deregulation was in the form of personal savings deposits, subject to interest rate ceilings. An increase in interest rates implied an outflow of funds. With the asset side being largely in FRPMs, whose payments are unaffected by short-term interest rate increases, and hold the potential of capital losses, thrifts faced losses through disintermediation, or deposit withdrawal. An increase in interest rates with an illiquid mortgage portfolio can create credit rationing, the liquidation of mortgages—with realization of capital losses—or borrowing funds from the FHLBB and other sources at higher market interest rates.

On the asset side, thrifts have been permitted to set the terms on ARMs, the consequence being the ability to shorten the maturity of the loan portfolio, and reduce the risk borne by the lender on interest rates and refinancing. Capital requirements for a thrift, in assets less liabilities, and in the ratio of assets to assets less liabilities, are lower than for commercial banks. The ratio of capital, or shareholders' equity, to total assets is stipulated at charter to be 3 percent, versus 6 percent for commercial banks. However, with high interest rates, nonperforming loans, and defaults, some thrifts may not have 3 percent capital ratios, or even negative capital, under GAAP. Lower interest rates need not improve the net worth of thrifts. There is no reason for lenders to be beneficiaries of high or low interest rates.

The balance sheet of the thrift is immunized if a given percentage interest rate change has no effect on shareholders' equity. If the average maturity of assets, in loans, exceeds that for deposits, the lender is vulnerable to interest rate risk, and may not be immunized.

The balance sheet of a thrift has a typical form:

**Balance Sheet, Thrift Institution, Date *t***

| **Assets** | **Liabilities** |
|---|---|
| Liquid assets | Liquid liabilities |
| Cash | Demand deposits |
| Securities (mortgage, other) | Plus: Time deposits |
| Plus: Illiquid assets | Plus: Borrowed funds |
| Mortgages | Equals: Total liabilities |
| Physical assets (equipment and real estate, historical cost) | Plus: Net worth |
| | Loan loss reserves |
| | Plus: Stock |
| Equals: Total assets | Plus: Retained earnings |
| | Equals: Net worth or general reserves equity |
| | Equals: Total liabilities and net worth |

Thrifts (savings and loan associations and savings banks), are subject to regulation on liquid asset ratios, that is, on the proportion of total assets held in cash and securities. Federally chartered thrifts, the large majority, are subject to FHLBB regualtion. State chartered thrifts are subject to liquidity regulation at the state level. Thrifts are regulated on both overall liquid asset ratios and the proportion of short-term liquid assets to the total. Liquid assets divided by savings deposits and borrowings maturing in one year or less are required to be between 4 and 10 percent by the FHLBB.

On the liability side, regulation focuses on net worth, alternatively described as general reserves. FHLBB regulations for FSLIC insured thrifts permit net worth to include all reserves for bad debts (counted as a liability), common and preferred stock, and retained earnings. These items arise on the historical cost balance shee as indicated. Net worth includes, for permitted regulatory purposes, appraised equity capital, income capital certificates, mutual capital certificates, and net worth certificates.

Appraised equity capital is the difference between the market value of physical assets and book value. Such an equity increase applies principally to real estate owned (REO), and is subject to appraisal issues. Income capital certificates are issued by the FHLBB to thrifts in financial difficulties. Mutual capital certificates and subordinated debt securities are issues where the holder has a claim analogous to that of an owner, as opposed to a depositor. Net worth certificates are also issued by thrifts in financial difficulties; these are exchanged for notes provided by the FSLIC or FDIC. From deposits, thrifts are required to hold reserves in noninterest bearing accounts at the Federal Reserve Bank.

On the flow side of the financial statements, the income and expense statement has the form:

**Income and Expense Statement, Thrift Institution**

Revenue
- Interest and payment income
- Plus: Points and loan fees
- Plus: Mortgage servicing fees (on ex portfolio loans)
- Less: Provision for loan losses
- Equals: Net revenue

Less: Expenses
- Interest expense
  - Interest payments on deposits
  - Plus: Interest payments on borrowed funds
- Plus: Operating expenses
  - Labor costs
  - Plus: Other expenses

Equals: Net income before taxes

Less: Income taxes
Equals: Net income after taxes

Less: Dividends paid
Equals: Retained earnings

Mortgage loans provide the largest source of revenue for thrifts, about two-thirds of the total. The revenue sources are in the interest payments received and in fees, such as points and penalties, for servicing the loans. Much of the rest of total revenue is interest received on liquidity holdings in cash and securities, with a large part of the latter in mortgage backed securities.

On the expense side, about four-fifths of the total expense is the payment of interest on borrowed funds, both to depositors, and from directly borrowed loans. Operating expense contains labor and other costs. The provision for loan losses and bad debts is encouraged by the tax laws. Under current tax regulations, a thrift can set aside up to 40 percent of taxable income as a provision for bad debts. A provision for bad debts is a deductible expense, and is treated in this manner as a subtraction from gross revenue.[4]

## Portfolio Loans

The effective rate of return to the ultimate holder of the mortgage can be derived. The lender can hold the loan in the portfolio, or sell to the secondary market. The effective rate of return developed here is applicable to this ultimate holder. It is assumed that the thrift maintains the loan in the portfolio.

The thrift, and other depository extender of loans, is the recipient of the points and interest rates and other fees. Consider a FRPM loan, with interest rate $r$, points $p$, prepayment penalty $q$, frequency of compounding $k$ per year, term $N$ in years.[5] In the first year, the thrift receives as income the points and loan fees, under cash as opposed to amortized accounting of these revenues. On a cash flow basis, the mortgage payment per period $k$ during the year is $M = m(r,N{:}T,k)B$, where $B$ is the loan balance. The term of the loan in periods is $N = Tk$, where $T$ is the number of years, and $k$ the frequency of compounding per year. For a 30-year term with monthly compounding and $k = 12$, $N = 360$. Over the term of the mortgage, the present value of cash flow in to the lender is $Z(r_e,N{:}p,T,k) = pB + MA(r_e,N{:}T,k)$, where $r_e$ is the effective rate of return to the lender, or ultimate holder. On a one dollar loaned basis, the cash flow in is

$$z(r_e,N{:}p,T,k) = p + mA(r_e/k,N{:}T,k)$$

It is convenient to convert the cash flow into a per dollar loaned basis, where $z = Z/B$, since $z$ is the price, in revenue received, per unit dollar provided to the borrower. The thrift or portfolio lender recognizes that the loan has a low probability of being held to term. Let the loan be prepaid at time $t$, $t \leqslant N$. The loan balance outstanding is $B_t = b_tB$, where $b_t = 1 - A_t/A_N$, and $A_t$ is the future value of a one-dollar annuity, given the frequency of compounding per year $k$ and contract interest rate $r$. The borrower can face a prepayment penalty. If the prepayment penalty is $C$ periods of interest

$$Q_t = (r/k)B \sum_{i=1}^{C} b_{t+i}$$

The prepayment penalty can fall to zero after some specific time. The balloon payment is $B_t$, the balance payable, and the prepayment penalty $Q_t$; and on a per dollar of initial loan basis, the penalty is $b_t + q_t$, where $q_t = Q_t/B$. This balloon payment is discounted to the date when the loan was initially extended, by $1/(1 + r_e/k)^t$. The initial date of the loan need not be used. The balance of the initial loan can be extended forward, as a future value, but the resulting estimate of the effective return $r_e$ is unaffected.

The lender is receiving a blend of interest and principal. If the lender counts "a buck is a buck is a buck," the mortgage payment is not decomposed. The present value, as of date of loan, of the cash flow in for the lender is,

$$z + p + mA(r_e,N) + \frac{b_t + q_t}{(1 + r_e/k)^t} = 1$$

for repayment at period $t$.

The cash flow statement for the lender, for economic purposes is

**Cash Flow Statement, Lender, Mortgage**
(present values as of date of loan origination, per dollar)

**Cash Flow Out** (disbursed to borrower)
Date of origination
Loan disbursed 1

**Cash Flow In** (received from borrower)
Date of origination
Points received $p$
Plus: Mortgage payments (present value) $mA(r_e,N)$
Plus: Balloon payment (present value) $(b_t + q_t)/(1 + r_e/k)^t$
Equals: Total cash flow in

The initial cash flow out of 1 is the dollar initially lent. The cash flow in for the lender contains three components. At closing on the loan, points $p$ are recovered. During the period of mortgage payments, the periodic payments are received as an annuity and converted to a capital sum by the annuity multiplier $A(r_e,N) = [1 - (1 + r_e/k)^{-t}]/(r_e/k)$. At the date of repayment, either from sale of the property or prepayment, the balloon payment is received as the sum of the outstanding balance and the penalty.

The effective rate of return for the lender solves the equation. Rearranging gives

$$1 - p = mA(r_e,N) + \frac{b_t + q_t}{(1 + r_e/k)^t}$$

the equation derived earlier for the borrower. The effective rate of return for the lender $r_e$ is solved iteratively.

The effective rate of return is $r_e(t{:}r,N,p,C,k)$, dependent on the date of repayment $t$, the contract interest rate $r$, the term $N$, points $p$, number of periods for interest penalty on prepayment $C$, and frequency of compounding $k$. The effective rate of return for the lender increases with the frequency of compounding per year, with the number of periods of prepayment $C$, and with the points $p$, all of which are initial parameters, unchanged regardless of when the loan is prepaid. The effective rate of return is increasing in the interest rate $r$, and decreasing in the term $T$, where $N = Tk$.

The effective rate of return is the appropriate revenue measure, on a financial definition, per dollar of loan extended. If the number of dollars of loan is a quantity, the effective rate of return is a price, and $r_e$ is decreasing in the period $t$. The return measures the revenue obtained from extending a mortgage loan. The economic or financial income statement will indicate $r_e$ as the revenue obtained, for a holding period of a mortgage to end at $t$. For a loan of balance $B$, the revenue recognized is $r_eB$.

Prepayment can occur in any period for $t = 1, \ldots ,N$, and the effective rate of return is not constant. One method of pricing is to assume that all prepayment occurs at a specified time, where this date is some measure of central tendency over historical repayment. If prepayment occurs at 12 years, a date used in actual calculations, then for monthly compounding where $k = 12, t = 144$. The prepayment date in the calculation is deemed to be some specific date $t$, but there is variation over this date. The effective rate of return varies with the term of the loan and the lender has no knowledge on when or whether prepayment occurs.

A more complete measure of the expected return for making a loan, for the lender, is to apply a probability distribution of repayments over time.

Let the density function of such repayments, over $t = 1, \ldots, N$, be $\Delta(t)$. The expected effective rate of return is

$$E(r_e) = \sum_{t=1}^{N} \Delta_t r_e(t)$$

The variance, and other aspects of $t$, can be determined. The density function $\Delta(t)$ is not dependent only on time $t$, but on the mortgage parameters. If market interest rates are below those in the contract $r$, the probability of prepayment increases.

For the lender using an effective rate of return method for pricing loans, revenue is $r_e B$, from a balance of loan $B$. Summed over all loans, total revenue is obtainable, in constructing complete financial statements.

In practice, lenders do not apply the effective rate of return procedure to calculating loan revenue. Rather, a strict cash-in-cash-out procedure applies. The income statements for the thrift or other lender report revenue as

**Income Statements, Reporting on Loan Revenue**

| | *Accounting* | *Economic* |
|---|---|---|
| Date 0 (date of loan extension) | $p$ (points) | $r_e$ |
| Date $i = 1, \ldots, t$ | $(r/k)b_i$ | $r_e$ |
| Date $t$ | $q_t$ | $r_e$ |

In the first year, if the compounding on the mortgage is monthly, the accounting income statement reports the points as revenue. Total revenue is $p + (r/12) \Sigma_{i=1}^{12} b_i$, from the loan per dollar. On the loan at 10 percent, with 2 points, the approximate yield in the first year is 12 percent. The economic or financial return is $r_e$, with all returns capitalized. The effective return $r_e$ depends on the holding period, but is less than 12 percent in the first year. Any other loan fees are treated analogously to points in the economic definition, but reported as income under the accounting definition.

During the loan period, the lender reports as interest income a portion of the periodic payment $M$. At date $t$, the prepayment penalty is reported as income. In the economic or financial procedure, the points are deferred and capitalized.

## Nonportfolio Loans

The lender does not need to hold the loan in its portfolio. It can sell the loan into the secondary market, either to an agency such as Freddie Mac, to a brokerage firm for packaging as securities, or as a whole loan to another lender or intermediary. On FRPM loans, there are well-developed secondary markets, because FRPMs are more homogeneous, more marketable, have fewer variables, and can be treated as long-term securities. Being long term, there is more time to amortize underwriting, pooling, and packaging costs. This secondary marketability provides lenders with an incentive to originate FRPM loans, and to be intermediaries. On ARM loans, there are less well-developed secondary markets. It is more difficult to package ARMs as securities, because of heterogeneity of the loans and conditions. The lenders face a higher probability of holding ARMs in the portfolio and carrying the risk. The lenders have less incentive to originate ARMs and become mortgage storefronts, taking the fees.

The advantage to the depository lender of selling a loan is the effect on the accounting, and economic financial statements. Regulation and supervision of thrifts focuses on capital adequacy. Capital of the thrift is the difference between assets and liabilities, using the accounting, historical cost balance sheet. Structures and equipment are reported at historical costs, below-market values where there has been real estate inflation. There is an incentive to realize these capital gains by sale of physical assets, even though economic balance sheets would indicate no change. Sale of a mortgage removes loan assets from the balance sheet and increases cash and reserves. Capital adequacy conditions are more easily met with sale of mortgages.

There remains servicing of the loan, collecting the payments and other fees. Let the fees be indicated as a percentage of the outstanding principal, or $r_f$, expressed on a periodic basis. A common rate of fees is 0.375 percent per year. For a monthly compounding, the rate of fees is 0.3125 percent per month, as $r_f$. The loan balance, per dollar of initial loan, at date $i$, is $b_i$. Revenue from a loan originated and serviced is

**Income Statement, Loan Originated and Serviced**

| | *Accounting* | *Economic* |
|---|---|---|
| Date of origination | $p$ | $r_e b_i$ |
| During loan service (revenue) | $r_f b_i$ | |
| During loan service (cost) | $c_i b_i$ | |

Reported as net income each period is $r_e$, the effective rate of return on servicing the loan. Cash flow in for the thrift or lender is $p + r_f \Sigma_{i=1}^{N}$ $(1 - c_i)b_i/(1 + r_e/k)i$, and the effective interest rate $r_e$ solves. If the thrift reports the points as current income in the year the loan is originated, income is overstated.

## Deposits

On the deposit side, for any one dollar deposited in a thrift, a reserve requirement is charged. The effect of reserve requirements is akin to points for the borrower. The depository institution is unable to gain access to the required reserves. If the reserve requirement is $S$ for deposits of a particular type, only $(1 - S)$ is available for lending. The interest rate paid on deposit $i$ is $r_i$, as an annual variable rate. The deposit insurance premium is $D$. The total cost of servicing the deposit is

$$C = r_i + RS + D$$

where $R$ is the opportunity cost of funds to the lender, used for discounting future incomes and expenditures and constant over time. The interest rate $r_i$ can fluctuate over time, depending on the maturity of the deposit. The depository institution remains having $(1 - S)$ to lend out per dollar deposited.

The deposit insurance premium and reserve requirement are set by regulation, respectively by the Federal Savings and Loan Insurance Corporation (FSLIC) and the monetary authority. The variables of choice to the lender are the target rate of return on funds $R$, and the interest rate paid on deposits $r_i$. The scope to change $r_i$ can be limited by market forces. Let the maturity be $t$. The present value of the cost for the deposit is, using a once annual compounding,

$$d = \sum_{i=1}^{t} r_i/(1 + R)^i + [RS + D]A(R,t)$$

## Deposit Insurance

Under both the FDIC and FSLIC, deposits at thrifts are insured for up to \$100,000 per account. Account holders include individuals, joint tenants, trustees, estates, partnerships, corporations, pension beneficiaries, escrow accounts, and governments. If the thrift should fail, the depositor is paid to the full amount of the insurance. For a thrift in difficulty—for example, with below the required GAAP net worth—the deposit insurance agencies have a range of options. They can make loans, purchase assets, or permit time for a merger or acquisition. Capital assistance can be provided. The regulatory authority of the thrift system is the Federal Home Loan Bank Board.

The basic premium structure levied by FDIC and FSLIC applies the same premium rate for all lenders and deposits. The annual premium is 1/12 of 1 percent of the total deposits. For FDIC insured institutions, this premium can be reduced by a rebate. After deducting operating expenses and insurance losses from the gross insurance assessment, the FDIC rebates 60 percent of remaining assessment income to the lenders. The rebate is the same for all lenders. The effective FDIC rate has varied between 1/30 and 1/13 of 1 percent.

Thrifts typically lend funds for residential mortgages in their home areas. Because of the absence of diversification, many thrifts face financial difficulties. If the FDIC and FSLIC acquire assets of thrifts, usually nonperforming (in that no payments on the loans have been made for 90 days), the management and disposition is turned over to the Federal Asset Disposition Association (FADA). FADA has the objective of disposing of owned real estate.

The rationale for government operated deposit insurance is that individuals are not able to acquire the financial information necessary to determine the risk or solvency of a particular depository institution. Deposit insurance reduces the possibility of a bank run. The presence of deposit insurance can lead the thrifts to lend to more risky lenders, since prudent management is not rewarded, there being no downside risk. Thrifts in problem regions of the country face short-run losses of deposits, or low-deposit bases. These higher-risk thrifts offer high interest rates nationally, effectively subsidized by the public insurance fund. A perverse incentive structure emerges.

With technological change—namely, electronic funds transfer and improved communications—consumers have the alternative of money market funds, which are not insured. These funds do not invest in risky assets such as mortgages, but rather in short-term government notes. The risk is internalized.

The beneficiaries of a structure with regionalized, or one-branch-unit, thrifts, that have national deposit insurance, are depositors lured by high interest rates and borrowers in the specific areas served. The losers are the larger and more successful thrifts, who cross-subsidize large banks, who are restricted from thrift deposits by law or who must pay higher interest rates to compete and taxpayers, who ultimately subsidize deposit insurance.

Since all deposit insurance premium rates are the same, thrifts and other lenders have an incentive to increase the risk of the institution. The amount of capital can be reduced relative to assets. Debt can be issued, and the proceeds distributed to shareholders. The portfolio can be decreased in diversification, and liabilities can be obtained by borrowing, through brokered deposits. A mismatching of maturities in assets and liabilities can arise. The insurance subsidy can be a deliberate strategy to induce state chartered banks to join.

Regulation of lenders by the FDIC and FSLIC applies the CAMEL criterion. The acronym, used to determine lender risk, means Capital, Asset Quality, Management, Earnings and Liquidity. One method of regulation on risk implies increasing the capital requirement, or assets less liabilities, for lenders with more risky portfolios. If deposit insurance were privatized, more risky lenders would pay higher premiums. The existence of public deposit insurance depends on there being a public goods characteristic, such as preventing damage and loss of confidence in the financial system.

Deposit insurance can be interpreted as a put option held by the thrift on the insurance fund. The exercise price is equal to the amount of insured deposits, relative to total liabilities. The exercise date is the date until the next audit. In the option pricing model of chapter 11, let $y_t$ be the value of the assets of the thrift, and $\gamma$ be the covered deposits. If assets fall below covered deposits, the put option is exercised, and the thrift seeks protection. The price of the option is

$$P_t = y_t - \gamma \qquad \text{if} \quad y_t < \gamma$$

$$= 0 \qquad \text{if} \quad y_t \geqslant \gamma$$

The expected price of the put option at exercise date $t$ is

$$E(P_t) = \int_0^{\gamma} [(\gamma - y_t)f(y_t)\, dy_t]$$

The current price of the put option is

$$E(P) = \gamma \exp\,[(-\rho t)N(\gamma 2) - yN(\gamma 1)]$$

where

$$\gamma 1 = \frac{\ln(\gamma/y) - t(\rho + \sigma^2/2)}{\sigma t^{0.5}}$$

$$\gamma 2 = \frac{\ln(\gamma/y) - t(\rho - \sigma^2/2)}{\sigma t^{0.5}}$$

$$= \gamma 1 + \frac{\sigma \tau^{0.5}}{2}$$

If deposits are guaranteed on principal and interest, the current value of deposits is $G = \gamma \exp(-\tau t)$, being the discounted amount of the guarantee, with $\rho$ being a risk-free interest rate. Then $\ln G = \ln \gamma - \rho t$, and $\ln \gamma = \ln G + \rho t$. Substituting $\gamma 1$ for $\ln \gamma$,

$$\gamma 1 = \frac{\ln (G/y) - \sigma^2/2}{\sigma t^{0.5}}$$

$$\gamma 2 = \frac{\ln (G/y) + \sigma^2/2}{\sigma t^{0.5}}$$

$$= \gamma 1 + \frac{\sigma \tau^{0.5}}{2}$$

where $G/y$ is the current deposit-to-total-asset ratio. Dividing the current price of the option by the current amount of deposit

$$E(P)/G = N(\gamma 2) - (y/G)N(\gamma 1)$$

where $E(P)/G$ is the value of the deposit insurance per dollar of deposit, or a risk-adjusted deposit insurance premium. The risk-adjusted deposit insurance premium depends on the difference between two cumulative standard normal distributions. This deposit insurance premium $E(P)/G$ depends on the deposit-to-asset ratio $G/y$, the time to next audit $t$, and the variance of the logarithmic change in assets $\sigma^2$. The risk-adjusted deposit insurance premium is increasing in the deposit-asset ratio $G/y$, and in the variance $\sigma^2$. As the risk increases, measured by the variance, the deposit insurance premium increases.

Some issues arise in the use of option pricing models in deposit insurance. Deposit insurance is not strictly a European put, being exercisable only at maturity. The thrift can make a claim on the fund at any time, implying an American put characteristic. The time to maturity is unknown, and the insurance does not have a specific time frame. The amount of deposits covered is not unlimited, so the amount of potential claim on the fund, that is, exercise price, is not known in the future. The variance in assets must be estimated based on past experience, which may not correspond to current or future risk of deposits.

### Interest Rate Risk

While some thrifts sell their FRPM loans into a secondary market, others hold them as portfolio loans, or are the secondary buyers. Thrifts are subject to both interest rate and refinancing risk. Regarding interest rate risk, as interest rates rise, the FRPM asset prices fall. There is disintermediation, if the deposits are unmatched with the mortgages; and the thrift faces an outflow of deposits underlying the mortgages.

There is refinancing risk. With refinancing, in the short run, the profit of thrifts rise, because loan fees, points, and processing costs are included as income in the current period, rather than being amortized over the life of the loans issued. Yields on the mortgage portfolios are reduced.

The method of matching and hedging both risks is for thrifts to use adjustable rate mortgages (ARMs). If consumers switch to FRPMs, the thrifts stand to bear both risks. In equilibrium, ARMs should carry lower interest rates, to compensate borrowers for carrying these risks. If the yield curve, or relationship between interest rates and maturities, is not steeply sloped, borrowers refinance, shifting from ARMs to FRPMs. Thrifts can reduce fees and points on ARMs to induce customers to take these loans. Thrifts are portfolio investors in mortgage backed securities (financial paper secured by mortgages). These securities are subject to interest rate and refinancing risk.

### Loan-Fee Earnings

Thrifts and other lenders report points and other loan fees as current income. They have an incentive to oencourage borrowers to refinance. There are Financial Accounting Standards Board (FASB) proposals to restrict the current reporting of loan fees as income. Loan fees include nonrefundable points, front-end management fees to initiate a loan, and loan service charges. Certain fee origination expenses that are currently deferred, or written off over up to 12 years, would have to be taken as current expenses.

The recognition of loan fees as current income overstates current income of thrifts. To the extent that lenders use some of the income to advertise or induce borrowers to refinance, there can be more loan activity than would otherwise be the case. The FASB would require thrifts to deduct internal costs immediately from points, while deferring costs billed from outside.

### Mortgage Banking Companies

Mortgage banking companies are nondepository institutions providing funds for mortgages. These firms attract funds from institutional investors, such as insurance companies, pension funds, and—in revolving form—payments by other borrowers on existing loans.

The largest mortgage banking corporations are Lomas and Nettleton, of Dallas, TX; General Motors Acceptance Corporation (General Motors Corporation); Norwest Mortgage (Northwest Bank), Minneapolis, MN; Manufacturers Hanover Mortgage (Manufacturers Hanover), Farmington Hills, MI; Weyerhaeuser Mortgage (Weyerhaeuser), Woodland Hills, CA; CrossLand Mortgage (CrossLand Savings), Los Angeles, CA; Commonwealth Mortgage (Commonwealth Savings), Houston, TX; Colonial Mortgage Services (Philadelphia National Bank), (Philadelphia, PA; Fleet Mortgage (Fleet Financial), Milwaukee, WI; Kissell (PNC Financial), Springfield, OH; and First Interstate (First Interstate Bancorp), Pasadena, CA. Parent organizations are indicated in parentheses.

Mortgage banking companies have an advantage of vertical integration, not only in providing home loans, but in obtaining an entree to providing other financial services, such as life insurance and revolving lines of credit. Financial service companies, such as banks, gain access to a list of mortgage clients.

For brokerage firms in mortgage banking, the business generates mortgages that can be packaged into mortgage backed securities for sale to other investors. One loan generates two transactions. Again, other financial and brokerage services can be sold.

For consumer firms, such as General Motors, Ford, and Chrysler, the mortgage lending base provides a source of potential buyers of other products, such as automobiles. The transactions occur in both directions. By providing financing through captive agencies, automobile companies increase the prices of automobiles, and subsidize the transactions through the credit company, at below-market interest rates. The credit company has access to a large number of potential mortgage borrowers. The borrower can obtain both automobile and mortgage loans at the same window.

The subsidized interest rates at the automobile credit companies are not available from other lenders. Other lenders do not have an automobile production facility to cover the loan losses. With their access to mortgage borrowers, automobile companies have access to the real estate market. The depository sector of the mortgage market argues that this is unfair competition, particularly as depository institutions are required to hold reserves at no interest rate, and have no access to the pool of potential borrowers generated by automobile companies.

Sales of appliances are positively correlated with sales of houses. Developments in this industry could involve appliance manufacturers providing direct financing, with the prospect of obtaining mortgage business as well.

Instead of lending to new home buyers from its own portfolio of internally and locally generated deposits, as do savings and loans, a mortgage banker is a strict intermediary. The mortgage banker finds money for mortgages by tapping sources of funds outside local regions. Historically, the demand for residential mortgages in the South and West exceeded the domestic capacity of local thrifts. The mortgage banker acts as an importer of funds from other areas. Any mortgage lender is a mortgage banker if it resells the mortgage to a second party, either separately or as part of a pool of loans. A mortgage banking company is a nondepository institution that performs the mortgage banking function. MBCs account for about 25 percent of new residential mortgages, second only to the thrifts.

Instead of earning money on the spread, or the difference between the cost of funds and the interest rate charges, the MBC relies on fees collected for originating the loan and for servicing. In servicing, a MBC acts as escrow agent for the payment of hazard insurance and real estate taxes, and collects principal and interest.

Realtors and builders are marketing agents for the MBCs. The MBC arranges short-term loans to finance the mortgages at a given rate. Once made, the mortgages are grouped for sale as a package to outside investors. Typically, the mortgages are insured by the Veterans Administration, the Federal Housing Administration, or private insurers.

Brokerage firms are sources of funds for the MBCs, for which they use proceeds from the sale of other mortgage backed securities. The volume of sales of mortgage backed securities is nearly half the total volume of new residential mortgages, so there is a large supply of funds from sale of such securities.

### Resale of Mortgages

Neither depository nor nondepository lenders retain large FRPM mortgage portfolios. The loans are sold to a secondary market, where a mortgage backed security is issued. Most mortgage backed securities are secured by FRPM mortgages, because of the length of term. Adjustable rate mortgages are usually retained in the portfolio by lenders. Once the mortgage has been extended, there are various options for the lender on selling the financing to the secondary market.

One alternative is the direct sale of the loan, as a whole loan, to an institutional investor, usually a life insurance company. With the proceeds of sale, the lender is able to extend additional mortgages.

Another alternative is to package a number of FRPM loans directly as Ginnie Mae modified pass-through securities, and to sell these to investors through brokerage firms. This mechanism of sale and packaging is used by mortgage banking companies.

The lender can sell the loans directly, for cash or guaranteed mortgage backed securities, to the Federal National Mortgage Association (FNMA, FAnnie Mae), or to the Federal Home Loan Mortgage Corporation (FHLMC, Freddie Mac). Mortgages are resold either through the traditional Ginnie Mae modified pass-through market, or packaged as collateralized mortgage obligations (CMOs).

## Concluding Remarks

Whichever altenrative is selected, the mortgage instrument is not an illiquid liability for a financial firm, depository or nondepository. Policy issues arise as to the competitive aspects of cross-subsidies of loans by consumer firms. Another issue regards the regulations faced by depository institutions—on reserve requirements and deposit insurance—while nondepository institutions do not face such restrictions. The issue could be resolved by increased regulation of the nondepository institutions. With the presence of money market funds, which do not carry deposit insurance, the individual depositor has other means of investing short-term funds. The money market funds purchase corresponding short-term paper, such as Treasury bills.

It is not appropriate for a lender to be funding long-term assets, such as mortgages, with short-term deposits. It is possible that if deposit insurance were not present, lenders would take fewer risks, and mortgage funds from depository institutions would be less available. Some of the slack would be taken up by the MBCs, and capital markets would be more efficient in the allocation of funds.

## Notes

1. Alternative risk-based premiums can include experience rating, where the premium is adjusted based on performance. Regulatory cost can be a source of regulation. Privatization is discussed in Kane [1985, 1986]. The issues raised in risk-adjusted premiums are discussed in the FDIC [1983].

2. Fees are received, but are neglected here to retain the calculations on a per dollar of loan basis. The loan fees received are a relatively small portion of total revenue, and may approximate the marginal direct cost—in staff, form filling, and application review—of processing the loan.

3. Merton [1977] has developed a model of deposit insurance as an option. The exercise price cannot be gauged accurately, because the amount of covered deposits, below the threshold, and its ratio to total liabilities, is not parametric, but fluctuates. Estimates of the variation in premium levies from risk-based deposit insurance have been presented by Ronn and Verma [1986].

4. The 40% permitted tax shield for the bad-debt provision is modified by certain adjustments. To be permitted any deduction for a bad-debt provision, an institution must have at least 60% of its assets in housing-related investments or in federal government or agency securities. To obtain the full 40% exclusion from income, a savings and loan institution must have 82% of its assets in these investments, losing 0.75% of the bad-debt deduction for each 1% below the threshold. The analogous parameters for savings banks are 72% and 1.5%. Thrifts are not permitted the 85% exclusion of income for dividends received from other corporations, which increases the incentive to hold mortgages and mortgage backed securities.

5. The specific characteristics of these securities are described in chapter 11.

## Bibliography

Allen, R. C. [1981]. *Nothing Down.* New York: Simon and Shuster.

Black, F., and Scholes, M. [1973]. "The Pricing of Options and Corporate Liabilities." *Journal of Political Economy* 81, 637–659.

Bradford, D. F., et al. [1984]. *Blueprints for Basic Tax Reform.* 2nd edition. Arlington, VA: Tax Analysts.

Brueggeman, W. B., and Stone, L. D. [1981]. *Real Estate Finance.* Homewood, IL: Richard D. Irwin.

Downs, A. [1986]. *The Revolution in Real Estate Finance.* Washington, DC: The Brookings Institution.

Federal Deposit Insurance Corporation (FDIC) [1983]. *Deposit Insurance in a Changing Environment.* Washington, D.C.: Federal Deposit Insurance Corporation.

Federal National Mortgage Association. *FNMA Yield Book.* Washington, DC: Federal National Mortgage Association, various issues.

Fisher, I. [1930]. *The Theory of Interest Rates.* London: Macmillan.

Government National Mortgage Association. *GNMA Price and Equivalent Yield Tables.* Washington, DC: Government National Mortgage Association, various issues.

Hulten, C., and Wykoff, R. [1981]. "The Measurement of Economic Depreciation." In C. Hulten (ed.), *Depreciation, Inflation and the Taxation of Income from Capital.* Washington, DC: Urban Institute Press.

Kane, E. J. [1983]. "A Six-Point Program for Deposit Insurance-Reform." *Housing Finance Review* 6, 269–278.

Kane, E. J. [1985]. *The Gathering Crisis in Federal Deposit Insurance.* Cambridge, MA: MIT Press.

McKean, H. P., Jr. [1965]. "Appendix: A Free Boundary Problem for the Heat Exchange Equation Arising from A Problem in Mathematical Economics." *Industrial Management Review* 6, 32–39.

McKean, H. P., Jr. [1969]. *Stochastic Integrals.* New York: Academic Press.

Merton, R. C. [1973]. "Theory of Rational Option Pricing." *Bell Journal of Economics and Management Science* 4, 141–183.

Merton, R. C. [1977]. "An Analytic Derivation of the Cost of Deposit Insurance and Loan Guarantees." *Journal of Banking and Finance* 1, 3–11.

Ronn, E. I., and Verma, A. K. [1986]. "Pricing Risk-Adjusted Deposit Insurance: An Option-based Model." *Journal of Finance* 41, 871–896.

Rosen, K. [1981]. "The Effect of Proposition 13 on House Prices in Northern California: A Test of the Interjurisdictional Capitalization Hypothesis." *Journal of Political Economy* 89, 191–200.

Smith, C. W., Jr. [1976]. "Option Pricing: A Review." *Journal of Financial Economics* 3, 3–51.

Tobin, J. [1969]. "A General Equilibrium Approach to Monetary Theory." *Journal of Money, Credit and Banking* 1, 15–29.

United States Department of the Treasury, Internal Revenue Service [1986]. Publication 436, Washington, DC: Government Printing Office.

Wilcox, R. [1983]. "Why Interest Rates Were So Low in the 1970s." *American Economic Review* 73, 44–53.

# INDEX

MIX
Papier aus verantwortungsvollen Quellen
Paper from responsible sources
FSC® C105338

If you have any concerns about our products,
you can contact us on
**ProductSafety@springernature.com**

In case Publisher is established outside the EU,
the EU authorized representative is:
**Springer Nature Customer Service Center GmbH**
**Europaplatz 3, 69115 Heidelberg, Germany**

Printed by Libri Plureos GmbH
in Hamburg, Germany